English Language Learners at School A Guide for Administrators

SECOND EDITION

Editors

ELSE HAMAYAN *and* REBECCA FREEMAN FIELD

with 75 Contributing Experts

D1301254

CASLON PUBLISHING

Philadelphia

Copyright © Caslon, Inc. 2006, 2012.
All rights reserved. Except for the
quotation of short passages for the
purposes of criticism and review, no part of
this publication may be reproduced, stored
in a retrieval system, or transmitted in any
form or by any means, electronic, mechanical,
photocopying, recording, or otherwise
without prior written permission of the
publisher.

CASLON, INC.
Post Office Box 3248
Philadelphia, PA 19130

caslonpublishing.com

9 8 7 6 5 4 3 2

Library of Congress Cataloging-in-Publication Data

English language learners at school : a guide for administrators / editors, Else Hamayan
and Rebecca Freeman Field ; with 71 contributing experts. — 2nd ed.
    p.   cm.
  Includes bibliographical references and index.
  ISBN 978-1-934000-04-5
  1. English language—Study and teaching (Elementary)—Foreign speakers—Handbooks,
manuals, etc. 2. Education, Bilingual—United States—Handbooks, manuals, etc. 3. School
administrators—United States—Handbooks, manuals, etc. 4. School management and
organization—United States—Handbooks, manuals, etc. I. Hamayan, Else V. II. Freeman,
Rebecca D. (Rebecca Diane), 1960–
  PE1128.A2E487 2012
  428′.0071—dc23   2011047822

CONTRIBUTING EXPERTS

Jamal Abedi
Professor of Education
University of California, Davis
Davis, California

Diane August
Senior Research Scientist
Center for Applied Linguistics
Washington, DC

Karen Beeman
Education Specialist
Illinois Resource Center
Arlington Heights, Illinois

Timothy Boals
Executive Director
World-class Instructional Design and
    Assessment (WIDA) Consortium
Madison, Wisconsin

Donna Christian
Senior Fellow
Center for Applied Linguistics
Washington, DC

Nancy Cloud
Professor and Coordinator of the M.Ed.
    in TESL Program
Feinstein School of Education and
    Human Development
Rhode Island College
Providence, Rhode Island

Nancy L. Commins
Independent Consultant and Curriculum
    Specialist
Bilingual ESL Network
School of Education and Human
    Development
University of Colorado at Denver
Denver, Colorado

H. Gary Cook
Research Director
World-class Instructional Design and
    Assessment (WIDA) Consortium
Madison, Wisconsin

JoAnn (Jodi) Crandall
Professor and Director, Language,
    Literacy and Culture Ph.D. Program
University of Maryland, Baltimore
    County
Baltimore, Maryland

James Crawford
President
Institute for Language and Education
    Policy
Portland, Oregon

Jim Cummins
Professor
Modern Language Centre
Ontario Institute for Studies in
    Education (OISE)
University of Toronto
Toronto, Canada

Jack S. Damico
Professor and Doris B. Hawthorne
    Eminent Scholar in Communicative
    Disorders
The University of Louisiana at Lafayette
Lafayette, Louisiana

Ester J. de Jong
Associate Professor of ESOL/Bilingual
    Education
School of Teaching and Learning
University of Florida
Gainesville, Florida

Lynne Díaz-Rico
Professor
College of Education
California State University San
    Bernardino
San Bernardino, California

Lynne Duffy
Bilingual and ESL Instructional
    Specialist
Community Consolidated School
    District 21
Wheeling, Illinois

Jana Echevarria
Professor Emerita of Education
California State University
Long Beach, California

Gisela Ernst-Slavit
ESL Program Director
Washington State University
Vancouver, Washington

Kathy Escamilla
Professor
Educational Equity and Cultural
   Diversity
University of Colorado
Boulder, Colorado

Kelly Estrada
Assistant Professor of Education
Sonoma State University
Rohnert Park, California

Shelley Fairbairn
Assistant Professor
School of Education
Drake University
Des Moines, Iowa

Rebecca Freeman Field
Director, Language in Education Division
Caslon Publishing
Philadelphia, Pennsylvania

Jack Fields
Director of Bilingual Education (Retired)
U-46
Elgin, Illinois,
Coordinator
Illinois Resource Center
Arlington Heights, Illinois

Monica Maccera Filppu
Bilingual Programs Developer/
   Coordinator
Office of Bilingual Education
District of Columbia Public Schools
Washington, DC

David Freeman
Professor of Reading and ESL
The University of Texas at Brownsville
Brownsville, Texas

Yvonne S. Freeman
Professor of Bilingual Education
The University of Texas at Brownsville
Brownsville, Texas

Robert Fugate
ESL Teacher
Greenfield Elementary School
Chesterfield County, Virginia

Patricia Gándara
Professor of Education
University of California, Los Angeles
Los Angeles, California

Erminda García
Teacher and Instructional Coach
MK Udall K-8 School
Phoenix, Arizona

Ofelia García
Professor
Ph.D Programs of Urban Education
Hispanic and Luso-Brazillian Literatures
   and Languages
City University of New York
New York, New York

Fred Genesee
Professor
Psychology Department
   McGill University
Montreal, Quebec, Canada

María Paula Ghiso
Assistant Professor of Literacy Education
Department of Curriculum and Teaching
Teachers College, Columbia University
New York, New York

Jeanette Gordon
Education Specialist
Illinois Resource Center
Arlington Heights, Illinois

Margo Gottlieb
Director, Assessment and Evaluation
Illinois Resource Center
Arlington Heights, Illinois
Lead Developer
World-Class Instructional Design
Assessment (WIDA) Consortium
Madison, Wisconsin

Else Hamayan
Independent Consultant and Editor
Córdoba, Argentina

Renea Hamilton
Former ESL Title III Coordinator
Delaware County Intermediate Unit
Morton, Pennsylvania

John Hilliard
Education Specialist
Illinois Resource Center
Arlington Heights, Illinois

Victoria Hunt
Assistant Principal
Emily Dickinson School, PS75
New York, New York

Stephaney Jones-Vo
ESL/Diversity Consultant
Starfish Education
Johnston, Iowa

Tamara King
Education Specialist
Illinois Resource Center
Arlington Heights, Illinois

Stephen Krashen
Professor of Education, Emeritus
University of Southern California
Los Angeles, California

Judah Lakin
English Language Learner Coordinator
   and Reading Specialist
KIPP King Collegiate High School
San Lorenzo, California

Jobi Lawrence
EASL Program Administrator
William Penn University
Oskaloosa, Iowa

Kathryn Lindholm-Leary
Professor Emerita
San Jose State University
San Jose, California

Robert Linquanti
Project Director
WestEd
Oakland, California

Joe Reeves Locke
ELL Program Teacher
Cohn Adult High School
Metropolitan Nashville Public Schools
Nashville, Tennessee

Paula Markus
District-wide Coordinator
ESL and English Literacy Development
Toronto District School Board
Toronto, Canada

Barbara Marler
Education Specialist
Illinois Resource Center
Arlington Heights, Illinois

Michele R. Mason
Doctoral student and research assistant
Washington State University Vancouver
Vancouver, Washington

Barbara Medina
Assistant Commissioner for Innovation
   and Transformation
Colorado Department of Education
Boulder, Colorado

Kate Menken
Associate Professor, Linguistics
City University of New York
Queens College and Graduate Center
New York, New York

Maritza Meyers
ELL Program Coordinator
Long Beach Public Schools
Long Beach, New York

Jill Kerper Mora
Associate Professor Emerita
School of Teacher Education
San Diego State University
San Diego, California

Lucía Morales
Dual Language Teacher
InterAmerican Magnet School
Chicago, Illinois

Cynthia Mosca
Former Director of ELL Programs
Cicero Public Schools
Cicero, Illinois

Monty Neill
Interim Executive Director
FairTest
Boston, Massachusetts

John Nelson
Graduate Program Director
TESOL M.A. Program
University of Maryland Baltimore
   County
Baltimore, Maryland

Ryan L. Nelson
Assistant Professor and Doris B.
 Hawthorne-BORSF Endowed
 Professor-I
The University of Louisiana at Lafayette
Lafayette, Louisiana

Diep Nguyen
Assistant Superintendent of Curriculum
 and Instruction
Evanston Township High School District
 202
Evanston, Illinois

Sharon M. O'Malley
Supervisor of ELL Programs
School District of the City of New York
York, Pennsylvania

R.C. Rodriguez
Director of Bilingual and ESL Education
Northside Independent School District
San Antonio, Texas

David Rogers
Executive Director
Dual Language Education of New Mexico
Albuquerque, New Mexico

Nadeen Ruiz
Chair, Bilingual Multicultural Education
 Department
California State University Sacramento
Sacramento, California

Karen Sakash
Clinical Associate Professor
University of Illinois at Chicago
Chicago, Illinois

Cristina Sanchez-Lopez
Education Specialist
Illinois Resource Center
Arlington Heights, Illinois

Nancy Santiago Negrón
School District of Philadelphia
Philadelphia, Pennsylvania

Deborah J. Short
Senior Research Associate
Center for Applied Linguistics
Washington, DC

Patrick H. Smith
Professor of Applied Linguistics
Programa de Lengua y Lingüistica
 Aplicada
Universidad de las Américas, Puebla
Puebla, Mexico

Holly Stein
Adjunct Professor
University of Maryland
Baltimore County and College Park
Baltimore, Maryland

Kimberly Thomasson
Manager, Multicultural Education
 Department
The School District of Palm Beach
 County
West Palm Beach, Florida

María Torres-Guzmán
Associate Professor and Program
 Coordinator
Program in Bilingual/Bicultural Education
Teachers College
Columbia University
New York, New York

Cheryl Urow
Education Specialist
Illinois Resource Center
Arlington Heights, Illinois

Suzanne Wagner
Education Specialist
Illinois Resource Center
Des Plaines, Illinois

Wayne E. Wright
Associate Professor
University of Texas at San Antonio
San Antonio, Texas

María Josefina (Josie) Yanguas
Director
Illinois Resource Center
Arlington Heights, Illinois

Judith Kwiat Yturriago
Assistant Professor
Teacher Education Department
Northeastern Illinois University
Chicago, Illinois

PREFACE

As with the first edition, the second edition of *English Language Learners at School: A Guide for Administrators* answers the questions that K–12 administrators and teachers are asking about meeting the needs of the English language learners (ELLs) in their schools. Seventy-five experts provide brief, accessible, and practical responses to these questions. This edition focuses explicitly on leadership, capacity building, and professional learning not only for administrators but also for general education teachers, literacy coaches, ESL/bilingual specialists, staff developers, and policymakers in ELL education.

Our use of the term *ELL education* is intentionally broad. By *ELL program* we mean the entire instructional program for an ELL at school, including the time an ELL spends in the ESL or bilingual classroom/program, the time s/he spends in the general education classroom, and the time s/he spends in specials and extra-curricular activities. This means that all teachers and administrators who have ELLs in their classes and schools are in fact ELL educators who need to be knowledgeable in ELL education. This broader notion of ELL education reflects an important shift in the education field: ELL education is no longer just the responsibility of the ESL or bilingual specialist. Improving instruction and achievement for ELLs is the shared responsibility of all educators.

PURPOSE

A confluence of factors has brought us to a tipping point in ELL education for administrators and teachers working in schools in many parts of the English-speaking world today.

- There has been unprecedented growth in the number of ELLs in schools and districts all across the United States, especially in suburban and rural communities that have not previously experienced such growth. While the general K–12 population grew 7.2% over the last decade, the ELL student population grew 51%. More than one half of states have experienced a growth of over 100% in their ELL populations during that same period (see National Clearinghouse of English Language Acquisition, 2011, for details). Most, if not all, teachers and administrators in the United States find ELLs in their classes and schools.
- There are federal accountability requirements that hold all public U.S. schools and educators responsible for the educational achievement of all students, including ELLs. All teachers and administrators must be *highly qualified* to work effectively with the ELLs in their classes and schools.
- State-mandated accountability data demonstrate that many of the ELLs in schools (especially those from low-income homes and

communities) are not attaining proficiency on state-mandated standardized achievement tests. There is a heightened sense of urgency to *close the achievement gap* for minority students (including ELLs) who continue to *lag behind* their white, middle-class, standard-English-speaking peers.

- There has been increasing awareness among administrators and general education teachers that most ELLs spend the majority of their instructional day in general education classes taught by teachers who have not yet learned to address ELLs' language and learning needs. There is a great demand for leadership and capacity building so that all teachers and administrators develop the necessary knowledge and skills to ensure that ELLs can participate and achieve at school.
- There is confusion and conflict at the local, state, and federal levels about what effective instructional programs and valid accountability requirements mean for ELLs.
- There have been severe budget cuts that require administrators and leadership teams to be creative in the ways that they use funding to address the challenges they face.

These factors present administrators and leadership teams with challenges as well as powerful opportunities to rethink the education of ELLs/bilingual learners.[1]

NEW TO THE SECOND EDITION

The second edition of *English Language Learners at School: A Guide for Administrators* maintains the popular structural features of the first edition. The book revolves around questions that administrators, teachers, and leadership teams are asking about effective education for the ELLs/bilingual learners in their schools, districts, and states. Experts (researchers and practitioners) synthesize the research and offer their expertise in brief, accessible, and practical responses to those questions. The questions are organized into chapters that focus on different topics. Each chapter begins with a set of Guiding Principles that apply in any educational context and ends with a Survey for Reflection and Action that invites administrators and leadership team members to identify the degree to which the Guiding Principles are implemented in practice in their schools. This new edition includes more than 20 new questions that we collected from the field, and we

---

1. All ELLs are bilingual learners, but not all bilingual learners are ELLs. An ELL is a student who has been designated as such by state-mandated English language proficiency tests. A bilingual learner is a student who uses two (or more) languages in his or her linguistic repertoire to learn. We use both terms in the preface and introductions to chapters to draw attention to two facts: (1) ELLs draw on all of the languages in their linguistic repertoire to learn, and (2) many students who are designated as English speakers are also bilingual learners.

have invited a number of new experts to share their expertise. All of the experts included from the first edition were invited to update their responses to reflect recent developments in research, theory, policy, and practice.

The second edition opens with a chapter on leadership and professional development. Staff developers have repeatedly asked us to share how we organize professional learning opportunities that promote leadership and foster shared responsibility around ELL education for administrators, teachers, and leadership teams in their districts and schools, not only in the United States but also in Canada, Latin America, and Europe. The new content and placement of this chapter is intended to facilitate this work for staff developers, especially for those who are relatively new to the field of ELL education. The guidance we provide is also intended to support ESL and bilingual education specialists who are increasingly called upon to provide leadership and professional development in ELL education. However, many of these specialists are new to the job of promoting leadership and structuring staff development for general education administrators and teachers.

Two important new strands run through the book. The first strand focuses explicitly on *bilingualism, biliteracy, home language, heritage language,* and *bilingual programs;* these questions are highlighted by the icon 🔍 in the table of contents. The second strand focuses on the notion of *data-driven decision making;* these questions are highlighted by the icon ▦. We take a broad view of *data* and of *data-driven decision making.* We know that a wide range of constituents, including students, parents, community members, teachers, administrators, and policymakers working at the school, district, state, and federal levels, all need to know how ELLs/bilingual learners/all students are performing and progressing relative to federal, state, and local standards, goals, and objectives. Answers to questions throughout this guide recommend how teachers and administrators can collect and use the right kinds of data (qualitative and quantitative, summative and formative) to guide placement, instruction, program and professional development, policy, and advocacy for ELLs.

The second edition of *English Language Learners at School: A Guide for Administrators* also features website resources that provide a space where professional learning communities (PLCs) of teachers, administrators, and leadership teams can interact with each other around their common mission and vision of improved instruction and achievement for ELLs/bilingual learners. Educators simply go to casloncommunity.com and register to use the site. Educators working individually or in PLCs are able to

- Download additional resources (e.g., PowerPoint slides and activities, outlines of professional development workshops). When a response in the book is accompanied by a resource (e.g., framework, guiding principles or questions, template, form) on the Caslon Community website, we include an icon ⌨ at that point in the text.

- Complete and share end-of-chapter Surveys for Reflection and Action.
- Link to other resources in the field.
- Participate in discussions within PLCs in their schools and districts.
- Participate in discussions within PLCs that connect schools, districts, communities, and states around common issues, concerns, and approaches
- Upload examples of innovative and effective practices that they have used in their schools and districts.

We continue to update website resources in response to burning issues in the field. Our intention is that administrators, teachers, and leadership teams will question each other about issues they face, learn together, and share examples of innovative policies, programs, and practices that they have developed or used. Because each Caslon title we publish is aligned with this mission, members of the Caslon Community can also find resources related to, for example, teaching for biliteracy, teaching adolescent ELLs, differentiating instruction and assessment for ELLs, special education considerations for ELLs, and implementing effective instruction for ELLs. (Visit caslonpublishing.com for a full list of titles.) Through our books and the Caslon Community (casloncommunity.com) we hope to contribute to the ongoing professionalization of the ELL education field and to grass-roots action regarding educational equity and excellence for ELLs/bilingual learners.

HOW TO USE THIS GUIDE

We hope that this guide will be useful in three ways: (1) as a quick reference for administrators, teachers, and leadership teams; (2) for specific program development and improvement at school and; (3) for pre-service or in-service professional development. For specific program development and improvement, the guide can be used by school-based collaborative teams to advise them as they choose an appropriate program for their school, plan a schedule or a grouping method for their ELLs, decide on an instructional approach, or reflect on how well their current programs and practices address the needs of ELLs in their school. For professional development, the guide can be used by administrators and others responsible for in-service training to help school staff expand their knowledge and skills in how children learn in two languages; policies and accountability requirements for ELLs; developing, implementing, and evaluating instructional programs for ELLs; classroom instruction and assessment; to meet challenges; and advocacy. The guide can also be used in pre-service programs for administrators who need a grounded introduction to this important aspect of their future work in schools. Often the needs of ELLs are addressed only cursorily in most educational leadership programs. Following are some specific examples of how this guide can be used.

- An administrator reviews an expert's response on a particular question that has arisen at school (such as, how long does it take ELLs to acquire English?).
- A staff member who is responsible for professional development uses one of the questions and responses as the basis for a discussion of how to address a particular challenge in their local context.
- An administrator, group of administrators, or a school-based PLC turns to the chapter on developing instructional programs for ELLs and begins with the Guiding Principles and Surveys for Reflection and Action to assess their school's strengths and needs relative to the topic. After completing the school-based survey, these educators might look for answers to the specific questions that arose as they worked through the survey, and perhaps use the conversations around this focal area to develop school-based strategies for action. Ideally, administrators will incorporate these strategies for action into their school improvement plans.
- A study group of administrators, teachers, or leadership team members develops an action plan that clearly articulates a problem or concern regarding ELLs at school with the help of the guide. This action plan should be incorporated into the district strategic plan or the school improvement plan.
- An administrator or staff member draws on the recommended resources (such as the suggestions for further reading, websites of professional organizations, or lists of useful resources) found on the Caslon Community website to follow up on an area that he or she wanted to explore in greater detail.

We hope that the research and practical recommendations in this guide (in the book and on the Caslon Community website) will prove helpful to administrators and staff in their efforts to help ELLs acquire English and achieve academically in all areas of the curriculum. And we look forward to seeing how administrators, teachers, and leadership teams use the Caslon Community website to engage with each other within and across educational contexts in their schools, districts, communities, states, and nations. Most of all, we hope that this guide enriches the lives of all students and staff in our schools.

CONTENTS

CHAPTER 4. DEVELOPING INSTRUCTIONAL PROGRAMS FOR ENGLISH LANGUAGE LEARNERS

1

LEADERSHIP AND PROFESSIONAL DEVELOPMENT

GUIDING PRINCIPLES
- We provide all educators with opportunities to develop the expertise and practices they need to create optimal learning environments for the English language learners (ELLs)/bilingual learners in our classes and schools. This includes central and school-based administrators, general education teachers, special education and reading specialists, bilingual and English as a second language teachers, support staff, parents, community liaisons.
- We consider the research base on ELL education as well as data about the ELLs/bilingual learners in our school to ground and inform the decisions that we make concerning our ELLs/bilingual learners. By *data* we mean information about our ELL/bilingual learners' strengths and needs as well as performance-based assessments of their content and language learning. These research-based, data-driven decisions form an integral part of all of the decisions that we make in our schools and throughout our school district.
- We organize collaborative leadership teams that focus on data to guide our school and district professional development plans.
- We implement professional development for all of our staff on ELL education that is comprehensive, focused in its delivery, and sustained over time.

INTRODUCTION

Administrators today are seriously challenged to ensure that all of their staff receive the professional development they need to educate the English language learners (ELLs)/bilingual learners in their classes and schools. More than a decade has passed since the No Child Left Behind (NCLB) Act of 2001 began its focus on accountability for all students in the United States, including ELLs. Today we see confusion and controversy on the Federal, state, district, school, program, and classroom levels about what effective education for ELLs/bilingual learners means as policymakers, administrators, teachers, parents, and community members try to make sense of contemporary debates about research, theory, policy, educational programs, in-school and out-of-school practices, and accountability systems. We find a critical need for knowledgeable leadership at every level of decision making (Federal, state, district, school, program, and classroom) that can help build capacity in ELL education in K-12 schools in urban, suburban, and rural communities not only in the United States but internationally.

We strongly believe that it is unrealistic for policy makers to expect to find a one-size-fits-all solution to the complex challenge of educating an increasingly linguistically, culturally, and socioeconomically diverse K-12 student population in rural, suburban, and urban districts across the United States in the 21st century. It is also unrealistic to expect educators to simply tweak a standardized system designed for monolingual English-speaking students and have it deliver results for ELLs/bilingual learners. Administrators and teachers working on the local level must step up and take the lead in developing and implementing sound educational programs and accountability systems that are aligned with state standards AND that are appropriate for the ELLs/bilingual learners in their particular districts, schools, and communities. The good news is that this kind of leadership and capacity building is already underway in many schools and districts today. Much work remains, and this guide is intended to help.

One direct result of NCLB is that every state in the United States has developed English language proficiency (ELP) standards and assessments, individually or in collaboration with other states (e.g., WIDA or World-class Instructional Design and Assessment), that focus attention on the range of oral and written academic language used for social and instructional purposes at school as well as in the content areas of language arts, mathematics, science, and social studies. Every ELL must be identified and their ELP level must be specified with attention to their listening, speaking, reading, and writing levels. Although we do find variation across state ELP frameworks (e.g., the number of ELP levels, the names of the levels), all state ELP standards and assessment systems reflect research findings on a continuum of second language development with attention to academic language and literacy development. These ELP standards and assessment systems offer a powerful basis for professional development in differentiating instruction and assessment for ELLs in any classroom setting, as well as a focus for collaboration among general education teachers and ESL and bilingual education specialists.

Furthermore, since NCLB was passed, all teachers and administrators working in U.S. public schools must be "highly qualified." Although we hear considerable debate about what highly qualified means, we do find increasing mandates and accountability requirements concerning professional development in the area of ELL education for all administrators and teachers, including elementary and secondary classroom teachers, literacy and special education specialists, and administrators in all parts of the United States today. More schools, districts, and states are now requiring all new hires to demonstrate competencies or show credentials in ELL education, and more teacher education and educational leadership programs in colleges and universities nationwide are providing some coursework in ELL education for all prospective teachers and administrators. At the same time, more districts and schools are providing in-service professional development in ELL education for all of their teachers and administrators.

The implications of all of these moves are that more teachers, administrators, program developers, and policy makers at all levels of decision making are beginning to understand how ELLs learn in two languages, and they are beginning to understand what is wrong with current policies and accountability requirements for ELLs. These educational leaders are also beginning to understand how to develop pedagogically sound, well-implemented instructional programs for ELLs/bilingual learners that can deliver realistic results in their diverse classrooms, schools, and communities.

How can administrators build capacity for ELL education in their districts and schools? The notion of a professional learning community (DuFour & Eaker, 1998) is fundamental. We know that school improvement occurs when

- educators develop a shared language and a common practice that is focused on improved instruction and performance of their ELLs/bilingual learners.
- educators engage in frequent, continuous, and increasingly concrete talk about student learning and teaching practice.
- educators frequently observe and provide feedback to each other.
- educators plan, design, and evaluate educational programs, materials, and practices together.
- educators use empirical evidence of student performance to guide instruction, inform program and professional development, influence policy, and strengthen advocacy.

Administrators must first assume responsibility for the education of the ELLs in their school and seek to further their own expertise and knowledge in ELL education. Administrators can encourage leadership teams in their schools and districts to function as professional learning communities that clarify and clearly articulate their mission and vision concerning linguistic and cultural diversity. Collaborative leadership teams can assess professional development needs, set goals, and develop and implement action plans to guide their work.

Perhaps the most powerful tool that an administrator has is to be a model to his or her staff by displaying positive attitudes toward linguistic and cultural diversity, keeping up to date on research on ELL education, and fostering a climate of professional learning. The principal sets the tone on the school level, and the superintendent sets the tone on the district level. Through grounded conversations about student learning, classroom practices, and program development, *all* educators can deepen their understanding of how to provide equal educational opportunities to ELLs/bilingual learners within the context of their regular practice.

This chapter begins by outlining structures that leadership teams can use to guide their ELL-focused work and identifying what different members of the staff must know and be able to do. The second half of the chapter provides insight into how effective administrators build capacity in ELL education. The chapter concludes with a Survey for Reflection and Action that administrators can use to review the strengths of the professional development opportunities that they make available to their staff and to identify action steps they may need to take in this area.

■ How can we help leadership teams develop and implement coherent programs for all students, particularly English language learners?
REBECCA FREEMAN FIELD

Knowledgeable educators understand that linguistic and cultural diversity are not problems to be overcome, but resources to build on. These educators work together to challenge the deficit orientation that has dominated policies and practices for ELLs/bilingual learners in the United States and to provide equal access to educational opportunities for all of their students. These educational leaders work to develop and implement effective instructional programs and practices for all students in their schools and communities, with focused and sustained attention on the needs of their ELLs/bilingual learners. They also use valid and reliable evidence of student performance to inform and defend their decisions about curriculum, instruction, and assessment; program and professional development; gifted, talented, and other types of special education; extra-curricular activities; parental and community outreach; and anything else that affects the educational achievement and social integration of ELLs/bilingual learners into the school community.

There is no one-size-fits-all approach to programming for ELLs. To meet the needs of the particular students in their district or school, administrators can organize ELL-focused leadership teams that use data, broadly defined, to guide their decision making. This means that leadership teams must collect and use authentic evidence of ELLs' growth and development relative to all standards and goals (e.g., academic growth and achievement, English language development and proficiency, biliteracy development) in order to counter the current state and Federal over-reliance on the results of state-mandated standardized academic achievement tests. Educational leaders must also present this evidence in ways that different constituents (students, parents, community members, teachers, school-based administrators as well as district, state, and Federal administrators and policy makers) can understand and use appropriately.

On the district level, ELL-focused leadership teams should include representatives of central, regional, and school-based administrators, teachers, and community members who collectively have or are prepared to develop expertise in all areas affecting the ELLs/ bilingual learners throughout the district, including curriculum and instruction, assessment and evaluation, special education, English as a second language (ESL), and bilingual education. On the school level, leadership teams should include (at least) the principal, a general education teacher, and specialists in literacy, math, special education, and ESL/bilingual education. Team members can work together as professional learning communities to develop an understanding of the strengths and needs of their students and communities, the research on ELL education, and the strengths, needs, resources, and constraints of their school and district. ELL-focused leadership teams must ensure that the programs they develop for ELLs meet the three-pronged Castañeda Standard (Castañeda v. Pickard, 1981). Programs for ELLs must be (1) research based and pedagogically sound; (2) well-implemented by highly qualified professionals using appropriate materials; and (3) periodically evaluated and restructured as necessary if they fail to deliver results.

Leadership team members can use the following questions to guide their collaborative work:

1. Who are our students?
    • Numbers of ELLs, heritage language speakers, English speakers
    • Student backgrounds: language, literacy, culture, education
2. What are our goals?
    • Academic achievement, English language development
    • Development of other languages and literacies
    • Other district/school goals and initiatives (academic, social, cultural)
3. How are our students performing relative to our goals? What evidence do we collect and how do we use that evidence to drive our decision making?
    • Results on mandated standardized achievement tests
    • Formative and summative evidence of student learning relative to all district/school goals to complement standardized achievement data
4. What supports do we have in place to ensure that our ELLs/bilingual learners can participate and achieve at school?
    • Policies, programs, practices, assessments, extracurricular activities
5. What are our strengths?
6. What challenges do we face?
7. What future possibilities[1] can we see for our students/school/district?
8. What action steps do we need to take to build on our strengths and address our challenges so that ALL of our students, particularly ELLs, including those with disabilities, can participate and achieve?
9. What resources will we need?

Leadership team members can use these guiding questions to help them look critically at what is happening with ELL education in their dis-

---

1. I use the term "future possibilities" instead of "needs" because it helps the conversation stay positive. Sometimes when groups focus too much on "needs," it can be challenging to move forward in positive ways.

tricts and schools in relation to research on ELL education so that they can develop context-responsive, pedagogically sound, well-implemented approaches that deliver results.

 TAMARA KING AND SUZANNE WAGNER

Successful, coherent, and comprehensive educational programs share a number of effective practices. One of these key practices is to organize instructional programs to effectively meet the literacy, academic, and language needs of the districts' English language learners (ELLs). A language education committee can be convened, composed of 10 to 12 members, representing district administration, building administration, bilingual/ESL teachers, general education teachers, special education teachers, parents of ELLs, and a member from the board of education. Including administrators and teachers from outside the ESL/bilingual department ensures that all language education program initiatives dovetail with other district initiatives. The goal of the language education committee is to create, maintain, and support an effective program for the districts' students that is research based and data driven. This program structure also serves as a way to communicate the goals and expectations to each educator who works with ELLs as well as to the local community.

The work of this newly convened leadership committee can be divided into three phases that loosely align with the three parts of the Castañeda Standard (Castañeda v. Pickard, 1981). In the first phase, the committee focuses on building the members' background knowledge regarding best practices in educating ELLs while learning about the current ELL services. By the end of phase one, the committee formulates an action plan for any needed changes to their programming for ELLs. During this year (or longer, if needed) of learning and strategic planning, the committee meets monthly. In the second phase, the committee meets every other month in order to guide the district through the action plan. The committee focuses their energy on facilitating the change process, solving problems, organizing professional development opportunities, and procuring resources. The third phase focuses on oversight and evaluation of the program. This phase may last for two years or more. At any time, the committee may decide to revisit phase one if the district's demographics have changed or the program needs to be restructured. Table 1.1 summarizes the committee's phases and tasks.

The committee structure provides a way to develop a common focus and a common language to talk about students and programs. The diversity of its members models a spirit of shared responsibility in the district's

TABLE 1.1 Outline of Language Education Committee Phases and Tasks (*Adapted from Wagner & King, in press*).

Task Force Phase	Members	Task	Frequency of Meetings
Phase 1: Strategic Planning	Representatives of all stakeholder groups	Build background knowledge of all committee members, data analysis, and action planning for next school year.	Monthly
Phase 2: Implementation	Same committee members as in Phase 1	Assure that the program is being implemented across the district with adequate resources (materials, staff development, etc.)	Every other month
Phase 3: Ongoing Analysis and Evaluation	Rotate one third of the committee out and replace with new repre- sentatives for that stakeholder group.	Review and refine language education programming each year. Monitor and analyze assessment and demographic data, exit and refusal numbers. At any time during this phase, the committee can decide to revisit phases 1 and 2 as a result of significant changes in the district.	2–4 times per school year

approach to educating ELLs. Like any other district committee, the language education committee oversees the district program, identifies and solves problems, plans professional development, and provides insights for future planning and changes. It serves as the hub of the Professional Learning Community language education network on ELL issues. As the various school teams implement the recommended changes, they can coordinate efforts and reflect about what works and what does not.

The new or restructured language education programs will remain strong over time when the district-level language education committee and school leadership teams share a mutual goal to provide standards-based comprehensible literacy, academic, and language instruction for all students, particularly ELLs (see Wagner & King, in press, for detailed discussion of these processes).

■ What kinds of knowledge and skills do administrators need in order to implement an effective program for English language learners?
BARBARA MARLER

The qualities of an effective leader will have particular relevance to administrators in the education of English language learners (ELLs). According to Marzano, Waters, & McNulty (2005), the following five operating principles come into play when establishing and maintaining a leadership team:

1. **Significance**—An administrator leads educators to address "questions that matter" so that new and existing work can be reviewed against goals and emerging issues in efforts to allocate resources appropriately.
2. **Quality**—The work and approach of teachers and administrators must exemplify the highest professional standards and withstand critical scrutiny. An administrator must hold all under his or her leadership accountable for both processes and results.
3. **Responsibility**—An administrator identifies, develops, and shares information and techniques that improve student learning so that educators can learn, grow professionally, and remain relevant in their work.
4. **Integrity**—The administrator is challenged to create and maintain an environment of trust, respect, and common values to produce maximum effectiveness among staff and students.
5. **Ethics**—An administrator's work and approach should reflect fair, just, and compassionate understanding and insight to produce opportunities for all children regardless of race, culture, language background, or socioeconomic status.
6. **Openness**—The decision-making process, led by an administrator, should be transparent to both internal and external audiences.

More specific to ELL education, an administrator needs to understand the basic process of second language acquisition and acculturation so that he or she can support teachers in their work with ELLs. To serve as an exemplary manager in this area, simple knowledge of the two processes is not sufficient. An effective administrator must know how to apply this knowledge to help support staff in creating and managing optimal school environments for learning. Such information should be used as a guide in decision making in such areas as planning for staff development for all educators (not just bilingual/ESL staff), allocating resources (staff, materials, and classroom space), crafting program design and supportive infrastructure (scheduling, language allocation, instructional priorities, collaboration opportunities), implementing policies and practices that will facilitate smooth student transitions (program entry, subject area transitions, and program exit), and designing parental involvement activities that will appeal to language minority parents (at home and school).

Additionally, an administrator needs to know the research in the area of effective instructional/assessment strategies for ELLs and the efficient use of standards-based data in order to serve as an instructional leader. Such knowledge allows the administrator to coach or direct teachers in creating and sustaining classroom environments that result in maximum academic achievement and linguistic progress for ELLs in the building or the program. This information also helps the administrator to accurately interpret student performance data in a way that has a meaningful impact on instruction and to communicate the data to a variety of stakeholders. Also, the administrator who is knowledgeable in these areas is a more effective and credible role model for staff as he or she demonstrates in his or her daily professional life what matters most in the education of ELLs.

Finally, an administrator needs to know the Federal and state law as it applies to ELLs. Many administrators are well versed in the legal requirements and legislation and court decisions pertaining to special education students. The law in relation to ELLs is less prescriptive and less prolific than the law in relation to special education. However, it does set minimum standards for education for ELLs and ensures the protection of the civil rights of language-minority students; it is therefore essential for an administrator to know this law.

The operating principles listed at the beginning of this essay set the foundation for the creation and maintenance of an effective program for all students. Knowledge and skills in the areas of second language acquisition; the process of acculturation; research in instruction/assessment strategies; and knowledge of relevant legislation, rules, and regulations move those principles into a cohesive and productive program for ELLs. *Perfect Match* (see www.thecenterweb.org/irc/ for information on this staff development program) pulls these principles, knowledge, and skills together to guide leadership teams in the creation of an optimal ELL program.

■ **What kinds of knowledge and skills do general education teachers, English as a second language teachers, bilingual teachers, and support staff need to implement an effective program for English language learners?**
JOANN (JODI) CRANDALL with HOLLY STEIN and JOHN NELSON

We begin by looking at the knowledge and skills needed by all teachers; then we address each of the specific categories of teachers, indicating what knowledge and skills they are likely to have as well as those for which they are likely to need special professional development. Finally, we discuss some special considerations for school personnel (guidance counselors, school secretaries, other support staff). We also provide a list of suggestions for professional development activities to promote better understanding and skills for providing effective instruction for English language learners (ELLs).

As indicated in Crandall (2000, p. 285), "there is substantial agreement within the educational community regarding the knowledge, skills, and attitudes (dispositions) that all teachers need to be able to effectively teach today's diverse students." One way of identifying these knowledge, skills, and attitudes is to look at the requirements for all teachers in states such as Florida or California, where there are large numbers of ELLs.

Florida requires all teachers to enroll in a university 3-credit course or participate in 60 hours of professional development focused on applied linguistics (first and second language acquisition and literacy development), cross-cultural issues, curriculum and materials, instructional methods, and assessment of ELLs. Elementary, reading, and secondary English teachers are required to enroll in 15 credit hours (one course in each of these five areas) or 300 professional development hours for their required ESOL (English for speakers of other languages) endorsement.

California (where more than one-third of all ELLs reside) requires all teachers to have an English Learner Authorization (or a Cross-cultural, Language, and Academic Development Certificate) on their teaching credential. To be awarded these, teachers need to know how and be able to apply principles of first and second language acquisition, literacy development, and effective instruction and assessment in teaching ELLs in their classes. This includes knowing how to select and adapt materials (including materials in the primary language) and how to use teaching strategies that support ELL's learning of English and subject matter content.

The following, then, are topics for pre-service teacher education or professional development for those who are already teaching ELLs:

- Knowledge of first and second language acquisition and literacy development.
- Knowledge of differences in cross-cultural communication and educational experiences and expectations concerning the appropriate roles of teachers, learners, and parents in school, as well as strategies for linking instruction with language and literacy activities in the home and community.
- Strategies for adapting materials and instruction to accommodate differences in language and literacy development (methodology for teaching ELLs both academic content and English) and for use of primary language resources.
- Appropriate assessment strategies.

GENERAL EDUCATION TEACHERS

There is a growing gap in the background, educational experiences, and expectations between teachers and the students in their classrooms. While national and state accreditation of teacher education programs may emphasize the importance of diversity and the need to "differentiate instruction" (which often translates as a need to provide for special education students), the majority of teachers have had little preparation for teaching students whose languages, cultures, and educational experiences differ substantially from their own. Thus, most mainstream teachers will need professional development in the following:

- Knowledge of how ELLs acquire and develop their first and second languages.
- Knowledge of how ELLs develop first and second language literacy.
- Knowledge of cross-cultural differences in communication.
- Skills in adapting instruction to accommodate students of differing levels of English proficiency (sometimes referred to as sheltered instruction, or specially designed academic instruction in English (SDAIE); see Echevarria & Graves, 1998; Fairbairn & Jones-Vo, 2010).
- Skills in providing instruction that is appropriate for different learning styles (oral/aural, visual, kinesthetic; a preference for working alone or in groups).
- Skills in conferencing with parents who may not speak English (such as finding and working with an interpreter) and who may have different expectations about the appropriate roles and responsibilities of parents and teachers in the education of their children.
- Skills in assessing learning (often referred to as "accommodations") that provide ELLs with an opportunity to demonstrate their understanding in a variety of ways, without relying on oral or written English that is above their level of the proficiency.
- Knowledge of the types of English as a second language (ESL) or bilingual programs and services offered to students and skills in working collaboratively with these teachers in co-planning or co-teaching lessons.

ESL TEACHERS
Novice ESL teachers usually have at least an undergraduate degree in TESOL (Teachers of English to Speakers of Other Languages) or, more typically, a graduate degree, in which they will have developed at least the following;

- Knowledge of the structure of English (pronunciation, grammar, vocabulary, register, genre, and so on) and skills in teaching that English structure to ELLs.
- Skills in helping ELLs to develop oral (listening and speaking) and written (reading and writing) proficiency in English.
- Knowledge of first and second language acquisition theories and their relevance to teaching English, through English, to ELLs with different English proficiency levels (it is not necessary to speak a student's language to teach that student English).
- Knowledge of how to assess ELL student learning of both language and content.
- Knowledge of the contribution of a student's first language to the development of English language, literacy, and content learning.

- Knowledge of cross-cultural communication and differences in learning styles and some skills in creating lessons for learners with diverse learning styles.
- Knowledge of the basic laws and regulations governing the education of ELLs.

They will usually have had experience learning and using another language, and they may have lived abroad or in diverse communities where they became interested in ESL. Thus, they will be prepared to have learners from different language and cultural backgrounds in their classes and to accommodate different levels of English proficiency in their instruction. Like all novice teachers, however, they will need the following:

- Knowledge of the policies and procedures related to ELLs in the school and district, including intake and placement procedures, the types of programs and services offered, regulations governing standardized assessments (exemptions and accommodations), and reports required.
- Knowledge of specific responsibilities, including whom to report to (principal, district supervisor, other).
- Knowledge of state or district curriculum and standards related to instruction for ELLs.
- Knowledge of the content taught in mainstream classes (through curriculum guides for the mainstream content areas or review of instructional materials) and skills for integrating academic concepts, texts, tasks, and tests into ESL instruction.
- Skills to work collaboratively with mainstream teachers in co-planning, co-teaching, or previewing/reviewing content in ESL instruction that effectively integrates academic content into the language focus.
- Knowledge of resources available to ELLs and their families and skills in accessing these resources, including working with district staff, guidance counselors, and district staff.
- Skills in communicating with parents, families, and community members from diverse languages and cultures.
- Skills in managing classes with a seemingly continual intake and outflow of students (resulting from the mobility of immigrant students and the differences in the rate of development of English language proficiency).
- Skills in working with students who have experienced severe shock or trauma as victims of revolution or war.
- If teaching in more than one school, knowledge of responsibilities and skill in functioning without the support of a school or even a regular classroom.
- If teaching in an elementary school, knowledge of scheduling and skill in negotiating time for ESL instruction.
- If teaching in a middle or high school with ELLs who have limited prior schooling or literacy, including students from countries in which a Creole variety of English is spoken, skills in teaching initial

literacy in English (Crandall, 2003; Crandall & Greenblatt, 1999; Hamayan, 1994).

Veteran ESL teachers will have most of the same knowledge and skills as novice ESL teachers, with the following exceptions: They may be teaching with methods and techniques that do not adequately focus on the academic concepts and language and literacy needs of their students, since a focus on integrating language and content instruction is relatively new in ESL teacher preparation. They may also be unaware of or resistant to standards developed for teaching ESL and will need focused attention on curriculum or lesson planning that reflects those standards.

Like all experienced teachers, they may also be suffering from burnout, which can be especially severe for teachers who have seen a constantly shifting population of learners from different parts of the world with different backgrounds and needs. Ways to provide needed professional development and refreshment include pairing these experienced teachers with novice ESL teachers, which can result in a mutually rewarding experience for both, and forming a relationship with a nearby university's TESOL teacher education program, which can bring teacher education faculty, teacher candidates, and graduate students in applied linguistics and TESOL as resources to the school (see Crandall, 2000). These teachers would also benefit from being able to attend a local or national TESOL conference.

BILINGUAL TEACHERS

Novice bilingual teachers who have a degree or endorsement in bilingual education have the knowledge and skills to teach content areas through the students' primary language. Being bilingual and bicultural themselves, they also share a great deal with their students and are able to provide emotional and educational support to students, who can continue to learn through their primary language while they are also learning English.

Novice bilingual teachers will have much the same knowledge and skills as ESL teachers but with the additional ability to teach through a student's primary language. They should also have preparation in teaching ESL, but they may have limited experience in doing so. They will need the following:

- Knowledge of the policies and procedures related to bilingual learners in the school and district, including intake and placement procedures, the types of programs and services offered, regulations governing standardized assessments (exemptions and accommodations), and reports required.
- Knowledge of state or district curriculum and standards related to instruction for bilingual students.
- Skills in working collaboratively with ESL and mainstream teachers, especially in transitioning students from bilingual classes to ESL, sheltered, or mainstream classes.
- Knowledge of bilingual resources available in the community and

skill in helping families, the school, and the district to access these resources, including help for guidance counselors, nurses, and other school staff who work with bilingual students.

- Skills in helping serve as a cultural interpreter for other school personnel.
- Skills in managing classes of students with diverse backgrounds, including differences in proficiency in the home language and English.
- Skills in working with students who have experienced severe shock or trauma as victims of revolution or war.

Like experienced ESL teachers, experienced bilingual teachers will need opportunities to learn new approaches and techniques for teaching bilingual learners and ways to align their instruction with new standards and assessments. They may also be experiencing teacher burnout and need a chance to work with a less experienced but enthusiastic bilingual teacher in a mentoring relationship from which both will benefit. They will also benefit from being able to attend local or national NABE (National Association for Bilingual Education) or other professional conferences, participate in teaching in-service programs focused on bilingual/bicultural students, or engage in other approaches to broaden their perspectives or provide an opportunity to share the wealth of their experiences with other teachers and school personnel.

SUPPORT STAFF

Effective schooling for ELLs requires understanding and assistance from all school personnel; however, most will have had little education or experience in dealing with students from a wide range of linguistic and cultural backgrounds. We discuss briefly some of the knowledge and skills needed by key personnel in the school. Experienced ESL, bilingual teachers in the school or district personnel who work with ELLs, and university faculty who teach in ESL or bilingual teacher preparation programs can all provide training and assistance to these personnel. If there is a large population of students from the same linguistic and cultural background, it may also be helpful to have a series of school-wide in-service programs focused on the language, cultural practices, educational experiences, and other important features of that community. A series of these programs will help all school personnel become more familiar and comfortable with the diversity of students in the school. Some schools have also provided classes in basic language instruction ("Spanish for Educators").

GUIDANCE COUNSELORS

Although guidance counselors have the knowledge and skills to interact with students and their families and to provide academic and other counseling, they are likely to have had almost no preparation for dealing with culturally and linguistically diverse students and families. They will need the following to help them tailor what they do for ELLs and their families:

- Understanding of basic differences in communication patterns (degrees of formality or informality, directness or indirectness, and so on) and the ability to present information in simple but noncondescending English.
- Knowledge of different educational systems and beliefs about appropriate roles and responsibilities of teachers and parents in schooling and skill in helping reluctant parents to participate in school events.
- Ability to work with an interpreter when needed.
- Knowledge of basic differences in beliefs and practices concerning mental and physical health and skills in interacting with culturally diverse students and families when discussing these topics.
- Knowledge of the ESL or bilingual programs offered in the school and skills in working with ESL and bilingual teachers in designing appropriate courses and schedules for ELLs.
- Knowledge of the educational systems and policies in the home countries of the ELLs or their parents and skill in helping both students and families to make the transition to American schools and colleges (Crandall & Greenblatt, 1999).
- For middle and high school, skills in helping ELLs to negotiate the complex path to college preparation, application, and financial aid, which may be especially difficult for students who are the first in their families to attend or even consider attending college (Crandall & Greenblatt, 1999; Cloud, Lakin, Leininger & Maxwell, 2010).

SECRETARIES

Secretaries are often the first to meet the families of ELLs, who may come to their neighborhood school to begin enrolling their children. These secretaries may have had no prior experience or training to help them in their role as the first point of contact for ELLs. They will need the following:

- Knowledge of the steps required for registration and placement of new ELLs.
- Knowledge of available resources for translation or interpretation within the school and the community, including a roster of language capabilities of all school personnel and students who can be called upon, especially for providing emergency translation or interpretation.
- Skills in greeting new parents and students and helping them feel welcome across language barriers.
- Skills in working with ESL or bilingual teachers.

NURSES

Nurses need to have a clear plan for how they will deal with emergency situations for all students, including ELLs. They will need the following:

- Knowledge of how to locate interpreters and translators for emergencies.
- Knowledge of whom to contact for translation of common forms or where translated forms are available.

- Knowledge of differences in medical practices and skill in explaining new medical practices to ELLs and their parents.

INSTRUCTIONAL AIDES/PEER EDUCATORS/TUTORS

Instructional aides are often a very diverse group. They may have high or limited levels of educational achievement; they may be members of the ELL's community or not. Depending on their background, they may be assigned different roles and will have different needs. It is important that administrators regularly assess the effectiveness of these indivudals, especially if they have a principal role in instruction of ELLs. At a minimum, they will need the following:

- Training in how to work to support ELLs in mainstream and ESL/bilingual classrooms.
- Basic knowledge of the cultural backgrounds of students and effective ways of interacting with them.
- Training in instructional strategies for teaching/tutoring ELLs that complement those used by the classroom teacher.

CUSTODIANS, BUS DRIVERS, CAFETERIA WORKERS

All of these personnel will need the following:

- Cultural awareness and sensitivity training to help them understand differences in student behavior.
- Basic instruction in modifying their language to make it understandable to ELLs (restating in simple language, demonstrating, using gestures, enlisting the aid of someone who speaks the student's language).

SOME PROFESSIONAL DEVELOPMENT APPROACHES FOR ALL TEACHERS

To help all teachers to develop greater understanding of and skills in meeting the needs of ELLs, the following professional development approaches may be useful:

- Peer observation, with mainstream and ESL or bilingual teachers observing each others' classes. This is particularly helpful if the teachers share some students and if the focus is on the students rather than the teachers.
- Collaborative curriculum development or lesson planning by ESL/bilingual and mainstream teachers. This is an excellent summer in-service program in which teachers work closely together and learn from each other.
- Team teaching. Opportunities for ESL/bilingual and mainstream teachers to co-teach, especially in the upper grades, can provide opportunities for teachers to learn instructional strategies from each other.

- Teacher inquiry or research groups. Small groups of teachers can be encouraged to engage in an extended program that focuses on better understanding the instructional needs of ELLs.
- Action research or reflective teaching groups in which both ESL and content teachers discuss their practice, modify their instruction, and share their results.
- Participation in a professional development school or similar internship site with a university that has a TESOL or bilingual teacher education program. This will increase the number of ESL or bilingual teachers in the school, provide opportunities for mainstream teachers to have an ESL/bilingual intern for part of the internship, and may lead to a longer-term collaboration focused on the needs of ELLs in the school.
- Courses co-taught by language and mainstream teachers or university teacher educators on topics such as how to teach and assess linguistically and culturally diverse students. It is important to develop collaborations among mainstream and language teachers to encourage sharing of knowledge, experiences, and concerns.
- Parent classes (especially in ESL) or after-school or weekend sessions for parents of ELLs and the ELLs focused on academic skills such as literacy or math, or community resources. Parents of ELLs may be reluctant to come to school or to participate in parent-teacher conferences or associations, but a program that focuses on their interests and needs can bring them to school and help make them feel more comfortable.
- Professional development programs focused on the culture and educational backgrounds of immigrant students in the school or district. These programs may include visits to community centers or students' homes, or a longer focus on the language, educational system, teacher and student roles and responsibilities, and parental expectations of the school. A good model for the latter is a semester-long program that brings students, members of the community, and teachers together in the learning process. Students can talk about their experiences, community members can explain cultural and educational traditions, and teachers participating in the program can tutor and learn from ELLs who need additional attention (see Crandall, 2003).

How do we ensure that teachers and staff have the professional development they need to implement an effective program for English language learners?
KIMBERLY THOMASSON

As the leader of a learning community with a population of English language learners (ELLs), one of my main concerns is that teachers have the knowledge to implement effective programs for ELLs. To ensure that teachers and staff have the professional development they need to implement such a program, there are four identified steps: needs assessment, timely and valuable professional development, evaluation, and reflection.

Once a clear vision is established, the next step is to find out what teachers and staff know and what they want to know. Conducting a needs assessment will provide valuable information that can be used to make a plan for professional development. By conducting a simple survey with questions about the kinds of training teachers have participated in and by asking what they want to know more about, staff needs can be quickly assessed. For training to be meaningful and valuable to teachers and staff, there should be a need and a desire for the information. After identifying the information that is needed by teachers and staff, administrators should arrange for high-quality professional development that will help teachers improve instruction for ELLs.

Time is always a challenge when it comes to professional development; therefore, short, structured, meaningful, and frequent staff development activities are most successful. Facilitators must create opportunities for teachers to internalize professional development so that information learned becomes a part of daily classroom practice. It is not just about sitting and receiving information. Information and new strategies learned in the course of professional development need to be implemented in the classroom. Teachers should have time to practice new skills and talk about how they have worked. For instance, professional development could be scheduled for two hours one afternoon a week for several weeks. Once a new strategy is presented, teachers are encouraged to practice it in their classrooms. During the following session the administrator and teachers talk about the implementation, address any concerns, and share successes. At the next session a new technique, and so on. This approach allows time for implementation in the classroom and continual support for teachers as they learn and try new approaches to teaching.

Once new practices for ELLs start being implemented in the classroom, it is time to evaluate whether or not those practices are having an impact on student achievement. Teachers are an integral part of this process. Their observations of student achievement, both academic and affective, give valuable information on student progress. The evaluation may include statewide test results, but other kinds of data gathered at the classroom level are likely to yield more meaningful information. Administrators should be cautious and remember that any changes worth making take time to become evident. After all, the goal is long-term student achievement.

Involving teachers in the entire professional development process is key to an effective ELL program, and it creates a vested interest among teachers in the success of ELLs in the school. Through this process, teachers become empowered. Empowerment is the way to ensure that teachers and

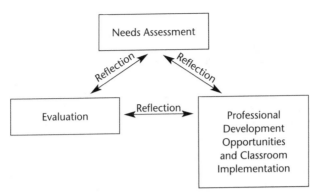

FIGURE 1.1 Fundamental processes in an effective professional development system.

staff have the professional development they need to implement effective programs for ELLs. The product is a self-sustaining system that is reflective, and a cycle for continuous improvement is created. This system is represented in Figure 1.1.

KELLY ESTRADA AND RENEA HAMILTON

In order to achieve the goals of an effective program for English language learners (ELLs), English as a second language (ESL) teachers, bilingual, and mainstream teachers must participate in professional development that equips them with the knowledge and skills they need to ensure that all of the ELLs in their classes develop comprehensive English language fluency, the types of academic English associated with specific content areas, and mastery of the content itself, whether it is in the native language or English.

START WITH THE END IN MIND

Effective professional development is outcomes based, where outcomes are tangible and result in significant improvements in student learning and achievement. We suggest setting attainable goals and designing a program of professional development that will provide teachers and other school personnel with the tools they need to meet these targets. It is equally important to solicit and support the participation of school administrators, who typically have a stake in closing achievement gaps between ELL and mainstream students. We have found that these administrators can provide the best grassroots leadership for schoolwide professional development efforts targeted to students such as ELLs.

BUILD CAPACITY

Since the numbers of ELLs are growing, sustaining and extending ELL professional development throughout the school and district setting is an opportunity for capacity building. Professional development for teachers of ELLs should target effective learning strategies that prepare all teachers to make grade-level content-area concepts comprehensible to ELLs from diverse language, literacy, educational, and cultural backgrounds. Such differentiated instruction and assessment strategies should result in improved achievement for all students, but they are especially effective for ELLs. Further, to be effective, professional development must be of the quality and duration to effect changes in classroom practice, changes that result in improvements in student learning. School administrators should therefore approach professional development as a long-term commitment. We recommend that schools develop an ongoing, sustained program of ELL professional development that incorporates core components of the school improvement plan. Using this approach, teachers will have the opportunity to translate professional development more effectively into classroom practice.

DEVELOP SHARED GOALS

Take advantage of the expertise represented in district teaching staff. For example, many districts employ full- or part-time ESL teachers who have specialized knowledge in the teaching of English to speakers of other languages. ESL teachers are excellent resources for content teachers and can provide high-quality support for lesson planning, instructional adaptation, and ELL student assessment. Also, we find that teachers work together best as special teams—small groups of teachers that engage in sustained professional development experiences with colleagues and expert others (university consultants, professional development providers). Various criteria can be used to form these teams—grade level, content area, high ELL classroom population, high desire for professional development experience, low ELL student performance in a content area, and so on. Once teams are assembled, they work closely (with the professional development provider if there is one) to develop a program that will complement and enhance existing or planned districtwide or schoolwide professional development activities. The ELL professional development program should do the following:

1. Address the highest priority needs with respect to improving ELL student outcomes.
2. Ensure that the focus of the ELL professional development program is an extension of the professional development focus for the entire school.
3. Target those "best practice" methods and strategies that will have the most impact on ELLs, both in their specialized classroom setting and in the mainstream and the wider school setting.

FOCUS ON PRACTICE

High-quality teacher professional development offers a variety of educational opportunities to learn, practice, and hone the skills necessary to improve ELL student learning. Thus, teachers need to participate in such professional development experiences as the following:

- Face-to-face sessions
- Classroom observation and feedback with respect to the focus of professional development
- Analysis of student outcomes (such as student work from lessons in which new strategies were implemented)
- Analysis of formative and summative student data (aligning instruction with classroom goals and objectives as well as with academic standards)
- Tracking of student progress over time in relation to instructional strategies implemented
- Participating in peer coaching and mentoring relationships

Teachers need ample time to modify, discuss, reflect upon, and analyze the results of changes in their practice. Various initiatives compete for the limited professional development time that is allocated for teacher learning. Therefore, it is critical that administrators provide ample time for teams of teachers to engage in all aspects of the professional development experience. This time should be set aside throughout the year or if possible over multiple years to allow for wider dissemination across the school or district and to promote in-depth exposure and broad coverage.

MARÍA TORRES-GUZMÁN AND VICTORIA HUNT

Assessment data can be used in various areas of decision making, including the assessment of professional development needs. When I (Torres-Guzmán) started collecting data on dual language programs in New York City, the school district and I decided to assess teacher needs in the areas of dual language education. We gave the teachers of all dual language schools a survey we had jointly constructed to ask them the following questions:

- Who are your students?
- What does your program look like?
- What instructional and evaluation issues are you facing?
- What is your educational and experiential background? How do you develop professionally, and in what areas?

Analysis of teachers' answers to these questions provided a grounded basis for decisions about program and professional development.

We looked at individual schools and at a subset of schools, and completed a comparative analysis of two types of schools. The subset consisted of literature-based dual language programs (that is, programs that are aligned with the research on effective dual language programs) that were stable. Stability was defined as being in existence for three or more years. Each of the three types of analysis gave us different information for decision making.

The data on individual schools gave administrators information about how the teachers in their schools characterized the students they worked with, whether they were on the same page with respect to the basic elements of the program they were implementing, what issues came up for them in instruction and in assessment, and how teachers saw their own development. The data from the subset of similar schools and the data from two different types of schools gave us information about the needs of dual language programs at different levels of development. Our analysis provided answers to the following important questions:

- Are the teachers' views of the students in the dual language program accurate when compared with the results that the school district provides? What would I (the administrator) have to communicate to the staff to get them to shift their understandings?
- If the way that the teachers described the dual language program in their school did not meet the literature-based criteria for dual language programs, what was obstructing the implementation of the dual language program? What else would be needed?
- Is a dual language program the best program option, given the staff and language distribution that was possible within the context of the school?
- Would it be more appropriate to acknowledge that the program implemented at the school was actually a second language/heritage language enrichment program rather than a dual language program?
- What instructional issues did the teachers raise, and how can I ensure staff development in the area of expertise they need?
- How might we transform the way staff development is done so that it becomes more teacher initiated?

Our analysis of teachers' answers to these kinds of questions led to the identification of three levels of staff development needs at the district level.

Schools that were in the beginning stages of a dual language program needed staff development on what a dual language program is and how to build one. Schools that were beyond the beginning stages needed to focus on instructional and assessment issues. Where the program was well developed instructionally, teacher-led, teacher-initiated types of professional development, such as teacher study groups and teacher inquiry projects, were important areas for staff development. When administrators use data on how their dual language programs are interpreted and implemented at the local school level, they can develop professional development activities that target the specific needs of teachers. Such a data-driven approach can ensure that schools that say they have dual language programs actually implement dual language programs that are aligned with research in the field.

With more established programs, ongoing reflection is necessary. Administrators and teachers must ensure that their program structure continues to focus on the needs of the students. Student needs change from year to year in a class, and larger demographic changes can affect a program over time. Further, any changes in state and city mandates also need to be considered. Therefore structures to support developing full bilingualism and biliteracy in both languages must be considered in our ever changing context.

Furthermore, opportunities for teachers to mentor each other in more established programs need to be created so that new teachers gain from the experiences of teachers who have been part of a program over time and who are often familiar with recurring challenges as well as with families that have multiple children in the school. New teachers are also a support for veteran teachers as they bring knowledge of recent studies from university programs and opportunities for dialogue about the why and how things are done. When there are few opportunities to support dual language or bilingual programs district-wide, mentor/mentee relationships that develop in a school are often essential in building long-term sustainability of the programs.

Finally, professional development in dual language programs in particular, or any program geared for language learners, must always consider language development and academic development at the same time. Ways to have academic development and language development support each other are crucial since bilingual learners are developing language proficiency at the same time as they are learning new concepts. Teaching the new language must be negotiated alongside the development of deeper academic understandings in literacy, math, and other content areas. Thus, professional development must address ways to support the development of a new language and academic progress simultaneously.

■ What are the implications of different ways of referring to these students (e.g., limited English proficient, English language learner, bilingual learners)?
OFELIA GARCÍA

Education systems throughout the world have increasingly turned their attention to developing the bilingualism of their students (see, for example, García, 2009a). This has to do with the increasing multilingualism of globalized societies, a product of advances in technology that facilitate communication and exchange of information, people, and goods. United

States classrooms are also experiencing an increase in bilingual students who speak languages other than English at home. And yet, instead of building on this national multilingualism, U.S. schools often focus only on students' monolingualism. Students who are bilingual, that is, those who are speakers of English and a language other than English (LOTE), are referred to as fluent English speakers, ignoring their bilingualism. And students who speak LOTEs and whose English is developing are referred to by the Federal government as limited English proficient (LEP) and by most educators as English language learners (ELLs).

An alternative way of referring to students whose English proficiency is developing is *emergent bilingual*, acknowledging that through school and through acquiring English, these children become bilingual. As I have argued elsewhere (García, 2009b; García and Kleifgen, 2010), when officials, school leaders, and educators ignore the bilingualism that these students can and must develop through schooling in the United States, they discount the home languages and cultural understandings of these children and assume their educational needs are the same as an English-speaking monolingual child. Thinking of these students as emergent bilinguals means that instead of being regarded as "limited" in some way or as mere "learners of English," as the terms limited English proficient and English language learner suggest, students are seen for their potential to become bilingual, and bilingualism begins to be recognized as a cognitive, social, and educational resource.

For school leaders and educators, working with these students as emergent bilinguals means holding higher expectations for these children and not simply remediating their limitations. The focus of administrators in creating school programs for emergent bilinguals should thus be the development of a challenging and creative curriculum that includes the development of academic English and literacy as an important component. In recognizing the emergent bilingualism of students, school leaders and educators of all kinds—whether bilingual, ESL, or mainstream teachers—would build on their strengths—their home languages and cultural practices.

Insisting that these children are emergent bilinguals also recognizes a bilingual developmental continuum instead of considering the children as falling within artificial categories of LEP/non-LEP or ELL/non-ELL. It reminds us that bilingual development is dynamic and interdependent (Cummins, 1979). That is, bilingualism is not linear—as the additive and subtractive models of bilingualism have led us to believe. Bilingualism is dynamic (for more on this, see García, 2009a) and bilingual development is uneven. Most of the time receptive abilities develop before productive abilities, but not always. And a bilingual student does not ever "have" two separate, autonomous languages. Instead, as a result of a challenging curriculum with committed educators, emergent bilingual students develop and use appropriate features in the school language to fulfill both social and academic needs, as they construct for themselves a single coherent communicative system and not just two separate languages.

In choosing to name these students, school administrators must be cognizant of the implications of naming these students as limited or as just learners of English. I have argued here that *emergent bilingual* is a term that better captures the richness and dynamism of the bilingual experience for these students, and that reminds educators to address their students' full linguistic and cultural complexity.

■ What levels of language proficiency in the language of instruction do bilingual teachers need to have in order to teach effectively in a bilingual program?
DAVID ROGERS

Since acquiring English is a primary goal (or one of the primary goals) of all programs for English language learners (ELLs), it is imperative that the instructor have a command of the English language as well as an intimate understanding of language acquisition, its steps, and the instructional strategies to facilitate acquisition. The teacher needs to make instructional input comprehensible, build on the student's background knowledge, and scaffold the academic concept and language of each lesson delivered.

If the ELL is fortunate to be supported by content instruction in his or her home language, the teacher delivering that instruction must possess native-like fluency and be academically proficient in the language of instruction. This is often overlooked as a primary concern in developing an effective program for the ELLs at school. Finding qualified instructors who can deliver quality instruction in the home language of ELLs can be a great challenge. Many teachers are socially fluent in the native language of their ELLs but do not possess the academic language or experience needed to be instructionally effective in that language.

Above all, the instructor who has the requisite native fluency and academic language level must have a clear understanding of the educational model (bilingual or ESL) selected by the school and must to be able to vary the use of the student's two languages in a way that fits into the long-term language plan for that student.

New Mexico offers the *La Prueba* examination for Spanish fluency, which all teachers must pass in order to complete and receive their bilingual endorsement. This endorsement permits them to deliver instruction in the language of their endorsement. The fifteen subtests of this comprehensive examination include fluency, grammar/conventions of the language, regional dialects, academic levels of language, and so on. It is not uncommon for a teacher to retake this test in order to successfully complete at least three of the four components of the test. Referred to as a "progressive" test, once the test is successfully completed, the site administrator can be confident that the teacher possesses a good foundation for instructing in the language. Instructor Proficiency Examinations now exist for both Navajo and Pueblo certified language instructors. There is also an Alternative Certificate for nondegree Native American language speakers teaching language and culture in New Mexico schools. This certificate is available for all tribes in the state.

■ How should administrators evaluate teachers when they are teaching in a language other than English?
JACK FIELDS

Few tasks required of a teacher supervisor are more intimidating than having to evaluate a teacher who is teaching children in a language other than English when the evaluator is a monolingual English speaker. Too often the evaluator opts to limit his or her observations to classes of English as a second language (ESL), which is unfair both to the teacher and to the children being served. Limiting observations to ESL lessons does not provide a full spectrum of observations in the process of retention or dismissal. As a bilingual program director working with many such principals and supervisors, I have identified a number of preparations and strategies that can help administrators provide more effective and relevant observations when first language instruction is being observed.

PREPARATION
Smaller districts with fewer resources usually depend on the building administrator to make evaluative decisions regarding staff. Even in large school districts where an ESL or bilingual director is employed by the district, evaluations leading to continuing employment or dismissal are usually the responsibility of the building administrator. This often makes administrators uncomfortable and threatens teachers, who feel they are being evaluated by someone who may not understand bilingual/English language learner (ELL) instruction. The risk of continuing the employment of an ineffective teacher because of discomfort with the language of instruction only endangers the teaching of more children for years to come.

The following *program questions* need to be answered before observing the teacher:

1. What is the philosophy and program design that are being implemented in your district?
2. What are the entry and exit criteria for children being served?
3. How is the appropriate language of instruction determined, and who determines it? (In my first job as a teacher, I simply switched

to Spanish whenever a supervisor entered the room, and they rarely stayed long. They almost never asked what I was doing.) In many rooms, the appropriate language of instruction may be different for different students in different subjects.

4. What academic performance does the English-only teacher expect from students transitioned into their rooms?

The following *classroom questions* need to be asked of the teacher when possible before the observation:

1. **The Observation**: What are the objectives of the lesson? How does the lesson fit into a series of lessons or objectives that are being taught? What activities will be used? How will the teacher evaluate the outcome of the instruction? If the language of instruction is a language that you do not know, having this information in advance will help you better understand what is going on in the room during the observation.

2. **The Students**: What assessment has been made of the students to establish the need for the instruction? What prior experience have the children had in preparation for the class? What special needs, if any, exist in the class? Obtain a seating chart so that in the follow-up conference you can refer to specific children in context with activities or behavior observed.

3. **The Teacher**: What professional preparation or teaching experience has the teacher had before entering the classroom? This background information may be helpful in developing later recommendations and providing support that the teacher needs.

OBSERVATION

The evaluator should arrive prior to the observation time to be able to observe how the class is initiated. Nothing is more frustrating for the teacher than the feeling that the evaluator missed something important at the beginning of the lesson that affected the observation later during the class.

Good instruction is normally good instruction, regardless of the language. We want to see classrooms where children are interactively involved in the lesson. The evaluator should observe children and their reactions to the lesson or the presentation. For conferencing later, the evaluator should also remember to make notes regarding specific situations using the seating chart and time.

BEHAVIOR

Does the children's behavior reflect that they know the class rules and follow them? Does the teacher have to constantly remind them of rules (not yet established or new for the visitor)? Do the children appear to be safe and comfortable in their interaction in the classroom? Or are they afraid to participate?

INSTRUCTION

Look for the qualities you see in any good classroom. Who does most of the talking? Are children asked to explain or clarify? Be aware of the length of children's responses. Short answers usually are an indication that lower-level questions are being asked. Do many or all children have the opportunity to participate? After an assignment is given, are the children able to do it? Move around the room when children are doing seatwork and ask children what they are doing. Observe the support the teacher offers children when they are doing seatwork.

CONFERENCE

Have the conference as soon after the observation as possible. This will allow the teacher to respond more meaningfully when you ask about the class. Ask teachers to evaluate their own lesson by sharing what worked well, what they would change, and so forth. The best teachers learn to evaluate their own and their students' work. Remember that "bilingual teachers" are often hired for their language skills and may have little background in research and instruction of ELLs. Much of the responsibility of the evaluator will fall in the area of determining what kind of a learner the teacher is and making decisions about the growth potential of the candidate and whether or not the candidate shows sufficient promise in his or her professional development for continuing employment. It is critical that the evaluator communicate a willingness to support the candidate in professional growth, using the evaluation process as a tool.

Begin the conference by having the teacher review the lesson plan (preparation) and the lesson implementation. Ask the teacher to share his or her own observation of the lesson or class. It is very important for teachers to develop the skill and willingness to self-evaluate. Using your notes and seating chart, ask the teacher to explain events or activities that were of concern to you or that you did not understand. If you are unsure of whether or not the appropriate language was being used in a particular lesson, ask the teacher to explain why the language was used or what other issues interfered with the teacher's doing what ideally should have been done. If you lack confidence in the teacher's answers, contact someone with expertise in the field so that your facility and students will develop appropriate instructional designs.

■ What are recommended resources for the professional development of teachers who work with English language learners?
NANCY CLOUD

One of the challenges administrators face in providing professional development to teachers and other personnel is locating resources for the great variety of staff development that is possible. Staff development can take many forms, including the following:

- Specialized graduate course work
- Attendance at conferences, learning institutes, or workshops
- On-site, sustained staff development provided by district experts or external consultants
- Networking among schools or programs
- Mentoring or peer coaching in classrooms
- School-based collegial circles or study groups
- Viewing of webinars and podcasts on topics of interest
- Hands-on working sessions among colleagues designed to improve assessment or curriculum

Staff development initiatives work best when they are focused on particular school improvement goals and in a format that would best respond to the personnel's level of expertise, role, and student population served. Teachers and other personnel need to feel that they are receiving valuable information that is advancing their practice. Quality staff development needs to be reality based, practical, and delivered from trusted sources. Administrators also need to provide incentives for participation in professional development, such as financial support (paying the cost of conference registration or course work), release time, or professional recognition (letters for their personnel file, acknowledgements in district newsletters).

Where can busy administrators go to locate useful resources for their local staff development purposes? The following listing is designed to assist with this process.

GRADUATE COURSE WORK AND NATIONAL BOARD CERTIFICATION

Graduate programs and course work can be used to substantially advance the knowledge or skills of assessment and instructional personnel, sometimes resulting in new teaching endorsements or licenses. Often course work can be offered on-site through continuing education at a reduced cost. As an additional incentive, cost-sharing arrangements can be implemented in which participants pay a portion of the cost and the school or district pays a portion. Teachers of English to Speakers of Other Languages (TESOL, www.tesol.org) maintains a directory of teacher education programs with course work specific to working with ELLs. Beyond delivering course work, college faculty working in these programs might also serve as partners for district- or school-based initiatives.

Another option for expert teachers is to seek national board certification. The National Board for Professional Teaching Standards (NBPTS, www.nbpts.org) has developed standards in English as a new language (ENL) for this purpose. Administrators can support teachers by providing access to support groups while teachers prepare their portfolios, release time to complete the requirements, or financial rewards upon completion.

PROFESSIONAL ASSOCIATIONS

A variety of associations provide professional development resources, most notably the National Association for Bilingual Education (NABE, www.nabe.org) and TESOL (www.tesol.org). The corresponding state affiliates of these two international associations offer parallel in-state professional development opportunities. In addition to conferences and institutes, professional associations provide Web-based discussion forums, online courses, and a variety of published professional development resources. Associations also exhibit professional development and classroom resources at conferences that can support local professional development initiatives, and they publish periodicals focused on best practices in teaching and assessment. Some journals are now offering continuing education units for reading and responding to topic-focused issues. All of these mechanisms can be used as specialized sources of professional development.

Other associations with specialized resources to tap include the following:

- The International Reading Association (IRA, www.ira.org)
- The National Council of Teachers of English (NCTE, www.ncte.org)
- The National Association for the Education of Young Children (NAEYC, www.naeyc.org)
- The Council for Exceptional Children (CEC, www.cec.sped.org), which periodically offers a Symposium on the Education of Culturally and Linguistically Diverse Exceptional Students)

STATE DEPARTMENTS OF EDUCATION AND FUNDED CENTERS

State education departments receive funding specifically earmarked for professional development. In addition to statewide institutes and workshops, state-funded personnel may be available to conduct in-house trainings. Grant- and foundation-funded centers also provide professional development resources. For example, the National Clearinghouse for English Language Acquisition (NCELA, www.ncela.gwu.edu) of the Office of English Language Acquisition, Language Enhancement and Academic Achievement for Limited English Proficient Students (OELA, U.S. Department of Education); the Center for Applied Linguistics/CAL (www.cal.org); and the Center for Research on Education, Diversity and Excellence (CREDE, http://crede.uscs.edu) are a few of the funded centers to offer online support, published materials, and professional development resources (videos, CD-ROMs) or special training events. A wonderful site for teachers, parents, and ELL program administrators is Colorin Colorado. It is filled with a wealth of resources, including topical webcasts delivered by national experts in the field that could be useful for in-house or online professional development. (www.colorincolorado.org).

SCHOOL/PROGRAM VISITS AND DEMONSTRATION TEACHING

Sometimes the best way to offer professional development is to visit a school or program in your region known to be effective. In this manner teachers and administrators can witness firsthand the type of assessment, curriculum, and instruction that makes a difference in the achievement of ELLs and can ask questions that help them better implement school-improvement initiatives. Similarly, demonstration teaching sessions conducted in live classrooms can often clarify for teachers how to implement research-based teaching approaches better than merely reading about them. Video-recorded teaching demonstrations also serve this purpose.

PUBLISHERS OF PROFESSIONAL DEVELOPMENT MATERIALS

Professional reading is a main contributor to professional development whether done in a collegial circle, in conjunction with credit-bearing course work, or independently. It would be impossible to mention all the publishers of this type of material, but, in addition to the professional associations and funded centers already mentioned, some representative publishers specializing in this type of material include Heinemann (www.heinemann.com), Hampton-Brown (www.hampton-brown.com), Pearson Education (www.pearsoned.com/us-school/index.htm), and Caslon Publishing (www.caslonpublishing.com). Publishers also offer professional development to schools and districts through consultants and representatives, particularly as it relates to their curriculum materials. Some offer online courses around their professional books or video-taped series designed to advance teaching skills in classrooms (see for example http://www.pearsonschool.com/index.cfm?locator=PSZ0B5, http://pearsonschool.com/index.cfm?locator=PSZ0Ay, and http://www.heinemann.com/PD/videowebbased.aspx).

SURVEY FOR REFLECTION AND ACTION

This survey reflects the guiding principles for effective leadership and professional development that were articulated in the Introduction to the chapter. Read the following statements to guide your survey of the leadership structure that is in place in your school and the professional development opportunities that are available to your staff. Indicate the extent to which each of the following applies to your school: DK—don't know; 1—strongly disagree; 2—disagree; 3—agree; 4—strongly agree. At the end of the survey, write down one to three strengths and future possibilities you identified through your school-based leadership and professional development survey. Then identify one to three concrete actions that you can take to improve the leadership structure and professional development opportunities at your school.

Everyone who works with the ELLs/bilingual learners in our schools has developed the expertise and practices they need to ensure optimal learning environments for these students within the context of the work that they do.

- Superintendent and school board   DK 1 2 3 4

- Central administration   DK 1 2 3 4

- School-based administration   DK 1 2 3 4

- Instructional coaches (e.g., literacy, math)   DK 1 2 3 4

- General education teachers   DK 1 2 3 4

- Bilingual education teachers   DK 1 2 3 4

- ESL teachers   DK 1 2 3 4

- Resource teachers (e.g., special education, reading)   DK 1 2 3 4

- Support staff (e.g., counselors, secretaries, nurses)   DK 1 2 3 4

- Parents and other household members   DK 1 2 3 4

- Community liaisons   DK 1 2 3 4

District and school-based leadership explicitly consider the research base on ELL education as well as data about our ELLs/bilingual learners (i.e., information about ELL/bilingual learner background strengths and needs; evidence of student learning from performance-based assessments) as an integral part of all decision making.

- Educational policy decisions in our district/schools explicitly   DK 1 2 3 4
  consider the data about our ELLs/bilingual learners relative to
  the research base on ELL education *before* policies are made.

- Curriculum decisions in our district/schools explicitly consider   DK 1 2 3 4
  the research base on ELL education as well as data about our
  ELLs/bilingual learners *before* the curriculum is selected.

- Decisions about instructional programming for ELLs/bilingual   DK 1 2 3 4
  learners explicitly consider the research base on ELL education
  as well as data about our ELLs/bilingual learners *as an integral
  part* of the general programming decisions that are made in
  our schools and throughout our district.

- Decisions about student assessments and school/district   DK 1 2 3 4
  accountability systems explicitly consider the research base on
  ELL education and data about our ELLs/bilingual learners' growth
  and achievement before assessment and accountability systems
  are institutionalized districtwide.

Knowledgeable collaborative leadership teams drive the professional development opportunities at our school and throughout our school district.

- Educators in our school/district engage in frequent, continuous, and increasingly concrete talk about student learning and teaching practice. DK 1 2 3 4

- Educators have developed a shared language and common practices that focus on improved instruction and achievement of ELLs/bilingual learners as an integral part of the work that they do. DK 1 2 3 4

- Educators use data on actual ELL/bilingual learner/all student learning (e.g., formative assessments) to guide professional development. DK 1 2 3 4

- Educators use data on actual teaching practice (e.g., videotapes and/or from observations of teaching) to focus professional development. DK 1 2 3 4

- Educators have ongoing opportunities to observe each other's practice with ELLs/bilingual learners/all students. DK 1 2 3 4

- Educators have opportunities to provide feedback about their practices with ELLs/bilingual learners/all students to each other in a supportive, nonthreatening environment. DK 1 2 3 4

- Educators cooperatively plan lessons, programs, materials, practices, and assessments for ELLs/bilingual learners/all students. DK 1 2 3 4

- Educators cooperatively review and evaluate lessons, programs, materials, practices, and assessments for ELLs/bilingual learners/all students. DK 1 2 3 4

Our professional development is comprehensively planned, focused in its delivery, and sustained over time.

- Educators in our school/district regularly assess professional development strengths and needs based on new developments in the field, reflective conversations about practice, evidence of student performance, and observation of teaching practice. DK 1 2 3 4

- We have developed comprehensive individual and collective   DK 1 2 3 4
  professional development plans with realistic and attainable
  goals to address our professional needs.

- Professional development focuses attention on specific   DK 1 2 3 4
  strategies that target specific goals and that are to be
  implemented in practice.

- We have opportunities to implement new strategies in our   DK 1 2 3 4
  practice.

- We have the opportunity to observe the implementation of   DK 1 2 3 4
  new strategies (self and/or peer observation).

- We reflect on the implementation of new strategies, using   DK 1 2 3 4
  classroom-based data on student learning and teaching practice
  to ground and inform our reflective conversations.

- We continuously identify professional development needs, and   DK 1 2 3 4
  the cycle begins again.

Strengths of our school district/school leadership and professional development

1. _____
2. _____
3. _____

Future possibilities

1. _____
2. _____
3. _____

Action steps

1. _____
2. _____
3. _____

2

HOW CHILDREN LEARN IN TWO (OR MORE) LANGUAGES

GUIDING PRINCIPLES

- Our instruction takes into account that English language learners (ELLs) are learning abstract content-area concepts in a nonproficient language and within a cultural context that may be unfamiliar to them.
- We make our pedagogical decisions based on the fact that it takes time for all students, particularly ELLs, to acquire the academic language and literacies they need for school success.
- Because a strong home language (including home language literacies) provides a solid foundation for cognitive development, academic achievement, and language and literacy development in English, we draw on and support the home languages of our ELLs/bilingual learners to the greatest degree possible at our school.
- Our programs and practices reflect an understanding of and sensitivity to the ways that culture influences all aspects of learning and teaching at school.
- Our program for ELLs/bilingual learners allows for variation in the ways that these students acquire English (and other languages) and achieve academically at school.

INTRODUCTION

Questions regarding how children learn in two or more languages must be at the base of any educational decision made about ELLs/bilingual learners at school. It is essential that program planning, curricula, and instructional strategies be based explicitly on what we know about how students learn a second language, how they develop literacies in a second language, and how they develop cognitively and learn academic content through a second language.[1] Yet many schools

---

1. Researchers and practitioners in the United States, the United Kingdom, and Canada have traditionally used the term *second language* when referring to *second language acquisition* research and *English as a second language (ESL)* programs, classes, or instruction. We increasingly find the term *additional language* replacing the term *second language* in the United Kingdom and parts of Canada, reflecting awareness that a student may actually be acquiring a third, fourth, or fifth language, or acquiring two or more languages simultaneously rather than sequentially. The use of the term *additional* also emphasizes an additive stance toward multilingualism in which the acquisition of a second or additional language does not lead to the loss of a first or home language. Given our primary focus on the United States context in this book, we retain the term *second language* in the introductions to chapters because of its continued prominence in the field today.

end up with policies and regulations that go against what is known about the most effective ways for children to develop proficiency in English, the language of instruction, while they are developing cognitively and acquiring knowledge and skills in the curriculum content areas through their second language.

For example, some districts restrict the time that an ELL may receive specialized English as a second language (ESL) support to one year. Yet, we know that it takes many children eight to ten years to develop the full range of oral and written academic English necessary to succeed in school (e.g., the language of mathematics, the language of language arts, the language of science, the language of social studies). Other districts prevent ELLs from learning the general education curriculum through their stronger primary or home language[2] while they are acquiring social, instructional, and academic language and literacies across content areas in English. Yet, we know that students who are in the early stages of second language acquisition develop cognitively and learn new abstract content-area concepts more effectively through their stronger primary language. Some districts, perhaps because of pressure from high-stakes testing, expect all students to master the same academic concepts at the same time (although there is no empirical evidence to support this approach). Because it takes more time for ELLs to develop advanced levels of academic English in all content areas than current accountability requirements permit, many ELLs/bilingual learners are deemed at-risk academically and given inappropriate remedial instruction. Yet, many students who do not demonstrate proficiency on standardized achievement tests in English, given more time and better instruction, would surely succeed a little later than their English-proficient peers.

Regardless of whether the instructional program for ELLs/bilingual learners provides some instruction in a language other than English (as in bilingual education programs) or uses English as the medium of instruction (as in sheltered English programs or in general education classes that serve ELLs), practitioners and policymakers must pay heed to how children learn in two languages. Not to do so is counterproductive at best.

This chapter briefly introduces administrators and leadership team members to research on how children learn in two languages so that they can look critically at Federal and state policies and accountability requirements and make principled decisions about the instructional programs they develop and implement for the ELLs/bilingual learners at their schools. Although there is considerable confu-

---

2. We find the terms *primary language, first language, native language, mother tongue, home language,* and *dominant language* used to refer to the language other than English in the linguistic repertoire of an ELL/bilingual learner. However, these terms reflect assumptions that may or may not accurately represent students' lived experiences. For example, in cases of simultaneous language acquisition, bilingual learners acquire more than one language at a time, calling into question what language is their first language. In cases of subtractive bilingualism, bilingual learners lose proficiency in their home language(s) while they acquire English, calling into question whether their first language is their dominant language. We use the term *home language* when we focus on the context of language use, and the term *stronger* or *primary language* when we focus on language proficiency.

sion and controversy in schools today about ELLs/bilingual learners, quite a bit is known about how children learn in two languages. We know why it takes so long for ELLs/bilingual learners to develop the academic language and literacies they need for academic success. We know that knowledge and skills developed in the primary language in oral and literacy domains transfer to English, the second language. We know that students can more readily learn abstract, cognitively challenging content-area concepts through their stronger language, and that ELLs must continue to develop cognitively while they are acquiring English in order to achieve academically at school. We know that universal concepts learned in one language do not need to be learned again in another language because they transfer. We know that it is easier to learn to read in a language that one is orally proficient in. Our understanding of this theoretical foundation has significant implications for how we teach content-area concepts to ELLs, and when and how we introduce second language literacy to these students. We also know that it is easier to acquire an additional language, and to learn in that language, in a familiar cultural context. Thus, cultural relevance must be central to the ELL classroom and school.

The responses offered by the experts in this chapter and throughout this guide are based on research on how younger and older students learn in two or more languages. To help administrators and leadership team members apply these research findings to their classrooms and educational programs, the chapter concludes with a Survey for Reflection and Action. Educational leaders can use this survey in their schools to determine whether their policies, programs, practices, and assessments are theoretically sound, and to address any discrepancies they find.

■ How long does it take for an English language learner to become proficient in a second language?
JIM CUMMINS

This question seems fairly straightforward until we probe a little deeper into what we mean by proficient and what aspects of second language proficiency we are talking about.

WHAT IS LANGUAGE PROFICIENCY?
As all administrators who have to deal with state standards and high-stakes assessments know, the term *proficient* can refer to widely different levels of actual competence, depending on the test and state standards. What counts as proficient in one state on a reading assessment, for example, may be far from proficient in another state. For purposes of thinking about English language learners' (ELLs') academic progress in English, however, we can define proficient in relation to the level of English competency of their native English-speaking peers. So the question can be rephrased as, How long does it take ELLs to catch up to their native English-speaking peers in English proficiency?

This brings us to the issue of what we mean by English proficiency. Although we commonly talk about "learning English" as though English proficiency were a unitary construct, we can all intuitively recognize some clear distinctions within that notion of English proficiency. These distinctions are apparent whether we are talking about native speakers of a language or second language learners. Specifically, we know that *conversational fluency* is quite different from *academic proficiency* in a language. The fast talkers in our classes are not necessarily the best readers. We also know that there are major differences between many of the technical or rule-governed aspects of a language, such as the rules for sound-symbol relationships (phonics), spelling, grammar, discourse, and so on, and the kinds of skills involved in reading comprehension. Thus, we can begin to distinguish three very different aspects of language proficiency: *conversational fluency*, *discrete language skills*, and *academic language proficiency*.

HOW LONG DOES IT TAKE FOR ENGLISH LANGUAGE LEARNERS TO CATCH UP ACADEMICALLY?

Very different time periods are required for ELLs to catch up to their peers in each of the three dimensions of proficiency. It usually takes about one to two years for students to become reasonably fluent in conversational English. About the same time is typically required for many ELLs in the early grades to acquire basic decoding skills in English to a level similar to that of their English-speaking classmates of similar socioeconomic background. However, research studies conducted in several countries show that second language learners usually need at least five years to catch up to native English speakers in academic English. Sometimes the catch-up period is much longer. Research conducted in Israel, for example, showed that Russian and Ethiopian immigrant students required about nine years to catch up to their peers in Hebrew academic skills.

These observations bring us to the next questions: What exactly *is* academic English? Why does it take so long for ELLs to catch up in this dimension of language?

WHAT IS ACADEMIC ENGLISH?

Academic English is the language of school success. As students progress through the grades, they are required to read, write, and talk about increasingly complex texts in the content areas of the curriculum (science, math, social studies, literature). Academic language becomes increasingly complex after grades three and four. The complexity of academic language reflects the following:

- The difficulty of the concepts that students are required to understand.
- The vocabulary load in content texts, which may include many low-frequency and technical words (primarily from Latin and Greek sources) that are rarely used in typical conversation.

- Increasingly sophisticated grammatical constructions and discourse structures that, again, are almost never used in everyday conversational contexts. By the upper grades of elementary school, students encounter the frequent use of the passive voice, embedded clauses, and extended noun phrases in a wide range of genres.

Not only are students required to read this language, they must also use it in writing reports and essays and in other forms of homework.

WHY DOES IT TAKE SO LONG?

One reason that catching up in academic English is challenging for ELLs, then, is the complexity of academic language. A second reason is that they are trying to catch up to a moving target. Native English-speaking students are not standing still waiting for ELLs to catch up. Every year, they make gains in reading, writing, and vocabulary abilities. So ELLs have to run faster to bridge the gap. In fact, in order to catch up within six years, ELLs must make fifteen months' gain in every ten-month school year. The average student makes just ten months' gain in every ten-month school year.

HOW CAN WE SUPPORT STUDENTS IN ACQUIRING ACADEMIC ENGLISH?

Understanding the nature of academic language points to some of the ways we can help students acquire it. If academic language is found in texts rather than in typical conversations, then we have to ensure that students are given ample opportunities and encouragement to read extensively. Thus, an administrative priority should be to ensure that school and classroom libraries are well stocked with engaging books. Encouraging students to write for authentic purposes is also crucial. Even recently arrived ELLs can create dual language books by writing stories or accounts of their experiences, initially in their first language and then working with peers, teachers, volunteers, older bilingual students, and even technology (Babel Fish or Google language tools) to translate and adapt their writing into English. (Two good web-sites with examples are http://schools.peel schools.org/1363/pages/dual.aspx and http:// www.multiliteracies.ca). Finally, some technology tools may be useful. An example is the the e-Lective Language Learning program, which provides supports to enable students to access the curriculum and to harvest the language of academic texts (http://www.dyned.com/products/el/).

H. GARY COOK

Two critical notions are behind these questions: "What do we mean by proficiency in English?" and "What do we mean by how long?" In the context of the No Child Left Behind Act of 2001 (NCLB), proficiency in English refers to the ability to (1) meet the proficient level of achievement on state assessments, (2) successfully achieve in classrooms where the language of instruction is English, and (3) participate fully in society. The presumption made by NCLB, and one supported by research, is that students proficient in English are more likely to be successful in school and in the community than those who are not proficient. We should also understand that when NCLB refers to English proficiency it means academic English language proficiency, which is the language needed to successfully communicate at school and in the workplace. NCLB requires that states use their English language proficiency (ELP) assessments (in part or whole) to determine English language proficiency. Specifically, the focus of ELP assessments is to evaluate the academic language needed to participate in school curricula that are based on states' academic content standards.

"How long" generally refers to how long in years, specifically school years. At the outset it should be understood that learning another language takes time, substantial time. In a study examining how long it takes to attain English language proficiency in two large California school districts, Hakuta (2000) writes,

> The clear conclusion emerging from these data sets is that even in two California districts that are considered the most successful in teaching English to LEP students, oral proficiency takes 3 to 5 years to develop, and academic English proficiency can take 4 to 7 years (p. iii).

In a national study on English language learners, Thomas & Collier (2002) found that there is not just one timeframe required for English learners (ELs) to attain proficiency. In their work, they compared how well English learners performed on academic content assessments compared with grade-level peers. They found that many factors determined how long it takes to perform like grade-level peers (a distant proxy for English proficient), e.g., exposure to education in the first language, type and quality of language instructional program, type of parental support, how English learners are supported when mainstreamed. Akin to Hakuta's work, Thomas & Collier write that it could take up to seven years for English learners to perform similarly to grade-level peers depending upon student background. Cook, Boals, Wilmes, & Santos (2008) analyzed ELP assessment data longitudinally across three states in order to support the establishment of annual measureable achievement objectives (AMAOs). They construed a principle: *lower is faster, higher is slower* (p. 7) regarding growth in language proficiency. Students starting at lower proficiency levels grow faster than students at higher proficiency levels. Likewise, students in lower grades grow faster than students in higher grades.

The bar chart in Figure 2.1 shows the percent of students in grades 3 through 5 who attain a Bridging (Level 5) score on the ACCESS for ELLs®

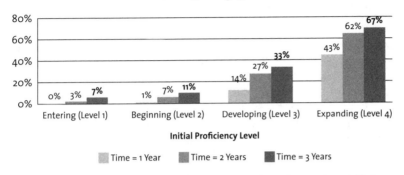

Grades 3 through 5

Initial Proficiency Level

■ Time = 1 Year   ■ Time = 2 Years   ■ Time = 3 Years

FIGURE 2.1 Percent of students in grades 3 through 5 who attain a Bridging (Level 5) score on the ACCESS for ELLs® assessment in a WIDA Consortium state.

assessment in a WIDA Consortium[3] state. Scores at Bridging or higher are used by many WIDA states to determine English proficiency. The chart displays four years of longitudinal data, starting from the 2005 school year. None of the students who started at the lowest proficiency level in 2005 (Entering) attained a Bridging score in one year. Only 3% attained this score in two years, and 7% attained it in three years. Even at the highest nonproficient level (Expanding), less than half of students (43%) attained a Bridging score in one year. As these data show, the language proficiency level a student starts at makes a difference in how long it takes a student to attain English proficiency.

Similar charts were created for other grade-level clusters in this state. As expected, students in low-grade clusters took shorter periods of time to attain a Bridging score; students in high-grade clusters took longer.

Back to our question: How long does it take for students who are English learners to become proficient in English? The answer is: it depends. It depends on the grade students start in and on their initial proficiency level. It also depends on their educational experience, their native language literacy, the type of language program they are in, parental involvement, and so on. Here are several rules of thumb to consider when asking the question, "How long?"

1. When looking at large numbers of students, across varying grades and proficiency levels, think up to seven years.
2. Younger students take less time.
3. Students at lower proficiency levels take longer.

3. WIDA (World Class Instructional Design and Assessment) is a consortium of states with the same set of ELP standards and assessments. ACCESS for ELLs® is the WIDA English language proficiency assessment for these states. For more information see www.wida.us.

4. Students' native language literacy and experience with education in their home country matters: The less, the longer.
5. The type and quality of language program matter.

There is a caveat to this discussion. The bar chart shown previously, Hakuta's findings, Thomas' & Collier's work, and Cook et al. describe what is observed. What is observed is not necessarily what should be. We can certainly do better. Maybe the timeframe to proficiency should be no more than five years. The optimal timeframe is yet unknown. But ultimately we must understand that what students start with influences how long it takes for them to develop English language proficiency.

■ What factors influence English language learners' success at school?
STEPHANEY JONES-VO and SHELLEY FAIRBAIRN

English language learners' (ELLs') success at school is impacted daily by a number of factors that influence whether the student receives consistent daily instruction appropriate for his/her language proficiency level and educational background, and whether the student feels welcome and at ease in the school community.

Administrators need to ensure that all teachers (not just the ESL or bilingual teachers) have the following information about the ELLs in their classes:

- **English language proficiency level:** One measure of English language proficiency (ELP) that all U.S. schools have is the ELP level of every ELL as determined through mandated ELP tests. The results of these tests include a composite ELP level and a separate level for each language domain (reading, writing, listening, speaking).[4] There are, of course, other ways to assess ELLs' proficiency in oral and written English.

  All teachers (general education, ESL/bilingual, literacy, and special education specialists) need to know what each of their ELLs can do in terms of reading, writing, listening, and speaking in order to provide appropriate instruction and assessment in *all* content areas. ELLs often have different ELP levels in different domains. For example, many ELLs' listening and speaking levels are higher than their reading and writing levels, which influences the kinds of instructional and assessment strategies that they need.

4. States use different English language proficiency standards and assessment systems (e.g., the WIDA Standards and ACCESS for ELLs are used by 26 states in the WIDA consortium; other states like California, Iowa, New York, and Texas use their own standards and assessments). All of these systems are based on research into stages of second language acquisition and academic English language and literacy development.

- **Educational/Literacy Background:** Academic achievement at school is about much more than English language proficiency. ELLs who have strong educational backgrounds possess a solid foundation on which their teachers can build. Students who have the benefit of first language (L1) literacy development are able to transfer that systematic knowledge/skill when learning the second language (L2). Alternatively, when a student of any age has not developed literacy in the L1 or has experienced gaps in her/his education, administrators must insist that teachers apply the same urgency and intensity often dedicated to teaching literacy skills to native English speakers in the early grades. This may call for special literacy programming designed for ELLs with low literacy skills or interrupted former schooling (as opposed to remedial instruction designed for native speakers of English).

Differentiating instruction and assessment according to English language proficiency level and educational/literacy background affords ELLs parity of access to the curriculum, holds them to the same content standards, and efficiently relies on the curricular content as the vehicle for learning English (Fairbairn & Jones-Vo, 2010).

Administrators must also lead staff in purposefully and appropriately responding to other critical student factors, including the following:

- **Immigrant/Refugee Situations:** Students from families who have come to the U.S. by choice vs. those who fled their homes due to threatening circumstances are likely to require different kinds of support.
- **Cultural Factors:** One key cultural consideration is the extent to which a student comes from a more collectivistic culture vs. the "typical" U.S. classroom culture, which is often more individualistic. Students with cultural backgrounds that vary from the cultural norms of their new classrooms will need support in learning how to function effectively in their new environment.
- **Prior Difficult Experiences:** Many students and families, whether immigrant or refugee, have faced difficulty prior to coming to the U.S. and/or in the journey to the U.S. These experiences will impact student readiness to participate in school activities.
- **Age:** Younger students benefit from not having as much ground to cover in "catching up" with their grade-level peers, while older students with strong educational backgrounds can transfer knowledge and skills to their learning in English-medium classrooms. The group facing the greatest challenge consists of older students who lack or have gaps in their prior schooling. These students need responsive and immediate programming designed explicitly to build their literacy from the ground up.
- **Language Distance:** Some languages more closely resemble English; therefore, speakers of those languages have a less daunting task in acquiring English than their counterparts who speak more

distant languages. For instance, speakers of Swahili or Spanish will have an easier time learning English than speakers of Japanese or Korean.

- **Social Distance:** This factor describes the extent to which a student is able to integrate into English-speaking society based on the practices of the student's Li group (e.g., a student who lives in an enclave community where English is not needed vs. a student from the only non-English-speaking family in the community).
- **Psychological Distance:** Issues such as culture shock and personal motivation comprise this factor. For instance, if the student desires to become a part of English-speaking society because of personal goals, her/his psychological distance is less; such a student is likely to learn English more readily than a student who sees her/his life in the U.S. as temporary and, as such, might be less motivated to learn English.

 Fairbairn & Jones-Vo (2010) provide a Student Background Information Sheet (Resource 1.1, pp. 35–36) and a Student Data Collection Checklist (Resource 1.2, pp. 37–38) that educators can adapt and use to guide their collection of this important background information, which can be kept in the ELL's cumulative folder for easy reference.

Administrators must expect and ensure that each teacher wholeheartedly instructs *all* students, taking into account all relevant factors. This charge cannot be shifted from teacher to teacher; this non-negotiable responsibility calls the administrator to hold all teachers accountable for the success of every ELL.

■ How do English language learners learn content-area concepts through their second language?
NANCY L. COMMINS[5]

To better understand the nature of learning through two languages, it can be helpful to think of the brain as a kind of "conceptual reservoir" as represented in Figures 2.2 through 2.5. This reservoir of knowledge can be accessed and added to through any language a person knows. The pathways in are receptive—listening, observing, exploring, reading, and imitating. The pathways out are the productive representations of thought and ideas—speaking, writing, artistic expression, and physical movement. In Figure 2.2 the arrows labeled *L1* (primary language) show these pathways going in and out of the reservoir. People can develop a shallow or a

5. Portions of this response originally appeared in Commins, N.L. (2011). Meaning is everything: Comprehension work with second language learners. In H. Daniels (Ed.) *Comprehension going forward: Where we are and what's next.* Portsmouth NH: Heinemann. Used by permission of the publisher.

Listening, watching, reading, and imitating

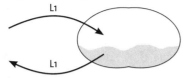

Speaking, writing, artistic expression,
physical movement, etc.

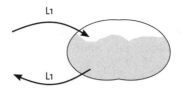

FIGURE 2.2 Adding to the reservoir through the first language.

FIGURE 2.3 Deepening the reservoir; strengthening the pathways.

deep reservoir, and as represented in Figure 2.3, as we learn more, the pathways in and out grow stronger.

As the pathways strengthen, the ability to take in and represent more information increases. Reading and writing are among the ways of accessing and adding to the reservoir, but they do not constitute the reservoir itself. Decoding is on the pathway; understanding an author's intent is in the reservoir. As educators, our job is to fill the conceptual reservoir as deeply as possible whether students can read and write or speak English— or not.

Monolingual speakers of any language will always add to their conceptual reservoir and represent what they know through their one and only language.

Whatever we know in one language we can learn to express through any language we learn. When people begin to learn a second language, they do not start a new reservoir—rather, they begin to express what they already know and understand through the new language. In Figure 2.4 and Figure 2.5, this is represented by the arrow coming out of the reservoir labeled *L2* (second language) at the top of each figure.

It is also possible to learn new information through a language you do not yet speak well, as is represented by the arrow labeled *L2* going into the

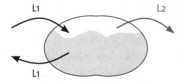

FIGURE 2.4 Learning a second language; taking from the reservoir.

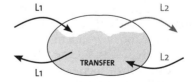

FIGURE 2.5 Using both languages.

reservoir at the bottom of Figure 2.5. To maximize students' potential for academic success means building on this understanding and seeing the relationship between the two languages as a springboard, not a deterrent. In linguistically diverse settings it should be our goal and intent to help students learn to deepen and express what they know through any language they can speak.

It is easy for teachers to overlook the fact that even if English is the only medium of instruction (as is the case for most ELLs in this country), second language learners are traveling with feet on both pathways. Students will always be attempting to make sense of the content through any language they know. In all settings, it is incumbent upon teachers to encourage students to take what they know in one language and express it through the other. All educators must affirm the importance of the primary language for learning regardless of program type—and recognize that learning through the primary language will strengthen learning through the second. In practice this means understanding and helping the students to consciously transfer what they are learning from one setting or language to another. While some individuals may sense this intuitively, many second language learners have the feeling they are starting from scratch, needing to learn once again to read, to write, to do math.

To successfully add to the conceptual reservoir through a second language takes the combined effort of learner and teacher. Particularly in the upper grades, teaching methods appropriate for native speakers such as reading textbooks and listening to lectures are still the main ways that students are expected to gain knowledge. This works for literate, motivated speakers of the language of instruction. However, if you do not speak or read the language of instruction well, other means are necessary that allow students to deepen their conceptual understandings while simultaneously learning the language. Teaching on the second language pathway begins with the concepts students have to learn and not what they will read to learn them.

Best practice for second language learners requires that teachers do whatever is necessary to make the content accessible and comprehensible while providing students the opportunity to interact with, connect to, act on, talk about, read about, and write about important ideas and information. To teach on the second language pathway is not to dumb down or reduce expectations or teach what is easy. Rather it requires differentiation along multiple dimensions, having determined how to make understandable for the students what is deemed most important for them to learn. This process will be advanced when educators advocate that family and community members continue to use their strongest language with their children—usually the primary language—to deepen understandings and help build schema.

■ What is the role of culture in language learning?
ELSE HAMAYAN

English language learners (ELLs) are faced with three significant challenges in school: they must learn new concepts (often quite abstract, especially above third grade), they must learn in a language in which they are developing proficiency, and they must learn in a cultural context that may be quite unfamiliar to them. This last challenge is the one that most educators pay the least attention to because it is not an explicit aspect of schooling and education (Cole, 1996).

Every bilingual learner brings subtle cultural norms and values to school. Many of these norms and values go beyond the superficial displays of folktales, fashion, food, and festivals, which are merely the tip of the iceberg (Figure 2.6). They consist of the ways in which each of us interacts

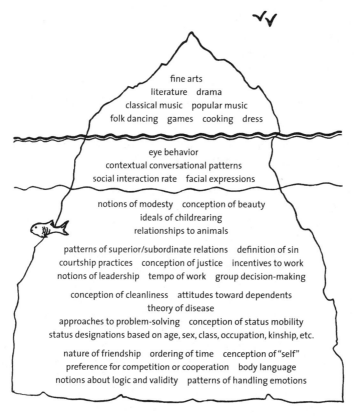

FIGURE 2.6 The iceberg model of culture (Illinois Resource Center, 1997).

with and makes sense of our surroundings, or what may lie just below the surface in the iceberg model. These norms and values govern how we do what we do. Notions of modesty, a preference for competition or cooperation, and approaches to problem solving, lie well below the visible surface. However, they permeate every aspect of the lives of ELLs at school. It is precisely for this reason that administrators need to consider cultural diversity in every aspect of the program that they establish for ELLs.

 Culture is tightly interwoven with not only language learning and use, but it is also a critical factor in learning in general (García, 2006). Learning is seen by many sociocultural theorists as an interaction between individual learners and the context within which that learning takes place (García, 2006; Rogoff, 2003). The culture of the classroom as well as the student's and his or her family's traditions play a vital role in helping or impeding the second language learning process. The way we interpret and interact with our environment can facilitate or inhibit learning. One way in which culture plays a role in the learning process relates to how well a student functions within the culture of the classroom. Students who are comfortable with the culture of the classroom and who behave according to the norms that govern the classroom are more relaxed learners than students who feel as though their behavior is off the mark. Often, students who are not acculturated into the culture of the classroom are not even able to articulate what it is that makes them different from the others. Students who stand too close to others or those whose norms of modesty are different from those of the general school population simply know they are uncomfortable, or that they are making others uncomfortable. As a consequence, they are likely to function at a lower level than their potential allows, and they may not be able to devote their full attention to learning.

Another way in which culture plays a role in learning is that culture serves as a key to understanding new concepts. An unfamiliar cultural context in which a new concept is being introduced can stand in the way of demystifying that concept. For example, during shared reading time, a story about a young child who is rewarded for showing great independence may be very confusing to a student who has been taught that reliance on parents and older siblings is not only acceptable but highly regarded. A classroom activity that is structured around competition and "winning" may be very hard to complete for a student who has learned to shun competitiveness and to value collaboration.

Our task as administrators and educational leaders is first to be aware of the diversity that exists among all students and to see that diversity as a source of enrichment for everyone in the school community. Second, we need to be open to learning, most easily from the students and their families, what their norms and values are. Next, we must think of ways of incorporating cultural diversity, in all of its complexity, into the everyday working of the school. In summary, the culture of the student must enter into the minds and hearts of teachers and administrators if the culture of school is to enter into the minds and hearts of the students.

■ What role does the home language play in an English language learner's life/schooling?
KATHY ESCAMILLA

The question of the role that a student's home language plays in their life and schooling is an important one and needs to be a central part of discussions of school programs and instruction even if English is the sole medium of instruction in the school.

First, it is important for school leaders and teachers to understand that a student's first language is not a barrier to learning a second language. A student's first language is a *scaffold* to learning a second language not an *impediment*. Examples to illustrate this statement are as follows. Results of the five most recent syntheses of research in our field have all come to the same conclusion that learning to read in the home language promotes reading achievement in the second language. That is, knowing how to read in a non-English language helps students learn to read in *English* (August & Shanahan, 2006; Genesee, Lindholm-Leary, Saunders, & Christian, 2006; Greene, 1997; Rolstad, Mahoney, & Glass, 2005; Slavin & Cheung, 2005; Willig, 1985). Perhaps we need to ban the word language interference from our vocabulary!

The above research results notwithstanding, it is clear that the vast majority of English language learners are in school programs where English is the only medium of instruction and students are not learning to read and write in their mother tongues. Even in these cases the native language plays a critical role in the student's life and academic career. Too often English-medium programs think that they must ban the use of students' native languages in order to accelerate the acquisition of English. It is important for educators to know that there is *NO* research to support this. In fact, the research indicates that banning the use of a student's native language in school may be counterproductive to learning English (Goldenberg, 2008). So how can native languages be used productively and strategically in English-medium programs?

Native languages can be used to clarify information and concepts to students. They can be used to help orient students to class activities and events and to manage classroom activities. In situations where there are students who share a native language, this language can be used between and among peers to clarify and process the teacher's instruction and to better comprehend classroom instruction. When students are beginning the process of acquiring English, a teacher who understands the native language may allow students to respond to teacher questions in their native languages thereby indicating that they have understood instruction even though they are not yet able to produce orally or in writing in English. Moreover, it is important for teachers and others to remember that even in English-medium programs, while English language learners are acquiring English, their native languages may still be the language in which they process information. Using a first language to process second language in-put is an important component of interlanguage and students should not be discouraged from using their first language resources to help understand their second language.

Aside from the classroom context, it is important for educators to understand that students' native languages are a primary means of communication in their families and ethnolinguistic communities. Native languages serve important social functions, and therefore students should not be discouraged from using their native languages in schools during recess, lunchtime, in the halls, or during other social situations in the school. Further, it is important for educators to understand that the native language will more than likely be the medium of communication in the homes of English learners. It is important that the school have mechanisms for communicating with parents in their native languages, no matter what the official school program is. It is further important that the school encourage parents to use their native languages as tools for communication with their children and that they encourage their children to continue using their native languages at home. Students with well-developed native language skills and registers also are more likely to learn these same skills in English quickly and well.

In short, educators are well advised to see native languages as resources to helping English language learners succeed in school. Native languages are scaffolds and bridges to English and are social and academic resources that aide the second language acquisition process. School programs should value, respect, and utilize these languages strategically.

■ How do English language learners acquire a second language at school?
FRED GENESEE

Effective English language and literacy instruction for English language learners (ELLs) takes multiple factors into account—factors in and outside school, as well as factors linked to ELLs' first language and English. Many of these factors are within the control of educators and should be considered seriously when planning English language and literacy instruction for ELLs.

My focus here is on factors within the school, but it is important to recognize that language experiences outside school can also facilitate English language and literacy development in school. In particular, literacy experiences in the home (such as being read to at home) and well-developed literacy-related skills that have been acquired in the home (such as knowledge of letters and letter-sound relations, decoding skills) facilitate ELLs' acquisition of literacy in English in school. This is true whether these experiences and skills are based on the home language or English. Thus, educators should encourage and support parents in providing literacy-related experiences and skills in the home, either in students' home language or in English. This can be done through home-based projects in which teachers send materials home to parents to work on with their children. The focus should be on language for literacy and higher-order cognitive purposes, not simply talk—for example, developing a wide range of vocabulary, knowledge of letters and letter-sound relationships, awareness of the purposes of writing, and the ability to think critically and inferentially about ideas and what is written. Many parents will need guidance in how to accomplish this, but this is entirely realistic if given help from the school. Encourage enriched experiences in the home language if parents are most competent in that language; otherwise, encourage literacy in English at home.

The development of literacy in English as a second language is similar in some important and fundamental respects to the development of literacy in English as a first language (Genesee, Lindholm-Leary, Saunders, & Christian, 2006). Both types of literacy development are influenced by learners' oral language skills, their acquisition of skills that are particularly relevant to reading and writing (depth of vocabulary, knowledge of letters, and relationships between sounds and letters), and their use of metacognitive skills linked to reading (such as phonological awareness, comprehension monitoring strategies, or inferring the meaning of unfamiliar words from context). Thus, teachers can use many of the instructional strategies that are useful with native English speakers with ELLs as long as they adapt them to the language level and needs of ELL students. At the same time, ELLs have a reservoir of skills, strategies, and knowledge that are linked to their home language. This reservoir of first language (L1) resources can help them bootstrap into English reading and writing, especially during the early stages of learning to read and write. This is true whether students are in English-only programs or in bilingual programs.

Educators should encourage and even train ELLs to see links between English and their home language and to draw on skills and knowledge acquired in the home language to comprehend or produce written text in English (such as knowledge of cognates or strategies for figuring out the meaning of unknown words in L1). Teachers should recognize that L1 influences on second language (L2) reading and writing are positive signs. When ELLs transfer their knowledge of L1 sounds or letters to English reading and writing or when they use cognates from L1 to interpret novel L2 words, they are actively using resources at their disposal to crack into the English system. Effective reading/writing instruction must take a multidimensional approach, focusing on the technicalities of reading/writing (such as decoding, spelling, and organization) while also teaching students to use strategies for comprehending, inferring, and so forth (such as using context and inferencing, monitoring comprehension, and invoking prior knowledge) and exposing ELLs to authentic texts that are adapted to their developmental needs.

PATRICK H. SMITH

Although much can be done to help learners master the language skills necessary for school success, increasing pressure for results can make the task seem a daunting one. I focus on three fundamental principles here: (1) understanding the basics of second language acquisition, (2) building on what learners can already do with language, and (3) providing opportunities for meaningful language use. School administrators who become knowledgeable in these areas can serve as educational leaders for English language learning.

UNDERSTANDING THE BASICS OF SECOND LANGUAGE ACQUISITION
Because learning and using our first language is part of our biological programming as humans, how we do these things is largely hidden from us. The automaticity of first language (L1) acquisition also blinds us to the facts of second language (L2) learning (Hall, 2005). Let us look at the key differences. Unlike first language acquisition, which virtually everyone masters without conscious reflection over a relatively fixed period of time, developing advanced proficiency in a second language often requires conscious effort, can occur in different sequences for different learners, and usually occurs over a greater time span. Another fundamental difference is that unlike L1 acquisition, L2 acquisition does not result in uniform outcomes: some people learn L2 more completely than others. This is especially true for academic language proficiency and literacy. Perhaps most important, in contrast to L2 acquisition, the quality and nature of the linguistic input do not seem to matter in L1 acquisition. No matter who talks to them, how, or how much, babies develop a first language. But to develop advanced proficiency in a second language we need a great deal of consistent and comprehensible linguistic input.[6] Finally, because second language learning frequently happens later in a person's life than first language learning, second language learners are generally more cognitively mature. Because they are older, they also have greater linguistic knowl-

6. There are some important parallels here for English speakers, especially those who speak vernacular varieties of English, in their acquisition of standard academic English.

edge and social experiences to draw on as they develop a new language in school. Understanding these fundamental differences between first and second language acquisition—and sharing this knowledge with teachers, parents, and learners—is critical for administrators who want to foster English language learning.

BUILDING ON WHAT STUDENTS CAN ALREADY DO WITH LANGUAGE

A second fundamental principle is to build on what students can already do with language. While some aspects of language, including cognates, may transfer across languages automatically, reading and other abilities require explicit guidance from skilled teachers. This is particularly true of speaking and writing because of the premium placed on conventional forms. This attention to form can be taught through specialized ESL strategies and by using the students' first language as a basis for building new language skills. Because literacy and other academic language abilities are differently understood across cultural contexts, knowledge about students' first languages and the ways schooling is organized in students' countries of origin is an especially useful tool for educators (Smith, Jiménez, & Martínez-León, 2003).

PROVIDE OPPORTUNITIES FOR MEANINGFUL LANGUAGE USE

Third, in order to develop oral and written language success, learners must use English to convey meaning. One way to do this is through a curriculum that pairs learners with more proficient speakers. Integrating English learners with native speakers of English in communicative tasks provides possibilities for language and cultural modeling, providing that all students are cognitively challenged.

ELSE HAMAYAN and REBECCA FREEMAN FIELD

Second language acquisition is a developmental process that takes time, especially the development of academic English and literacies in English. There is also considerable variation in the ways that English language learners (ELLs) acquire the spoken and written English that they need in order to participate and achieve at school. This variation depends both on the language and literacy expertise that the ELL brings to school and on the language and literacy contexts that the ELL participates in at school, home, and in other places in his or her everyday life.

While we know that second language and literacy development is not a linear process that is the same for all students, we also know that there is considerable uniformity in the stages that ELLs go through (Krashen & Terrell, 1983). Five stages have been identified: preproduction, early production, speech emergence, intermediate fluency, and fluency. As Table

2.1 summarizes, each level of English production is associated with student characteristics that can be observed, descriptions of how students learn at that level of proficiency, and the most effective language for literacy development and content-area instruction. The continuum of second language development reflected in current English language proficiency (ELP) standards and assessment systems is grounded in this early second language acquisition research. That is, preproduction and early production roughly correspond to Level 1 on most current state standards, speech emergence roughly corresponds to Level 2, and intermediate fluency roughly corresponds to Level 3. There are more ELP levels in the state-mandated ELP systems, reflecting a developing understanding in the field of what academic language proficiency is and how long it takes for ELLs to develop academic language proficiency.

When many general education teachers and administrators learn about Krashen's (1982) notion of a "silent period" (the preproduction stage), they often breathe a sigh of relief as they begin to understand why some of their ELLs do not talk to them for what may seem an uncomfortably long time. According to Krashen, what language learners need at this stage is a focus on meaningful communication or comprehensible input in a low-anxiety environment without being forced to produce the language. This is what Krashen and Terrell (1983) called the natural approach. The key here is comprehensibility: when beginning language learners are immersed in an environment that is rich in oral and written language, and when they can make sense of that language, they acquire that language.

Educators also need to recognize that there is considerable variation in how long it takes for different ELLs to move through the preproduction (silent period), early production, and speech emergence phases. This is very similar to infants and young children acquiring their mother tongue. Some children begin talking at the age of one; others do not start to talk until they are well into their second year. Jim Cummins earlier in this chapter noted that it typically takes ELLs about one to two years to develop what he calls conversational fluency, or what is called intermediate fluency in Table 2.1. Some learners exhibit a longer silent period than others, and the same student may talk more in some contexts than others or more about some topics than others. Individual factors such as age, learning style, personality, motivation, background knowledge, as well as contextual and sociocultural factors, such as the relationship between the participants in the interaction, and the setting in which the interaction takes place, can all influence the quality and quantity of ELLs' talk.

ELLs at school need to do more than just acquire English; they also need to learn complex content-area concepts so that they can achieve academically, and the pressure is on for these students to perform at grade level in English. Although intuitively it may make sense to think that spending

TABLE 2.1 Learning English: The stages (Illinois Resource Center [1999]; adapted from Krashen and Terrell [1983])

Level of English Production	Student Characteristics and Needs	How Students Learn	Most Effective Language for Instruction
Preproduction	Silent period: no speaking Responds to instructions and commands (e.g., "put on your coat") Needs environments where they can understand teachers and peers	Learns by listening and watching Points, gestures, draws, or recreates something to show understanding	First language
Early Production	Speaks using one or two words Gives "yes" or "no" answers May mix languages (this is a normal part of language development) Needs environments where s/he can understand teachers and peers	Learns by listening, watching, and speaking using one or two words Points, gestures, draws, recreates, or responds to questions with one or two word answers to show understanding	First language
Speech Emergence	Speaks using more than one or two words to express a thought and can retell a story or event Responds to open-ended questions Ready for formal reading and writing instruction in English Needs environments where s/he can understand teachers and peers	Begins to ask questions Utilizes basic literacy skills Participates in discussions and responds to questions using emerging syntactic structures (grammar)	First language
Intermediate Fluency	Ready for more advanced reading and writing instruction in English Needs considerable help with vocabulary development in math, science, social studies Needs environments where s/he can understand teachers and peers	Utilizes more advanced literacy skills Builds on content learned through discussions using more advanced syntactic structures	Sheltered English and first language
Fluency	Language and learning skills are comparable to those of a native English speaker		English and first language

more time in English and less time in the primary language at school would enable ELLs to acquire the academic English they need for school success more quickly, this is actually not the case. According to comparative longitudinal research on ELLs in different types of programs in the United States (e.g., Lindholm-Leary, 2000; Collier & Thomas, 2009), the most effective language for literacy and content-area instruction when students are beginning to acquire English is their native language. Virginia Collier also emphasizes that "the main reason for teaching instructional material in Li is the crucial role that cognitive development in Li plays, and the fact that cognitive development in Li needs to continue nonstop through around age 12 to ensure academic and cognitive success in L2" (personal communication, 2005).

Finally, intermediate fluency is a very broad category. Educators must be careful not to assume that when students *sound* like they can speak English (that is, they have what Cummins calls conversational fluency, or what here is called intermediate fluency), they have acquired the oral and written academic English they need to participate and achieve without support in the all-English mainstream classroom. Sheltered (Echeverria, Vogt, & Short, 2008a) and differentiated (Fairbairn & Jones-Vo, 2010) instructional strategies in English with primary language support are most effective for complex content-area instruction for ELLs at this stage in their second language development.

In sum, this 5-stage model allows educators to begin to understand in a very general way characteristics of ELLs at different stages of second language acquisition, and it suggests which languages are most effective for literacy and content area learning. This 5-stage model is the foundation for the continuum of second language development reflected in descriptions of what ELLs can do with reading, writing, listening, and speaking in state English language proficiency frameworks. At the same time, educators must be sure to observe their particular ELLs closely to understand and document how they are acquiring English at school, and how the school best can support these processes.

How does first language literacy development relate to second language literacy development?
DIANE AUGUST

Researchers have explored the relationships between first language literacy and second language literacy for word-based components (word recognition, vocabulary, and spelling) and text-based components (reading comprehension, strategy use, and writing). Taken as a whole, researchers find evidence of both negative and positive transfer (Nakamoto, Lindsey, &

Manis, 2008; Manis, Lindsey, & Bailey, 2004; Cárdenas-Hagan, Carlson, & Pollard-Durodola, 2007; Fashola, Drum, Mayer, & Kang, 1996; Gholamain & Geva, 1999; Jimenez, García, & Pearson, 1996; Lanauze & Snow, 1999; Nagy, McClure, & Mir, 1997; Reese, Garmier, Gallimore, & Goldenberg, 2000). More specifically, the following has been found across a wide range of ages:

- Word recognition skills acquired in a first language transfer to the second language.
- There is positive transfer of vocabulary knowledge for words that are cognates.
- Children use spelling knowledge in the first language when they spell in their second language, and errors associated with first language spelling disappear as students become more proficient in their second language.
- There is evidence of cross-language transfer of reading comprehension in bilinguals of all ages, even when the languages have different types of alphabets.
- For comprehension, there is also transfer from student's second language to their first; bilingual students who read strategically in one language also read strategically in their other language. Moreover, the more students use strategies in reading, the higher their reading performance.
- For writing, the studies suggest there are cross-language relationships for writing, but levels of first language and second language proficiency may mediate these relationships.

The studies as a whole indicate that it is important to consider factors other than the components of interest in thinking about cross-language relationships. The nature of the written systems involved—the kind of alphabet and its orthographic complexity—and how alike they are in how they influence children's ability to take advantage of their first language for some components of literacy. For example, several studies suggest that there is transfer for spelling only in cases where the two languages are somewhat alike. The proficiency of the learners in both their first and second language is an important variable. For example, in the area of metacognition, some research suggests that children need to have attained a threshold of second language proficiency before they can apply first language strategies to the second language. In the area of writing, there appears to be transfer for older students, but only for those who are orally proficient in their first language but not in their second. Finally, while many studies have found transfer from the first language to the second, others have found that there is also transfer from the second language to the first. For example, in the area of writing, students instructed exclusively in their second language may apply the second language writing skills when writing in their first language.

✏ ■ In what language should an English language learner begin to read and write?

FRED GENESEE, NANCY CLOUD, and ELSE HAMAYAN

It is preferable that English language learners either learn to read and write in their home language first, or continue literacy instruction in their home language, while they are learning to read and write in English. There are several reasons for this.

- Research shows that ELLs with emergent or developed skills in reading and writing in the home language learn to read and write in English more easily than ELLs who lack such skills because literacy skills, especially the foundational skills of literacy, transfer readily from the home language to English.
- The development of reading and writing skills calls on a host of skills and knowledge, including world knowledge, vocabulary, sentence grammar, knowledge of letter-sound relationships, and phonological awareness. Many of these are skills and sources of knowledge that ELLs have already acquired in the home language. Thus, beginning literacy instruction in the home language allows teachers to draw on literacy-related skills and knowledge that ELLs have already acquired, and it allows ELLs to take advantage of resources linked to the home language that are already available to them.
- Acquiring literacy skills in more than one language contributes to ELLs' overall bilingual competence, which research has shown is, in turn, related to cognitive advantages in the ability to focus on, inhibit, activate, and integrate information.
- ELLs with well-developed literacy skills in two languages enjoy personal and career advantages because knowing how to read and write in two languages gives them access to information in more than one language and gives them a competitive edge for many jobs in the increasingly globalized work force.
- Extensive research has shown that ELLs who participate in dual language programs achieve the same and in many cases higher levels of English language reading and writing skills than ELLs in English-only programs when evaluated on standardized or state-mandated tests of literacy (Genesee, Lindholm-Leary, Saunders, & Christian, 2006). Research indicates further that ELLs who participate in extended dual language programs—those that begin early, continue throughout the elementary grades, and provide at least 50% instruction through the home language—are especially likely to achieve such high levels of proficiency in reading and writing in English.
- Engagement is an important ingredient of effective literacy instruction. Using the home language of ELLs as the language of initial instruction in school, or as an active support for literacy, classroom teachers are better able to engage ELLs who come to school with emergent or developed literacy skills in the home language. Learning to read and write in a language they are still acquiring makes it more difficult for students to engage in literacy activities.

- Using the home language along with English is a way in which classroom teachers can promote the metalinguistic, including phonological, awareness of ELLs (see Cloud, Genesee, & Hamayan, 2009 for specific strategies). Metalinguistic and, especially, phonological awareness have been shown to be important predictors of the acquisition of initial literacy skills, especially word decoding.

Promoting literacy skills in ELLs' home language should begin in the home and with parents. Parents of ELLs should be encouraged (and provided guidance where necessary) to use language in the home in ways that will support their children's literacy development. This can include activities involving written language, such as reading story books to their children or giving children the responsibility of checking off items from a shopping list as items are placed in the cart. Parents can also use oral language, which research has shown to support the acquisition of literacy skills, in activities such as storytelling, conversations in which children are encouraged to organize information in a logical or sequential order or to analyze and think critically about what they have seen (on television, for example) or they have just witnessed (such as day-to-day events), rhyming, and other children's games in the home language.

Supporting ELLs in the development of literacy skills in the home language (along with English) can be provided in the home (as noted), in community libraries with large ELL populations, and in schools by offering the option of bilingual or dual language programs.

■ Does learning in a native language delay the acquisition of English?
ELSE HAMAYAN and REBECCA FREEMAN FIELD

The quick answer to this question is yes and no. For the longer answer, we can turn to what is known about early childhood bilingualism, and then separately to what is known about the acquisition of a second language at a later time.

Let us start with early childhood bilingualism, by which we mean learning two languages from birth or in the first year of life. There is some evidence that children who grow up with two languages show some delay in language production. When language does appear, there may be mixing of the two languages, at least in the early stages of language development. However, both of these occurrences, delay and mixing, have no long-term effects and are not related in any way to observable developmental issues. Given high-quality exposure to both languages, children who grow up bilingually develop proficiency in both languages. Proficiency in the two languages may develop equally or to different levels depending on the continuity of exposure to and use of the two languages, as well as a few other variables (Bialystock, 2001; Genesee, 2003; Genesee & Nicoladis, 2007).

There is evidence that this type of early additive bilingualism, in which both languages are valued and nurtured in a quality environment, is advantageous for children. Bilingual children show earlier concept development than their monolingual peers, and they also show more creativity in problem-solving tasks. Whether these occurrences have any long-term effects is questionable. However, if nothing else, this jump-start that bilingual children experience may lead to high expectations and a positive self-image, both desirable conditions for young children (Hakuta, 1986).

As for later acquisition of a second language, some delay in learning the new language may be observed in the earlier stages of second language development if the learner is continuing formal instruction in the primary language. Students who are taught in their primary language while beginning to learn English as a second language may develop proficiency in the second language at a slower rate than students who are immersed in English with little or no support in their primary language. However, this early boost quickly levels off, and students who receive intense instruction in English as a second language early without support for their primary language often begin to fall behind, and many do not attain a high enough level of proficiency to survive in an academic setting where English is the language of instruction. This subtractive type of bilingualism has adverse effects on second language acquisition. Conversely, students who continue to learn through their primary language may have a slow start in learning English as a second language; however, their development in English continues steadily until they reach a high level of proficiency that allows them to learn new abstract concepts through that language.

SURVEY FOR REFLECTION AND ACTION

This survey reflects the guiding principles about how children learn in two or more languages that were articulated in the Introduction to the chapter. Use this survey to review how your policies, programs, practices, and assessments reflect fundamental assumptions about how linguistically and culturally diverse students learn. Indicate the extent to which each of the following applies to your school: DK—don't know; 1—strongly disagree; 2 —disagree; 3—agree; 4—strongly agree. At the end of the survey, write down one to three strengths and needs you identified through your review. Then identify one to three future possibilities that you can see to make your policies, programs, practices, and assessments more theoretically sound. Finally, identify one to three concrete actions that you can take to build on the strengths you have identified in order to realize those future possibilities.

We understand that our ELLs are learning abstract content-area concepts in a nonproficient language and within a cultural context that may be unfamiliar to them.

- Our policies for ELLs reflect an understanding that they are   DK 1 2 3 4
  learning abstract content-area concepts in a nonproficient

language and within a cultural context that may be unfamiliar to them.

- Our instructional programming for ELLs reflects an   DK 1 2 3 4
  understanding that they are learning abstract content-area
  concepts in a language that they are still acquiring and within
  a cultural context that they are still learning about.

- Our classroom practices reflect an understanding that our ELLs   DK 1 2 3 4
  are learning abstract content-area concepts while they are
  acquiring social and academic English and within a cultural
  context that are still learning to participate in.

- Our assessments take into consideration ELLs' language   DK 1 2 3 4
  proficiency level and other background factors so as to allow
  learners to demonstrate content-area knowledge and skills.

We understand that second language acquisition, especially the acquisition of academic language and literacies needed to participate and achieve at school, is a developmental process that takes time.

- Our policies for ELLs reflect an understanding of how ELLs   DK 1 2 3 4
  acquire English for social and academic purposes.

- Our instructional programming for ELLs allows them the time   DK 1 2 3 4
  that they need to develop academic language and literacies
  across the content areas.

- Our classroom practices provide opportunities for ELLs to   DK 1 2 3 4
  develop social and instructional language as well as the oral
  and written language they need to succeed in all content areas.

- Our assessments allow ELLs to demonstrate their English   DK 1 2 3 4
  language development across content areas over time.

We understand that a strong home language, including literacy in that language, provides a solid foundation for cognitive development, academic achievement, and language and literacy development in English,

- Our policies support the maintenance and development of   DK 1 2 3 4
  ELLs'/bilingual learners' home language to the greatest degree
  possible.

- Our instructional programming for ELLs/bilingual learners   DK 1 2 3 4
  supports the maintenance and development of ELLs'/bilingual
  learners' home language to the greatest degree possible.

- Our classroom and school-wide practices support the   DK 1 2 3 4
  maintenance and development of ELLs'/bilingual learners'
  home language to the greatest degree possible.

- Our assessments support the maintenance and development   DK 1 2 3 4
  of ELLs'/bilingual learners' home language to the greatest
  degree possible.

We understand that culture influences all aspects of learning and teaching at school.

- Our policies reflect an understanding of and sensitivity to the   DK 1 2 3 4
  cultural backgrounds of all of the students in our school and
  community.

- Our educational programs reflect an understanding of and   DK 1 2 3 4
  sensitivity to the cultural backgrounds of all of the students
  in our school and community.

- Our classroom practices reflect an understanding of and   DK 1 2 3 4
  sensitivity to the cultural backgrounds of all of the students
  in our school and community.

- Our assessments reflect an understanding of and sensitivity to   DK 1 2 3 4
  the cultural backgrounds of all of the students in our school
  and community.

We understand that there is considerable variation in the ways that ELLs acquire English (and other languages) and achieve academically at school.

- Our policies allow for variation in the ways that ELLs/bilingual   DK 1 2 3 4
  learners are expected to acquire English and achieve
  academically at school.

- Our educational programs are designed to address the variation   DK 1 2 3 4
  that we find among the ELLs/bilingual learners in our school in
  ways that build on the linguistic, cultural, and educational
  resources that these learners bring with them to school.

- Our classroom and schoolwide practices build on the diverse   DK 1 2 3 4
  strengths of the ELLs/bilingual learners in our classes as we
  differentiate instruction to address their varied language,
  literacy, and learning needs.

Strengths we can identify

1. _____

2. _____

3. _____

Future possibilities we can see

1. _____

2. _____

3. _____

Action steps we can take

1. _____

2. _____

3. _____

3

POLICIES AND ACCOUNTABILITY REQUIREMENTS FOR ENGLISH LANGUAGE LEARNERS

GUIDING PRINCIPLES

- We address all Federal, state, and local goals, mandates, and accountability requirements regarding English language learners (ELLs).
- We have developed an authentic accountability system for ELLs that is integrated into the system created for their English-proficient peers.
- We explicitly articulate local school district and school language education policies and procedures for ELLs/ bilingual learners that are aligned with the procedures created for their English-proficient peers.
- We use valid and reliable data on the academic achievement and English language development of ELLs to inform our policies and accountability requirements for these students.

INTRODUCTION

The Civil Rights Act of 1964 mandates that U.S. public schools provide equal educational opportunities for all students. Educators are challenged to ensure that their English language learners (ELLs) have the support that they need in order to access the educational opportunities to which they are legally entitled. More than forty years of Federal, state, and local legislation has led to the development of a wide range of policies, programs, and practices that are intended to support this effort. And more than thirty years of research on the educational experiences and outcomes of ELLs in a range of program types has contributed to our understanding of what is and is not effective for these students.

Since the passage of No Child Left Behind in 2001, U.S. schools have been held accountable by the Federal government for the academic achievement and English language proficiency of ELLs in their classrooms. The good news is that the largely underserved ELL population has been moved from the margins to the mainstream of U.S. educational concerns and ELLs are no longer invisible in our schools. For example, every state has developed English language proficiency (ELP) standards and assessment systems that reflect a research-based continuum of oral and written social and academic language development, and every ELL is to be identified and assessed in the domains of reading, writing, listening, and speaking to determine their current level of English language proficiency. We also see more focus on pre-service and in-service professional development of teachers and administrators who work in the academic mainstream than we have ever seen before this time.

However, the bad news is that current Federal and state policies and accountability requirements for ELLs do not reflect what we know about how children learn in two languages. *Data-based decision making* has been interpreted narrowly to mean the results of standardized tests of academic achievement in English, which experts agree is not a valid or reliable assessment of academic achievement for ELLs who are still acquiring academic English. Under the current accountability system, ELLs are treated as a monolithic disaggregated subgroup that in many schools across the United States is not making adequate yearly progress (AYP), with little to no attention paid to the tremendous variation within the category of ELL and how this variation relates to success in school. Teachers, administrators, and schools are labeled as failing when they fail to make AYP under the current accountability system. Unfortunately, in many schools and districts across the United States ELLs are seen as more of a "problem" than they were in the past.

Teachers and administrators in schools and districts in every part of the United States have serious questions about how they can meet Federal and state accountability requirements for their ELLs. This chapter seeks to address many of those questions and encourages administrators and leadership team members to look critically at their local policies and accountability requirements in relation to (1) what the research says about how children learn in two languages and (2) what their data, broadly defined, say about how their ELLs/bilingual learners are performing and developing relative not only to state standards but also to local district, school, program, and community goals. By data, we mean all types of information about students and their households, the learning environment at school, and the larger sociopolitical and economic context surrounding the school. We strongly believe that an accountability system that fails to take into consideration the research base on what we know about effective educational programs, practices, and assessments for ELLs/bilingual learners, and that fails to take into consideration valid and reliable empirical evidence of student learning over time, and that punishes teachers and schools for not being able to do what is oftentimes simply impossible, is a very harmful accountability system indeed.

The chapter begins with a brief historical overview of the Federal policy context surrounding the education of ELLs today. Then we consider some of the problems and challenges of the current accountability system for ELLs and present empirical evidence of ELL achievement on the national level since NCLB as well as in states that passed English-only laws nearly a decade ago. The majority of the chapter reflects a broader notion of accountability for ELLs/bilingual learners/all students. Experts clarify what an authentic accountability system for ELLs needs to include and outline ways that educators working on the state, district, and school levels can use valid and reliable evidence of ELLs' growth and achievement to drive their decision making. Finally, we consider how a district or school can develop a language policy that is appropriate for their context to structure this important work. The chapter concludes with a Survey for Reflection and Action.

School district and school administrators can use this survey to review their current policies and accountability requirements for ELLs and identify the strengths of and future possibilities for these policies and procedures. Equipped with this information, administrators can take the necessary action steps to ensure that their ELLs have equal access to the educational opportunities they offer all students at their schools.

■ How have laws regarding English language learners evolved in the United States?
KATE MENKEN

Policies regarding the education of children who speak languages other than English are far from new in the United States. Historically, such policies have been decided by a combination of legislation, court mandates, and Federal, state, and local educational policies that have shifted with the ebb and flow of immigration waves to this country. When the U.S. Constitution was written, linguistic diversity was the national norm, and instruction was multilingual in schools. Bilingual German-English schooling was authorized by law first in Ohio in the nineteenth century, and this was followed by several other states adopting a bilingual education law. Bilingual education also flourished unofficially elsewhere, and other European languages were taught in response to pressures from immigrant groups (Crawford, 1992). More than a dozen states passed legislation for schooling in languages other than English, either as a subject or as the medium of instruction.

With the arrival of the second great wave of immigrants to the United States in the early twentieth century, however, anti-immigrant sentiment increased, and the dominance of English grew. The "Americanization" campaign of this period corresponded to increased restrictions placed on the use of languages other than English. After the United States entered World War I in 1917, several states passed laws and decrees banning instruction in languages other than English from public and private classrooms and other places (Crawford, 1999). Similar attempts were made to prohibit the teaching of Japanese, Chinese, and Korean in California and Hawaii, and Spanish in New Mexico. In 1923, Congress considered a bill to make English the official national language. Although this bill did not pass, and anti–foreign language laws were eventually overturned, they had a great impact on public sentiment. From the period of mass immigration into the United States during the early twentieth century until the 1960s, few or no special services were offered to emergent bilingual[1] students in schools where English was the sole language of instruction.

---

1. Following García (2009b), I adopt the term 'emergent bilingual' in lieu of 'English language learner.'

It was after the Civil Rights Act of 1964 that the need to provide language support for emergent bilinguals, and the recognition that language is tied to educational inequity, were first explicitly addressed in Federal education legislation. The Elementary and Secondary Education Act is the main Federal law funding K-12 public education in the United States, and it has been reauthorized numerous times since its initial passage in 1965. The law provides guidelines with which states must comply in order to receive Federal education funding, including provisions for emergent bilinguals, and these guidelines change each time the law is reauthorized.

The recognition that language support programming must be provided to emergent bilinguals in school was first enacted in the 1968 passage of Title VII of the Elementary and Secondary Education Act, entitled the Bilingual Education Act. The Bilingual Education Act acknowledged the challenges posed by the linguistic diversity of U.S. public schools and authorized the funding of innovative programs for emergent bilinguals, such as bilingual education and English as a second language (ESL).

Programs to meet the needs of emergent bilinguals, however, were only truly implemented in U.S. public schools after the *Lau v. Nichols* case of 1974. The suit was brought by Chinese parents in San Francisco who asserted that a child named Lau was unable to access the academic content needed to succeed in school due to his limited English. The Supreme Court ruled in this case that "*identical* education does not constitute *equal* education under the Civil Rights Act." As a result, school districts across the country were required to take "affirmative steps" to address the educational challenges for emergent bilinguals due to language (for example, by implementing bilingual education or ESL programs).

In the wake of these mandates, a wide array of program models addressing the needs of emergent bilinguals has been implemented. These models are divided between those which are bilingual (wherein instruction is in English and another language) and those in which instruction is solely in English. Although bilingual education programs proliferated after the 1960s, in recent years programming options for emergent bilinguals have been increasingly limited (Menken, 2008, 2011).

More immigrants arrived in the United States during the past two decades than ever before, and there has been a backlash against the growing immigrant population and the languages they speak. With funding from Ron Unz, a millionaire software entrepreneur, anti–bilingual education ballot measures have passed at the state level in California (1998), Arizona (1999), and Massachusetts (2002) prohibiting bilingual instruction in those states despite research showing the effectiveness of bilingual education.

Marking the end of the Bilingual Education Act, the Elementary and Secondary Education Act was reauthorized in 2001 and renamed No Child Left Behind (NCLB). Eliminating the term 'bilingual' altogether from its name, Title III of NCLB replaced Title VII and was renamed "Language Instruction for Limited English Proficient and Immigrant Students." The law mandates that emergent bilinguals be included in state assessment systems for accountability purposes and requires that these students make "adequate yearly progress" toward mastering academic content and English proficiency—with only passing mention of bilingual education or native language use. As such, this law implicitly promotes an English-only policy, pressuring school districts to ensure emergent bilinguals take and pass high-stakes tests in English or risk sanctions, such as loss of Federal funding or school closure (Menken, 2008).

In 2010, the Obama administration awarded funding to selected states through a grants competition program called "Race to the Top" that propagates the myopic emphasis on high-stakes testing of NCLB. These states need to show evidence of the following: advancing standards and assessments, developing systems for gathering and analyzing data to measure student progress, ensuring teacher effectiveness, and improving failing schools. All of these areas are unforgivingly measured by scores on tests in English, creating the unfortunate situation in which schools and teachers serving large numbers of emergent bilinguals are disproportionately likely to be labeled failures. Taken together, anti–bilingual education mandates and the test-and-punish approach of NCLB and Race to the Top indicate a return to a period of language restrictionism like that seen during the Americanization campaign of over a century ago (Menken, 2008). While reauthorization of NCLB is on the horizon, it appears that its overreliance on high-stakes testing will remain.

On the other hand, states such as Connecticut, New York, New Jersey, Illinois, Indiana, Texas, and Wisconsin currently mandate bilingual education in schools where there are twenty or more students who speak the same language other than English. Likewise, in 2010, Illinois became the first state to mandate bilingual education in preschool. Other states such as Washington mandate bilingual education when 'practicable.' Certain states, among them New Mexico and Michigan, effectively mandate bilingual education by funding only this type of program. And several states, including New Mexico, Oregon,[2] Rhode Island, and Washington, have adopted what they call "English Plus" mandates. This is best described in New Mexico's legislation:

> NOW THEREFORE BE IT RESOLVED . . . Proficiency on the part of our citizens in more than one language is to the economic and cultural benefit of our state and the nation, whether that proficiency derives from second language study by English speakers or from home language maintenance plus English acquisition by speakers of other languages. Proficiency in English plus other languages should be encouraged

2. At the time of writing, Oregon has introduced a bill to make English the state's official language, which will be voted upon by the state senate in the coming months.

throughout the State. (House Joint Memorial 16, New Mexico legislature, 1989).

Although bilingual education is more common in states with policies that explicitly mandate or fund it, legislation is no guarantee that funding will be provided; for instance, although policies mandating bilingual education remain in New York City, the policy is being disregarded in many schools and the number of programs has dramatically declined since the passage of NCLB (Menken, 2011). Finally, programs using students' native languages in order to maintain those languages or as an instructional strategy can also be found in classrooms across the United States, even in states where native language instruction is not promoted (García, 2009).

■ What are the problems with standardized testing for English language learners?
MONTY NEILL

English language learners (ELLs) face the same issues with standardized testing as do all other students, and they face additional problems. While tests can provide some useful information when properly used, high-stakes uses have produced many damaging consequences.[3]

Tests used to evaluate students and schools under No Child Left Behind (NCLB) are narrow, overwhelmingly multiple-choice instruments. Current reading tests fail to measure real thinking skills or richer content knowledge, while emphasizing lower-level skills measured through decontextualized short reading passages.

Teachers and administrators cannot rely on the tests to adequately inform them how well students really can read or do math. Because of the huge pressure to boost scores, schools increasingly focus what they know is tested and on the format in which it is tested. This leads to less instruction in untested subjects. Intense drill on rote aspects of learning and multiple-choice test practice crowds out important teaching and learning. This process de-motivates many students.

The ability of teachers to adapt instruction to the needs and interests of their students while ensuring attention to meaningful standards is further undermined when schools turn to scripted curricula, the constant use of externally mandated mini-tests, and similar techniques to raise (inflate) scores. These problems are more intense in schools with student groups such as ELLs that score low because those schools are most vulnerable to NCLB-mandated sanctions. Thus, ELLs suffer greater harm from the misuse of these narrow instruments. Administrators must help change harm-

---

3. The evidence on the points made here is vast. See, for example, Neill et al. (2004) and other material at http://www.fairtest.org; and Baker et al. (2010).

ful policies while doing their utmost to ensure high-quality curricula, instruction, and assessment despite the power of the tests.

ELLs face additional issues. Subject area tests often have less accuracy for ELLs than for other students. Linguistic complexity in test items can hinder students' ability to demonstrate their knowledge. Particular terms may be confusing, as happens, for example, between similar-seeming but different Spanish and English words. Students may grasp the math but not the language of the math question. Tests with simplified language have shown some ability to overcome some of these problems, but administrators need to be extra wary of using test results in evaluating ELLs. In addition, a student may receive content instruction primarily or wholly in English. S/he may have insufficient English to be fairly assessed in English. However, assessment in the native language (if available) may not be helpful if the student is not literate in that language or has learned content in English (e.g., math) but has not acquired enough academic English to be fairly assessed in that language.[4]

Finally, while tests of language proficiency have improved, the Federal government does not yet seem to view them as adequate. In any event, no one test should be used as a stand-alone basis for a decision when other information, such as student classroom work and teacher evaluations, is available.

Careful student evaluation by teachers is educationally more important and can fulfill many assessment needs that cannot be met by standardized tests. The critical question, then, is how to ensure teachers are skilled, accurate assessors. For this, ongoing professional learning, particularly collaboratively within schools, is essential. It will pay off not only in improved assessing, but better teaching and ultimately stronger learning.

■ What kinds of accommodations are appropriate when assessing English language learners?
JAMAL ABEDI

To provide fair assessment for every child in the nation, both Federal (e.g., NCLB Act of 2001, P.L. 107-110) and state legislation require the inclusion of all students, including English language learners (ELL students) in national and state assessments. States are then required to consistently and accurately assess these student's content knowledge and level of English proficiency by providing appropriate accommodations that help them present a more valid picture of what they know and are able to do.

However, if the accommodations used for these students alter the focal construct, then the assessment outcomes for these students may not be

4. See Neill (2005) for more discussion and references for this section.

valid and may not be combined in the analyses and reporting of the assessment results. Therefore, accommodations used for ELL students should be examined based on the following criteria: (1) effectiveness, (2) validity, (3) differential impact, (4) feasibility, and (5) relevance.

Accommodations are effective if they make assessments more accessible for ELL students. As for validity, the level of impact of accommodations on the mainstream student population should be examined. If accommodations change the performance of non-ELL students for whom accommodations are not intended, then the accommodations may have altered the focal construct. If so, they should either be removed from the assessment system, or if they improve the assessment quality for all, they should be provided to all students.

With respect to the differential impact of accommodations, student's background characteristics should be considered when assigning accommodations. For example, accommodations that may be useful for ELL students who are more proficient in English or have been enrolled in English-only classes may not help ELL students at a lower level of English proficiency.

The feasibility of accommodations is also an important factor in accommodation decisions. Accommodations that are difficult to implement may not be applicable regardless of how effective and valid they are. For example, one-on-one testing as a form of accommodation would be a burden for the test administration.

Relevance is another criterion for evaluating accommodations. Many of the accommodations currently used for ELL students were created for and used by students with disabilities. For example, providing *multiple test breaks* or *marking answers on the test booklet* may help students with certain disabilities but may be of less help for ELL students. Similarly, language-based accommodations, such as a customized dictionary, that are useful for ELL students may not help students with significant cognitive disabilities.

Based on these five criteria and the research literature on accommodations for English language learners, the following are examples of accommodations that are deemed relevant for ELL students:

1. Bilingual Version of the Tests. This accommodation is used to reduce the impact of language factors on the assessment outcome of ELL students when the language of instruction and language of assessment are aligned.

2. English/Bilingual Glossary. English and bilingual glossaries, with a brief individual definition or a paraphrase, provide definitions of non–content-related terms that appear in the test.

3. Customized English/Bilingual Dictionary. A customized dictionary is a literal cut-and-paste of actual dictionary entries which only includes terms that are (1) in the test and (2) non–content related. It is logistically feasible, as it is only a few extra pages attached to the test rather than the entire volume of a dictionary.

4. English/Bilingual Commercial Dictionary. Providing a dictionary (English and bilingual) is another commonly used accommodation; however, it may provide unfair advantage because of explanations, definitions, pictures, and examples of terminology if content-related terms are included.

5. Linguistically Modified Assessment. Linguistic modification involves taking existing assessments and simplifying the linguistic features that are considered irrelevant to the content and unnecessary in the assessment.

6. Computer Accommodation. Different forms of accommodations for ELL students can be provided via computers. For example, instead of looking up the definition of a word in a dictionary, a pop-up glossary can provide the definition to a student instantly during the test.

■ Has progress been made in raising achievement of English language learners since the passage of No Child Left Behind in 2001?

WAYNE E. WRIGHT

Title III of NCLB is designed to hold states and districts accountable for raising the achievement of English language learners (ELLs). Nonetheless, reports from and commissioned by the U.S. Department of Education (DOE) reveal that few states have met their Title III ELL student performance goals, and that achievement data are unable to document increased ELL student performance.

Under Title III, school districts must set annual performance goals (annual measureable achievement objectives) based on increases in the number or percentage of ELLs in (1) learning English, (2) attaining English proficiency, and (3) passing Title I mandated state reading and math tests. In a 2008 report to Congress, the DOE reported that none of the states met all of their Title III ELL performance goals in 2006. In 2010, the American Institutes for Research (AIR), in a DOE-commissioned report, found that only 11 states met their ELL performance goals in 2008 (Boyle, Taylor, Hurlburt, & Soga, 2010). Nonetheless, the authors and ELL experts cited in the report declared "it's not possible to conclude that the increase over two years from no states to 11 states reaching their goals means that the achievement of such students is improving" (Zehr, 2010, p. 10).

The AIR Report outlines why achievement data cannot demonstrate ELL student progress.

- As many as 17 states failed to report sufficient data to determine if they met each of their performance goals.
- Expected performance levels in learning and attaining English varies widely because each state sets its own goals. For example, in 2008:
  - Performance targets for student progress in learning English (goal 1) ranged from 20% (KS and NM) to 85% (IL).

- Performance targets for students attaining English proficiency (goal 2) ranged from 0.5% (SC) to 70% (NJ).
- Expected performance levels on reading and math tests vary widely because each state sets different targets for passing rates for each grade level and test. For example, in 2008:
  - Passing rates for 8th grade math ranged from 33% (ME) to 86% (TN).
- State language and content-area tests vary widely in content and level of difficulty, thus making meaningful comparisons impossible.
- State definitions of "progress in learning English" and "attaining English proficiency" vary widely, even among states that use the same proficiency tests.
- Even within single states, progress cannot be determined because most states have revised their tests and/or performance targets.
- Nineteen states (as of 2007) have not imposed accountability actions on school districts due to delays in creating English language proficiency standards and assessments and doubts about the validity of their performance target determinations.

Based on these and other findings, the AIR Report concludes, "This lack of stability, consistency, and transparency surrounding the implementation of Title III performance objectives raises concerns that states' Title III accountability systems may not be effectively informing and motivating improvement at this time" (p. 19).

While NCLB failed to show ELL improvement based on its own mandated measures, research has shown that NCLB's narrow focus on high-stakes testing frequently leads to narrowed test-preparation curricula and programs and instruction that are ill-suited to meeting the language and academic needs of ELL students (Menken, 2008; Olsen, 2010; Wright 2005, 2007; Wright & Choi, 2006). ELLs are, however, capable of making tremendous progress in learning English and academic content when provided with high-quality programs and instruction tailored to their linguistic and academic strengths and needs (August & Shanahan, 2006; Genesee, Lindholm-Leary, Saunders, & Christian, 2006; Wright, 2010).

■ **Has progress been made in raising the achievement of English language learners since the passage of English-only laws in California, Arizona, and Massachusetts?**
PATRICIA GÁNDARA

In 1998 Proposition 227 was passed in California, effectively banning bilingual education for most students in that state. The premise of the initiative was that English language learners (ELLs) were performing poorly because bilingual education had impeded their academic progress and that an English-only instructional policy would accelerate their acquisition of English. Proposition 227 was followed, in Arizona, by Proposition 203, a similar but slightly more restrictive initiative, which passed in 2000. Then in 2002, Massachusetts was the third state to pass legislation built on the same model, which came in the form of Question 2. In every case the promise was that ELLs would rapidly become fluent in English, "not normally intended to exceed one year," and make significant academic progress.

With as much as a decade's worth of data on the outcomes for ELLs in these states it is now possible to say with certainty how this mandate for English-only instruction has turned out. Parrish et al. (2006) concluded in a 5-year study funded by the California Department of Education that "since the passage of Proposition 227 . . . the performance gap between English learners and native English speakers has remained virtually constant in most subject areas for most grades" (page viii), and "we estimate the probability of an EL being redesignated to fluent English proficient status after 10 years in California to be less than 40 percent" (page ix). Thus, neither the ELL students' acquisition of English nor their achievement appeared to be accelerated significantly as a result of the passage of Proposition 227. A second study conducted at Stanford University came to similar conclusions four years later: "On balance, it seems fairly certain that the sledgehammer approach to dismantling bilingual education in California disrupted any coherence that may have existed in the system, harmed students in the immediate term, and on average created no overall benefit" (Wentworth et al., 2010, p. 47). An additional reason that there were no striking differences in the performance of ELLs in the aftermath of Proposition 227 is that more than 70% of ELL students in California were *already* in English-only instructional programs before Proposition 227. The idea that bilingual instruction could have been the reason for poorly faring students was specious.

Studies conducted in Arizona to determine the effects of Proposition 203 in that state had similar findings but with an additional twist. Mahoney and her colleagues (2010) concluded "the gain [in test scores] experienced before Proposition 203 was nearly identical to the gain after Proposition 203" (p. 61). It is also notable that in Arizona, as in California, a small minority of students were enrolled in bilingual instruction prior to passage of the law; only 21% of ELLs were assigned to bilingual instruction in Arizona in 2000 when the initiative passed.

A study of the impact of Proposition 203 on special education placement in Arizona was conducted by Artiles and colleagues (2010), concluding that "after 2002 [the year Proposition 203 was enacted], ELs had a greater risk than their English proficient peers of receiving special education services . . ." (p. 112). The researchers further questioned if schools were "increasingly relying on special education as a way of coping with the unrealistic requirements of these restrictive language policies or the lack of preparation of teachers to meet these students' needs" (p. 114).

Finally, researchers in Massachusetts examined the data in that state to determine if Question 2 had met its promise of increasing achievement for their ELL students. The great majority of ELLs are found in the Boston Public Schools (BPS), and so the researchers relied on these district data. Uriarte and colleagues (2010) found that "the achievement gaps in both math and ELA, but especially in math, widened between ELs and . . . students in general education . . . " (p. 83), and " . . . although drop out rates increased across BPS . . . between 2003 [when Question 2 passed] and 2006, the magnitude of the increase for ELs was significantly larger than among students in general education . . . " (p. 83). Like California, the researchers found that the abrupt closing of bilingual programs and the shift to English-only instruction created significant disruptions in the education of the ELL students that persisted for years in BPS.

To summarize the long-term outcomes for ELLs under the English-only instructional regimes imposed by California, Arizona, and Massachusetts: Propositions 227 and 203 and Question 2 have not delivered on the promise of accelerating English proficiency or academic achievement, and in each state there have been additional negative consequences for ELLs. There has been no narrowing in achievement gaps between ELLs and non-ELLs in any of the states, and there appears to have been a widening of the gaps in Massachusetts as well as a disturbing increase in drop out, especially among younger ELL students. There are indications in Arizona that more ELLs are placed in special education in a misguided effort to meet students' needs.

■ What does a valid and reliable accountability system for English language learners need to include?
JAMES CRAWFORD[5]

Seven years after passage of the No Child Left Behind Act, it is clear that the law is failing English language learners (ELLs). While NCLB's system of "holding schools accountable" has brought increased "attention" to these students, the effects have been more harmful than beneficial. By relying on arbitrary achievement targets and invalid assessments, the law cannot make accurate determinations about school quality. Moreover, the high-stakes nature of its accountability system has had perverse effects that contradict everything we know about best practices for ELLs. Though portrayed as a "civil rights" measure by supporters, NCLB has proven to be the exact opposite. Its one-size-fits-all approach ignores what is unique

5. This piece was originally published as Crawford, J. (2009). *No Child Left Behind. A Failure for English Language Learners* (www.elladvocates.org). Copyright 2009 by the institute for Language Education Policy. It is reprinted here in its entirety with permission of James Crawford.

about ELLs, contradicting the basic principles established by the U.S. Supreme Court in *Lau v. Nichols* (1974). In practice, NCLB has reinforced a two-tier educational system, in which ELLs are taught a substandard curriculum that stresses basic skills in the two tested subjects while more privileged students receive a challenging, all-round education that fosters the creativity and critical thinking needed in college and professional careers.

NCLB's accountability framework depends on standardized test scores to make high-stakes decisions about schools. But valid and reliable assessments of academic achievement are not widely available for students whose English is limited. And it is doubtful they ever will be, considering the diversity of ELLs in levels of English proficiency.

- No one even pretends that achievement tests designed and normed for English speakers are valid or reliable for ELLs. Simply put, when children do not understand the language of the test, they are unable to demonstrate what they have learned.
- "Accommodations," such as allowing extra time or providing bilingual dictionaries, can sometimes raise ELLs' scores, but English-language tests with accommodations have not been proven valid or reliable in measuring what students know.
- In some states, tests of English language proficiency—which are more likely to be valid or reliable—were initially used under NCLB to assess ELLs in language arts. But the U.S. Department of Education has blocked the practice because these tests are not "aligned" to state standards and has mandated the use of achievement tests given to fluent English speakers.
- Native-language assessments are sometimes a solution, but only in a minority of cases. Currently, such tests are unavailable in most languages other than Spanish. Some are simply translations of English-language tests, which are neither valid nor reliable. Native-language assessments are also inappropriate for the vast majority of ELLs today who are being taught academic concepts, knowledge, and vocabulary in all-English programs.

NCLB requires states to set targets for "adequate yearly progress" (AYP) that are the same for all students, regardless of the educational challenges they may face. This approach, which has no basis in research or practice, makes no sense for students in general and for ELLs in particular.

- Students in the ELL "subgroup" are highly diverse in language and cultural background, socioeconomic status, amount of prior schooling, initial level of English, and other factors that determine how long it takes them to acquire English and transfer to mainstream classrooms.
- As a result, there are wide variations in their academic progress. Research has shown that it can take from one to six years for ELLs to become proficient in oral English and four to seven years to become proficient in academic English.

- Judging ELLs against arbitrary and unreasonable AYP standards only sets them and their schools up for failure. In effect, NCLB "holds schools accountable" for the demographic profile of their students—not for the quality of instruction.

The ELL subgroup, as currently conceived, is an inappropriate category for accountability purposes. By NCLB's own definition, the subgroup is composed of students who have difficulties reaching the proficient level on state standards because of language barriers. Sooner or later, all schools with an ELL subgroup are destined to be labeled failures and subjected to punitive sanctions. Here's why:

- The subgroup's composition is constantly changing, creating a "treadmill effect" in which ELLs' performance, on average, can never advance very far. As new students arrive speaking limited English, the effect is to pull down average scores. As students acquire English proficiency and leave the subgroup, again the effect is to pull down average scores.
- Thus, in this case, NCLB "holds schools accountable" for failing to achieve what is mathematically impossible—not for the quality of instruction.

The Bush administration has acknowledged some of these problems, but its regulations allowing schools additional "flexibility" in ELL assessment procedures and AYP calculations do not offer any real solutions. Specifically:

- Exempting newly arrived ELLs from language-arts assessments for 12 months has no scientific support—i.e., no research evidence to indicate that all-English assessments will be valid or reliable after that point. As noted above, studies show that it takes considerably longer for the average student to acquire a second language for academic purposes.
- Counting former ELLs for up to two years in calculating AYP is equally arbitrary and unscientific. At best, it will slightly postpone a school being labeled "needs improvement" on the basis of inaccurate information.

Despite NCLB's emphasis on "scientifically based" instruction, the law's flawed accountability system creates incentives for schools to abandon best practices developed through research and professional experience. Instead, it has encouraged practices known to be harmful for ELLs. These include:

- dismantling bilingual education programs and otherwise limiting native-language instruction because of pressures to raise ELL scores on English-language tests;
- narrowing the curriculum to language arts and math, the two subjects that count for AYP, at the expense of everything else in the school day;

- stressing test preparation and other drills that stress remediation in low-level skills instead of the enrichment opportunities open to mainstream students;
- replacing sound strategies for second-language acquisition with an excessive and inappropriate emphasis on English language arts;
- promoting a heavily phonics-based approach to win Reading First funding, even though it is neither supported by research nor tailored to ELLs' needs;
- encouraging "educational triage"—that is, focusing attention on children perceived to have a chance to score at the proficient level on tests, while ignoring those deemed hopeless as well as those likely to pass;
- retaining high-school ELLs in grade, allowing them to drop out, or even pressuring them to do so, merely to raise average test scores;
- discouraging school administrators from enrolling ELLs at all, because they are seen as a downward drag on scores that could lead to punitive sanctions;
- demoralizing dedicated educators and, all too often, driving them from the profession by the unfairness and irrationality of NCLB's accountability system.

What's the alternative? Schools should be held accountable for serving ELLs using a system that is accurate, equitable, flexible, and tailored to the unique needs of these students. It should also be based on long-established principles of ensuring equal opportunity.

- An appropriate accountability system would consider "inputs" as well as "outputs"—not just test scores but also financial resources, ELL program designs, qualified teachers, appropriate materials, challenging curricula, state-of-the art instructional methods, and so forth.
- Such a system already exists. The *Castañeda v. Pickard* (1981) test, designed to determine whether school districts are meeting their obligations to ELLs, has been a cornerstone of Federal civil-rights enforcement for more than 20 years. It provides that:
  - Instructional approaches for ELLs must be based on an educational theory recognized as sound by experts.
  - Resources, personnel, and practices must be reasonably calculated to implement the program effectively.
  - Programs must be evaluated and restructured, if necessary, to ensure that language barriers are being overcome.
- NCLB explicitly avoids requiring any particular instructional approach for ELLs. Thus it provides no guidance whatsoever about appropriate "inputs." *Castañeda* addresses this question—not through prescriptive requirements but through a set of criteria for decision making. It could be effectively incorporated into a state-administered accountability framework that would offer districts flexibility while ensuring that ELLs receive the appropriate services they need and deserve.

DIANE AUGUST AND ROBERT LIQUANTI

A valid and reliable accountability system at the school and district level should include longitudinal data on current and former ELLs, tracking them over time from school entry until they leave the state's school system. It is important to monitor the progress of both current and former ELLs for several reasons. First, maintaining a consistent subgroup designation for former and current ELLs yields more accurate information about performance and progress of the subgroup, thus enhancing program evaluation and improvement efforts. Second, continuing to monitor the progress of ELLs throughout their school careers recognizes the developmental nature of second language acquisition and allows better service delivery to students at all levels of English proficiency. Finally, calling increased attention to long-term ELLs ensures these underserved students receive additional instructional supports.

Data that are important to collect and report for each student include demographics, the context in which he or she has been educated, and English-language proficiency (ELP) and academic assessment results, including the student's initial ELP level. The demographic data might include the number of family members, parental occupation and levels of education, child's country of origin, and languages spoken in the home. Data related to instructional context might include the languages in which the child has been schooled and the percent of time the child has spent in content classes by language of instruction (e.g., second-grade math instructed in Spanish). Other student-related data that should be collected to monitor the progress of all students who begin school as ELLs includes number of absences and special education services, including gifted and talented services.

Students should be assessed to determine their levels of first and second language proficiency and content knowledge in core academic subjects in the languages in which they are schooled. All assessments should be developed using universal design principles to ensure that as many students as possible can fairly and accurately demonstrate their knowledge and skills. Additionally, because language is a key barrier to assessing second language content-area knowledge, appropriate accommodations should be provided to ELLs as necessary to give them linguistic access to the test items. However, this must be done without invalidating the test construct by giving ELLs an unfair advantage. While the research on specific accommodations for ELL students is limited, state policies specify a range of available accommodations for content assessments but they need to be selected carefully to ensure that they support each ELL's particular linguistic needs. In defining accommodations for ELLs several factors need to be considered, including the fact that ELLs are a heterogeneous population and not all ELLs benefit from the same accommodations (e.g., an ELL at an early stage of learning English and with limited literacy skills in English will not benefit from the availability of a dictionary as might an ELL who has an intermediate or advanced level of ELP). Accommodations for ELLs also need to be clearly distinguished from those intended for special education students. Assessment practices that can increase the validity of inferences made from content assessments given with accommodations include (1) monitoring accommodations provided for each content assessment; (2) examining student achievement data to evaluate effectiveness of each accommodation; and (3) disaggregating these data by students' levels of English language proficiency to assess the extent to which particular accommodations support students at different ELP levels.

Ideally assessment data should help teachers plan instruction for their students—that is, it should be formative in nature. In this era of standards-based reform, we suggest the data collected align with the state's content standards. In reporting outcomes, data should be disaggregated by ethnic background, ELP levels, and time in English instruction so that school personnel can track the progress of individual students according to these variables.

For additional information about valid and reliable accountability systems we suggest consulting the recommendations of the Working Group on ELL Policy, a group of researchers with extensive experience in the education of ELLs and a substantial understanding of the research on effective strategies for this population. The Working Group's mission is to bring a research perspective to developing recommendations, sharing information, and fostering dialogue among educators, policy makers, and other stakeholders about current policy issues affecting ELLs (http://ellpolicy.org/).

■ **How can we provide valid and reliable evidence of English language learner student growth and how can we use that evidence for decision making?**
MARGO GOTTLIEB and DIEP NGUYEN

There are several assessment issues embedded within this question, and as administrators, you need to disentangle what constitutes reliable and valid evidence for English language learners (ELLs) from its application and use. That is, unless there are proven reliabilities and validities attached to your assessments, the data are not meaningful, resulting in inappropriate or erroneous decisions about students. And, the higher the stakes for the assessment, the stronger the psychometric qualities must be. So let's tackle these issues one by one.

First, let's consider the reliability of the assessment. Reliability refers to dependability; assessment data collected from performance tasks must be consistent in scoring, interpreting, and reporting. Second, there's the validity of the assessment; that is, realistic and meaningful inferences must be drawn from results that match the measure's intended audience(s). In other words, instructional assessment tasks or measures administered to ELLs have to be mindful of the students' characteristics when being designed, tried out, refined, and implemented. Only then can administrators have confidence in the data and use it as a source of evidence of student performance.

Now, let's see how to accrue evidence of student growth for decision making. When speaking of ELLs, remember there are always two constructs to consider: growth in language development and growth in achievement. Therefore, as administrators, you always need to work with various data sources. In working in dual language settings or in language education programs where a language in addition to English is the medium of instruction, evidence must mirror the language in which the subject areas are taught.

The information gathered on ELLs should always be contextualized in light of the students' historical backgrounds and educational experiences. In doing so, we suggest using what we refer to as a Balanced Assessment System, Inclusive and Comprehensive, or the BASIC Model (Gottlieb & Nguyen, 2007), where data are pooled from multiple levels of implementation, including those from the state, district, language education program, school, and classroom, to create a profile of student learning. Built from shared educational goals, a unified vision, and commitment by teachers and school leaders, the evidence, by being directly related to teaching and learning, is both valued and valid. The BASIC model is represented in Figure 3.1.

The BASIC model includes both formative and summative assessment in order to produce the range of data needed for decision making within programs for second language learners at the classroom, program, dis-

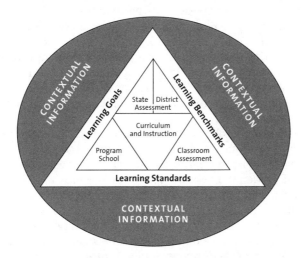

FIGURE 3.1 The BASIC model (Gottlieb & Nguyen, 2007).

trict, and state levels of implementation. Grounded in contextual information, framed by learning goals, standards, and benchmarks, and anchored in curriculum and instruction, these complementary data sources offer teachers and administrators powerful tools to measure student performance throughout the year. Implementation of the model calls for extensive planning and the development of an assessment framework that delineates the process of data collection, analysis, and reporting. Gottlieb and Nguyen (2007) lay out a step-by-step process that teachers and administrators can use to guide their work.

Finally is the issue of how evidence might be used for decision making. There are several considerations to keep in mind. (1) The application of data needs to match the purpose of the assessment. (2) Data ought to be current and timely to use as defensible evidence. (3) Stakeholders' perspectives should be included in the decision- making process. By establishing a baseline and then systematically gathering reliable and valid data on ELLs at regular intervals, you will be able to measure student growth over time and make appropriate decisions to optimize student achievement.

NANCY L. COMMINS and BARBARA MEDINA

Valid and reliable assessments for English language learners (ELLs) must address both English language proficiency level as well as academic achievement based upon identified standards. The challenge of assessing academic proficiency must be met using standards and assessment tools that provide a "truthful" measure of student content proficiency.

Current academic assessments are tools designed for native English speakers. For ELLs these assessments become tests of English language proficiency, not necessarily academic proficiency. In such a system, teachers and schools that serve linguistically diverse populations are often penalized when judged solely on whether their students meet benchmarks set for native English speakers. In moving away from a "one-size-fits-all" approach to a comprehensive standards and assessment system we can improve the validity and reliability of the data that inform your decisions as an instructional leader.

The first step is to recognize the need for instruction that supports English language development while also providing access to academic content. It is unwise—and not necessary—to wait 3 to 5 years for the full development of academic English language before providing ELL students with access to content instruction. Such decisions sustain an achievement gap and promote academic failure.

The second step is to identify standards that link language and academic proficiency. In Colorado, the newly adopted WIDA English Language Proficiency Standards provide developmentally appropriate standards for English language development while delineating a "pathway" that leads to Colorado student content and performance standards.

The third step is to build an assessment system that documents student progress in meeting grade-level standards. The Colorado Growth Model[6] moves beyond a single point assessment to document student growth compared to a cohort of students with similar scores. This kind of growth model provides a mechanism to identify where students begin and how they have progressed and allows educators to use assessment data in a more dynamic way to monitor achievement, make predictions, and suggest areas for improvement of instruction. Even though Colorado uses assessments designed for native English speakers, the use of a dynamic and statistically robust growth model provides substantial data for discussion to identify instructional strategies that result in student gains.

The growth model of assessment like the one used in Colorado is different from a "value added" model that is used to judge teachers. Using a complex statistical analysis, the data tells a story rather than providing a de-contextualized score. The student growth scores allow us to ask: Is the score one that we would have expected relative to other students who started with the same score previously? Is the score higher or lower? How much growth will students need to make in order to catch up or keep up on the road to academic proficiency? The individual student "stories" provide robust data for discussion of effective or ineffective instructional decisions at the classroom, school district, and even state level. The data provide a foundation for the identification of appropriate benchmarks across proficiency levels.

Another way that assessment can inform decision making is by using data from different sources in a collaborative approach to accountability. In this kind of system, educators identify desired student outcomes and the common assessments that will be used to measure them. This approach is exemplified by the BASIC model described in detail by Gottlieb and Nguyen (2007). The cornerstone of the BASIC model is a "pivotal portfolio." This portfolio system includes summative assessments required for evaluation of student achievement as well as formative assessments that are used to periodically measure student outcomes and inform instruction at the classroom level. They recommend that assessments include measures of oral language proficiency, literacy development, and academic learning. It is a model that can be adapted to programs that serve linguistically diverse populations at both the school and district levels.

A complement to such assessment systems would be a means for developing and disseminating indicators that students are learning, differentiated by language proficiency level. Teachers and students would benefit

6. The Colorado Growth Model was designed using an "open source" platform that is available to other states or entities that wish to use it. More information is available at https://edx.cde.state.co.us/growth_model/public/index.htm

greatly if exemplars of differentiated assessments and instructional activities that meet the needs of students at all levels of language proficiency were widely available. Schools, district, and even statewide collaborations could be initiated whereby individual teachers and schools could contribute to a centralized repository that could be accessed and shared.

SUMMARY

The challenge for educational leaders is to use dynamic assessment systems to develop statistically valid and reliable frameworks that link differentiated assessments with instructional and curricular innovations. The reward is the valid and reliable demonstration of student knowledge and skill that can inform ongoing decision making about effective curricular and instructional practice.

Implementing the kinds of approaches described previously reflects an asset orientation to linguistic and cultural diversity. It is predicated on the belief that all students, regardless of language proficiency level, can meet rigorous standards when provided with appropriate instruction and the means to display their knowledge.

TIMOTHY BOALS

English language learners (ELLs) need to develop their English language proficiency *and* their academic knowledge and skills. While all students typically take academic tests, including state and Federally mandated testing in reading and mathematics, ELLs must also be tested annually for progress in learning to listen, speak, read, and write in English. This is known as English language proficiency (ELP) testing.

ELP testing has changed greatly in recent years. Prior to the passage of the No Child Left Behind Act (2001), how schools tested ELLs for English growth was typically a local decision. Most states did not mandate one particular test. Some had a list of suggested tests and many permitted "informal assessments" based solely on teacher observation. Teacher observations of progress can be very valuable within classrooms, but if strict and consistent guidelines are not followed it is difficult to confirm the validity, reliability, and comparability of teacher observations. Commercially available ELP tests have been used for decades to add consistency to this process.

The recent Federal requirements for reporting ELP progress and attainment introduced new demands on ELP testing instruments that have led to a new generation of tests that provide higher levels of validity and reliability. The older assessments were fine for the purposes for which they were used. Teachers needed a basic English identification and screening tool for program placement. ELP tests were purchased and kept on hand to fill those needs.

Now the annual ELP tests resemble large-scale academic tests in many ways. Unlike the box kit teachers had on hand before, these assessments arrive at the district and must be held securely and administered during a state-determined testing window under strict administration guidelines. Certainly this is more time consuming for school staff and more costly for states. But these safeguards, along with design changes in the tests provide the stakeholders at all levels from the classroom up to the U.S. Department of Education the opportunity to see more clearly how the progress of these students is unfolding. Jamal Abedi (2007) notes the following characteristics of the new annually administered ELP assessments:

- They provide reliable scores across grades and across language progress levels, giving us a better picture of how and where growth is occurring kindergarten through high school within and between schools, districts, and states.
- They are aligned to State approved English development standards, which are in turn linked to State academic content standards, ensuring that the tests measure the specific academic English needed to succeed in school.

In addition to more reliable and valid ELP testing, our field is also grappling with how to better assess ELLs' content knowledge and skills. Current academic tests, even with allowable testing accommodations, are not giving us the best picture of student progress at low to intermediate levels of English language proficiency. This is because the lack of English knowledge "gets in the way" of performance on academic tests. We cannot be sure if the student is missing the question because he or she does not know the content or simply does not understand the question as presented. We are capable of developing better content tests that minimize the language barrier, allowing us to see what ELLs know and are able to do and clearly measure their progress even at lower levels of English language proficiency. Here's to hoping that we do it sooner rather than later.

BARBARA MARLER

Data or evidence-based decision making is essential for making appropriate decisions regarding services for ELLs. The use of data eradicates rules of thumb, tradition, custom, reliance on a single observation, and the notion of "the way it's always been done" as a basis for practice and establishes a research foundation as well as a collaborative and shared responsibility orientation toward policy. The steps in the process are as follows:

1. The administrator should lead the process of gathering valid and reliable data/evidence regarding academic achievement and language proficiency. This includes academic and language

proficiency testing, both standardized accountability measures and local measures such as common assessments. Additional demographic and needs assessment data are frequently helpful as well.

2. Once a tipping point is reached, i.e., sufficient data is amassed to make logical observations, the administrator should guide the process of data/evidence interpretation and analysis. Analysis must take into account research in the field of ESL/bilingual education (trends and specific studies), legal parameters, compliance requirements, local circumstances, student characteristics (cultural background, previous schooling, personality, and family dynamics), professional judgment (training, education and experience in the area of ELS/bilingual education), and professional preferences (values, beliefs, vision, and mission such as those established through professional learning communities). Good data management systems can increase the efficacy of collection and analysis.

3. After interpretation and analysis, the administrator should assert influence in the process of making observations about ELLs' performance and/or progress made to make certain that these observations reflect what is known with regard to linguistically and culturally responsive education. Observations must be confined to the school or district's sphere of influence—what educators can actually accomplish, change, or do during the school day—and not include what the students and or parents need to do differently.

4. Observations lead to the development of hypotheses of practice or HOPs. The administrator should model the practice for extended validation for the HOPs; they can be furthered validated or invalidated by continued collection, review, and interpretation of data/evidence. HOPs form the foundation for goal setting.

5. Goals should cluster around the following areas: improving instructional practice, meeting legal compliance, crafting program design, and setting policy. The administrator should hold all educators accountable for organizing goals around these areas. The ultimate goal is always to improve ELLs' academic/linguistic performance and/or progress.

6. Once a goal or a set of goals is determined, an action or game plan is developed to put the goal(s) into practice. Monitoring implementation of the action/game plan is an ongoing process that provides evaluation of intended outcomes and allows for revision and a cycle of continuous improvement. The administrator should establish the process for monitoring the action/game plan that allows for his /her continued influence to promote and sustain valid and reliable decision making for ELLs.

Data-based or evidence-based decision making assures that administrators and teachers craft and implement effective and efficient language-assistance services for ELLs that are responsive to students' needs, legally compliant, reflective of "best practice," and sensitive to local concerns and issues. The Perfect Match workshop series, offered by the Illinois Resource Center in partnership with the World-Class Instructional Design and Assessment (WIDA) Consortium, provides professional development for the implementation of these steps. In the *Perfect Match* workshop, participating leadership team members learn the steps in the process and the necessary strategies for implementation to assure that valid and reliable data/evidence drives the decision-making process with regard to ELLs.

■ How do we use evidence on program effectiveness to inform policy?
JUDITH KWIAT YTURRIAGO

In the spring of 2004, the Evanston School District 65 (SD 65) School Board in Evanston, Illinois took a vote that drastically changed the bilingual program for English language learners (ELLs) in the entire district. The board voted to eliminate the pull-out, transitional bilingual education (TBE) program from kindergarten through fourth grade for the fall of 2004. What made this vote so unusual is that unlike many other districts that were eliminating TBE programs in favor of English-only programs, this board voted to establish a dual language education program for all Spanish-speaking students in the district. This decision did not come about overnight and was the result of four years of local data gathering and planned use of concrete evidence of the success of a program model, namely, two-way immersion (TWI), which was the type of dual language program offered in the district. The first two TWI kindergarten classrooms were started in two elementary schools in the fall of 2000.

This pattern of improved achievement has continued and is documented in Table 3.1 and Table 3.2, which detail the academic achievement of Hispanic students in SD 65. The majority of Hispanic students in SD 65 (over 95% in any given school year) begin in the TWI program in the primary grades and continue in the program until at least fifth grade. In Illinois, all school districts are mandated to not exit a student from a TBE or TWI program until that student has achieved specific scores in the categories of literacy and overall on the WIDA ACCESS Test for ELLs. In Illinois, TBE or TWI students must remain in a program until they have achieved a score on the ACCESS Test of 4.2 in the literacy category and 4.8 in the overall category.

TWI students continue to develop Spanish language proficiency in the middle grades in specially developed Spanish for Spanish speakers courses in grades six through eight. In addition, Hispanic TWI students are carefully monitored and receive specialized sheltered instruction services in the content areas throughout the middle grades.

TABLE 3.1 Percentage of the SD 65 TWI Hispanic 2005 Cohort Students Who Met or Exceeded Standards on the Illinois Standards Achievement Test (ISAT) from 2005 through 2010: Source www.district65.net.

Hispanic 2005 Cohort of TWI Students	2005 Grade 3	2006 Grade 4	2007 Grade 5	2008 Grade 6	2009 Grade 7	2010 Grade 8
ISAT Reading	50% met or exceeded	70% met or exceeded	80% met or exceeded	71% met or exceeded	70% met or exceeded	82% met or exceeded
ISAT Math	70% met or exceeded	81% met or exceeded	77% met or exceeded	86% met or exceeded	83% met or exceeded	90% met or exceeded

Prior to the decision to end the SD 65 TBE program and replace it with the TWI program, SD 65 had three program models to serve ELLs: (1) transitional bilingual education, (2) transitional program of instruction (TPI) which is a sheltered English instructional model, and (3) two-way immersion. When the TWI program was started, about 7% of the Spanish-speaking students were enrolled in it, with the rest enrolled in the TBE program. The transitional program of instruction program had about 25% of ELLs in it from thirty countries who spoke twenty-seven languages. The TBE program was a half-day pull-out program that had been in existence for more than twenty years. The academic performance of students who were in that program was consistently low year after year as measured by local curriculum-based assessments in reading and math, as well as by state standardized tests. After the first year, the ELLs in the TWI program outperformed the Spanish-speaking TBE students on the three local kindergarten assessments in Spanish used to gauge readiness for first grade. Results were similar during the 2001–2002 school year for the same two groups on the district assessments for first graders going on to second

TABLE 3.2 Percentage of the SD 65 Hispanic Eighth Grade Students Who Met or Exceeded Standards on the ISAT from 2001 through 2010: Source www.district65.net.

Hispanic Students	2001 8th Graders	2002 8th Graders	2003 8th Graders	2004 8th Graders	2005 8th Graders	2006 8th Graders	2007 8th Graders	2008 8th Graders	2009 8th Graders	2010 8th Graders
Math	49	41	47	52	53	84	76	71	90	90
Reading	67	45	46	48	56	77	77	72	77	82

grade. Other measures used to gauge teacher and parent opinions of the TWI program also demonstrated overwhelming satisfaction.

These data were presented to the school board with great fanfare, and the first significant vote that the board took was to expand the TWI program in the fall of 2002 to four kindergartens and two first grades in two schools. The TBE program continued to serve students in grades two through five. Local assessments in math and reading in the spring of 2003 again showed a significant difference in the scores of the Spanish-speaking TWI and TBE second-grade students. The TWI students consistently outperformed the TBE students on all measures. That spring, the school board again voted to expand and consolidate the TWI program in two schools.

The following spring, test results showed the same advantage for Hispanic students in the TWI program. Spanish-speaking TWI students outperformed their peers in the TBE program, and, most impressive to the mostly English-speaking school board members, the TWI English-speaking students performed the same as or better than their English-speaking peers in the general education classrooms in the same school. This increase in academic achievement for TWI students was despite the fact that the English-speaking student group in the TWI program was as racially and economically diverse as the general education students in this same school.

Spanish-speaking ELLs who had been in the TBE program in the second and third grades were placed in the TWI program for third and fourth grade in fall 2004. This program change resulted in three TWI third grades and three TWI fourth grades with eight or nine English speakers in each class along with eleven to twelve Spanish speakers. In years past, the numbers of English speakers and Spanish speakers in each class had been more equal. The ratio of English speakers to Spanish speakers in the lower grades did remain equal. While the program was expanded each year, Spanish-speaking fifth- through eighth-grade ELLs were still served in a TBE program simply because TWI had not yet reached fifth grade. In 2005 after the TBE program was eliminated, the TWI program was stabilized in five elementary schools and the academic achievement of the Hispanic students in the program began to steadily improve as previously documented in Tables 3.1 and 3.2.

The TWI program is now in five elementary schools and serves 331 Hispanic students, 212 white students, 44 Black students, 32 multiracial students, and four Asian students. In these five schools, TWI is now in six kindergartens, six first grades, six second grades, six third grades, six fourth grades, and six fifth grades. By fifth grade, over 96% of the Hispanic students have been reclassified as English proficient based on the ACCESS Test for ELLs. The bilingual program in the three middle schools now serves only 12 Hispanic students who entered the TWI or bilingual programs in the later grades. The expansion of the TWI program in SD 65 by the policy makers in the district was a result of making data-driven decisions based on the evidence of program effectiveness over the last ten years.

■ How do we develop a language policy that is appropriate for our school and community context?
REBECCA FREEMAN FIELD

Since the passage of the No Child Left Behind Act of 2001, administrators have been challenged to ensure that all of their constituents (teachers, support staff, parents, students, community partners) understand and support the ways that they organize their bilingual and English-medium programs and practices for English language learners (ELLs) at the local level. The effort to clearly articulate how ELLs are to reach the same high standards as all students in the school or district is complicated by the confusion, controversy, variation, and change that we find in the United States today about effective programs, practices, and assessments for ELLs. A school district or school language policy and implementation plan can help educators navigate this complex challenge.

A school language policy identifies areas in the school's scope of operations and programs in which language problems exist. It sets out what the school intends to do about areas of concern and includes provisions for follow-up, monitoring, and revision of the policy itself in light of changing circumstances. It is a dynamic action statement that changes along with the dynamic context of a school (Corson, 1999).

An effective language policy and implementation plan should (1) comply with all Federal, state, and local policies and accountability requirements, (2) respond to local community needs, interests, and concerns, (3) promote the development and implementation of educationally sound programs for language learners (ELLs and/or English speakers) that deliver valid and reliable results, (4) be understood and supported by all constituents (administrators, teachers, students, parents, community members), and (5) drive decision making on the local level. The language policy should begin with a mission statement that clearly articulates the school district's or school's stance toward languages other than English. School districts and schools that are committed to maintaining and developing languages other than English, not only for ELLs but also for English speakers, must reflect this mission in all of their policies and procedures. This is critical, given the increasing English-only orientation that we find throughout the United States today, particularly in low-income contexts.

Most schools and school districts today do not have one explicit, coherent language policy that is endorsed by the school board and supported by a written implementation plan that includes procedures guiding all aspects of education (in a readily accessible format). However, all schools with language learners do have language policies that guide practice at the local school level. In some cases the language policies are not explicitly written but are implicit in practices that we can observe within and across schools in the district. In other cases the policies are explicitly written but the practitioners working in classrooms throughout the school or the district are unaware of the existence or meaning of these policies, which leads to inconsistencies in implementation. In many cases we find gaps, confusion, or contradictions in policies and procedures that are to guide the education of language learners, including but not limited to ELLs.

Administrators and leadership team members can lead the effort to develop coherent language policies and implementation plans for their schools and school districts. For example, they can organize a retreat or an institute where they clarify the mission and vision of the school district or school around linguistic and cultural diversity, and articulate the goals, outcomes, and timetable for this language planning process. Participants in this process will need to (1) review existing policies and procedures guiding all aspects of program development, implementation, monitoring, and evaluation, (2) identify gaps, inconsistencies, confusion, or contradictions in those policies and procedures, and (3) make recommendations for coherent policies and procedures that are aligned with what the research tells us about effective programs and practices for ELLs/bilingual learners to address these areas of concern. Participants in the development of the language policy and implementation plan should represent the multiple levels of institutional authority in the school district (such as central, regional, and school-based administrators, teachers, counselors, and community liaisons) and the range of linguistic and cultural groups served by the schools. Including participants with this wide range of expertise and interests is essential because it increases the likelihood that the language policy and implementation plan that emerges will be understood and supported by all constituents throughout the school or district and community.

Since writing a language policy and implementation plan is a large task that takes time, it is useful to divide into task forces with specific, clearly defined charges such as:

- defining programs for language learners that are approved in the district (bilingual, English-medium, heritage language, world-language) with reference to the research base that supports these program models;
- listing instructional approaches that should be found in all classes that serve bilingual learners (e.g., sheltered instruction, differentiated instruction);
- describing the components of the district's assessment and accountability system with attention to the needs of language learners;

- identifying special challenges (e.g., students with limited former education, struggling readers and writers, long-term ELLs, special education needs);
- planning professional development;
- setting up outreach and advocacy.

The task forces first collaborate on their particular tasks, and then share their work with all constituents in the school district and community. The

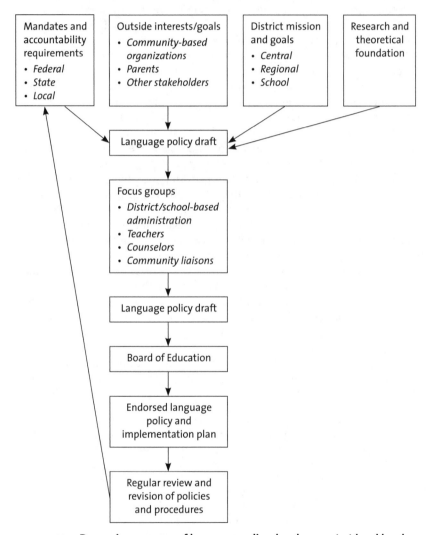

FIGURE 3.2 Dynamic processes of language policy development at local level.

language policy that emerges should be a short, concise document that lays out general goals, definitions, and principles, and it should be submitted to the school board for approval. The implementation plan will be a much longer document that includes all of the policies and procedures that different constituents (administrators, mainstream teachers, ESL/ bilingual teachers, literacy/special education specialists, parents, support staff) need to follow in order to realize the mission and vision of the district language policy.

Prior to submitting the language policy to the school board for approval, the language policy and implementation plan must be understood and supported by the various constituents. Administrators may choose to organize a series of focus groups, for example, with district administrators, school principals, teachers, and community representatives to review and respond to the proposed language policy draft. Administrators may choose to consult with external partners, for example, from a university or resource center, to ensure that the policy and implementation plan is in fact aligned with all of the relevant federal and state policies and with research on effective programs, practices, and assessments for ELLs. Once this has been accomplished, the language policy is ready for board approval.

To ensure that the policy and implementation plan is actually implemented in practice, district and school administrators must regularly monitor its use and address program and professional development needs as they arise. To ensure that the policy and implementation plan changes with the dynamic context of the school—as Federal, state, or local mandates are revised or developed, or as school or community demographics change, or as student performance or program effectiveness data yield important new insights—the policies and procedures must be regularly reviewed and revised. Administrators may choose to institutionalize an annual review of all data, policies, and procedures to ensure that the written policies and procedures actually drive decision making on the local level. Figure 3.2 represents the dynamic processes of language policy development at the local level.

SURVEY FOR REFLECTION AND ACTION

This survey reflects the guiding principles for policies and accountability requirements for ELLs that were articulated in the Introduction to the chapter. Read the following statements to guide your survey of the policies and procedures for ELLs that are in place in your school/district. Indicate the extent to which each of the following applies to your school: DK—don't know; 1—strongly disagree; 2—disagree; 3—agree; 4—strongly agree. At the end of the survey, write down one to three strengths and future possibilities you identified through your review of your policies and procedures for ELLs. Then identify one to three concrete actions that you can take to improve those policies and procedures.

The school district/school has a language policy for ELLs and an implementation plan that includes the following:

- A mission statement that (a) aligns the district's/school's policies, programs, and practices with all local, state, and Federal mandates and (b) clearly articulates the district's/school's stance on languages other than English.   DK 1 2 3 4

- Procedures ensuring that ELLs have access to all programs and services that are available to all students, and that ELLs' needs are considered in all aspects of district/school programming (e.g., curriculum, instruction, assessments, promotion and retention, special needs services).   DK 1 2 3 4

- Procedures governing the uses of languages in the school system, including issues of language choice, translators and interpreters, and languages of tests.   DK 1 2 3 4

- Defining criteria of the type(s) of program(s)—sheltered content-area instruction (SI)/specially designed academic instruction in English (SDAIE), English-as-a-second-language (ESL)/English language development (ELD), bilingual education (transitional bilingual education, dual language education), heritage language programs—that is/are implemented in the district/school.   DK 1 2 3 4

- Procedures for the allocation of languages for instructional purposes at every grade level (i.e., how much English as well as instruction in the primary/partner language is included at different stages of language proficiency in each type of program).   DK 1 2 3 4

- Procedures that enable the identification of students who are eligible for ESL/bilingual/heritage language services.   DK 1 2 3 4

- Procedures governing the assessment and placement of ELLs in appropriate program(s).   DK 1 2 3 4

- Procedures for the recruitment, retention, and professional development of all teachers, administrators, and staff who work with ELLs.   DK 1 2 3 4

- Procedures governing all aspects of program implementation   DK 1 2 3 4
  from placement to proficiency, including testing
  accommodations, exit criteria based on multiple measures,
  promotion and graduation requirements, and ways to address
  ELLs' special needs.

- Procedures governing the collection, analysis, and use of   DK 1 2 3 4
  standardized and alternative assessment data on English
  language development.

- Procedures governing the collection, analysis, and use of   DK 1 2 3 4
  standardized and alternative assessment data on home
  language development (when home language development
  is a goal of the program).

- Procedures governing the collection, analysis, and use of   DK 1 2 3 4
  standardized and alternative assessment data on the academic
  achievement of ELLs in the language(s) used for instructional
  purposes.

- Procedures governing program monitoring and evaluation.   DK 1 2 3 4

- Procedures for the ways that summative and formative data are   DK 1 2 3 4
  used to inform instruction, program, and professional
  development and to determine the effectiveness of different
  types of programs for ELLs.

- Procedures for informing parents of all aspects of program   DK 1 2 3 4
  development, implementation, and evaluation.

- Procedures for articulating with community-based   DK 1 2 3 4
  organizations and institutions of higher learning to support all
  aspects of program development, implementation, and
  evaluation.

- Procedures governing how components of the language policy   DK 1 2 3 4
  and implementation plan are reviewed and revised on a regular
  basis.

- Procedures for how individual schools and the school district   DK 1 2 3 4
  overall can obtain the resources they need to make
  implementation of the language policy a reality.

Strengths of our school district/school policies and procedures

1. _____

2. _____

3. _____

Future Possibilities

1. _____

2. _____

3. _____

Action steps

1. _____

2. _____

3. _____

DEVELOPING INSTRUCTIONAL PROGRAMS
FOR ENGLISH LANGUAGE LEARNERS

GUIDING PRINCIPLES
- We understand that English language learners (ELLs) are everyone's responsibility.
- We assess the strengths and needs of our ELLs/bilingual learners.
- We clearly articulate our goals for ELLs/bilingual learners and the means of assessing student performance and development relative to those goals.
- Our instructional program for ELLs/bilingual learners is aligned with state content and language proficiency standards and based on sound educational and language learning theory.
- We ensure that our instructional program for ELLs/bilingual learners has adequate resources for implementation.
- We use an authentic assessment and accountability system that yields the range of data we need to inform all of our decision-making regarding the ELLs/bilingual learners in our schools.

INTRODUCTION

Although English language learners (ELLs) must ultimately reach the same high educational standards that all students must reach, there is no one-size-fits-all program model that schools can uncritically implement to accomplish this goal. Schools vary tremendously in terms of the student and community populations they serve, local goals for ELLs/bilingual learners, and the school's human and material resources and constraints. Administrators must assess the specific strengths and needs of their students and school. They can then turn to more than thirty years of research on and practice in a range of English-medium and bilingual programs that have been developed for ELLs/bilingual learners. This research base yields strong converging evidence about critical features of effective programs. Administrators can draw on this research base to inform their decisions about the specific programs that they develop for their school and community contexts.

The goal is for schools to develop educationally sound instructional programs that everyone (parents, teachers, district personnel, community members) understands and supports, and to implement those programs effectively so they can deliver results for ELLs/bilingual learners. By instructional programs for ELLs, we mean all of the instruction that an ELL receives in a day, not just time spent with an ESL or bilingual specialist. Program coherence is key. Unfortunately, too few schools develop coherent programs for their ELLs/bilingual learners, and too many ELLs/bilingual learners lag behind their English-speaking counterparts. This chapter guides administrator and leadership team efforts to meet this challenge and plan instructional programs that are appropriate for the ELLs/all learners in their schools.

The chapter begins with defining features of effective programs for ELLs/bilingual learners in any context. We then move to general questions about prototypical bilingual and English-medium programs that we find in U.S. public schools today, and about the research base on the effectiveness of these different kinds of programs. The majority of the chapter addresses more specific questions about program development. The responses that experienced educators provide to these questions give insight into the decision-making processes of effective leaders in diverse school and community contexts. The chapter concludes with a Survey for Reflection and Action that administrators and leadership teams can use to identify strengths of and future possibilities for the programs for ELLs that they have developed in their schools/districts.

■ What are defining features of effective programs for English language learners?
NANCY L. COMMINS

Programs for English language learners (ELLs) differ according to the number of students served, the languages they speak, the available human and material resources and—quite important—public policy and the political will of the community. In some programs all content-area instruction is in English, while others use students' primary language for the reinforcement of content-area concepts or for initial literacy instruction. In ideal circumstances, programs aim for full academic bilingualism through in-depth and ongoing development of both literacy and content in students' primary language and English (Miramontes, Nadeau, & Commins, 2011). An important goal of each kind of program must be to produce academically proficient English speakers. The availability of primary language instruction will affect the following:

- The length of time it takes for second language learners to function academically at the same level as native English speakers.
- The extent to which teachers will need to modify their instruction to make the curriculum understandable to all students.
- Students' potential for lifetime bilingualism.

The less access students have to learning through their primary language, the longer it will take to reach full English proficiency (Thomas & Collier, 2002). English-medium programs, far from being the easy solution, take more concerted efforts on behalf of all the teaching staff to ensure that second language learners achieve success. In addition, students in English-medium programs are much more likely to lose their first language.

While programs for second language learners can vary dramatically, they all should be guided by certain basic principles and understandings. It is very important that students receive planned, daily instruction in English as a second language and that teachers do whatever is necessary to make content-area instruction understandable through all learning modalities. The following critical features can guide educators' efforts to address the needs of their ELLs, regardless of program type.

Create a Climate of Belonging

- Utilize materials that value students' home language and culture.
- Reach out to parents and community members.
- Encourage parents to interact with their children in their strongest language (usually not English).

Implement Standards-based Instruction

- Organize instruction around a common body of knowledge, with attention to differentiation in the methods of delivery.
- Identify enduring understandings and essential vocabulary and highlight them in instruction.
- Gather curriculum materials at a wide range of reading levels.

Use Data to Inform and Shape Instruction

- Find out who the learners are and what they bring to instruction.
- Assess students' academic and literacy skills in their primary language, whether or not it is used in instruction.
- Use multiple forms of assessment to document students' progress as well as attainment of benchmarks.

Elevate Oral Language Practice

- Provide constant opportunities for interaction in order to increase student talk and decrease teacher talk.
- Determine the language structures required for participation in instructional activities, and provide students with opportunities to practice them aloud.

Deliver Meaning-based Literacy Instruction

- Use text to represent ideas and concepts that students understand and can say.
- Incorporate language experience approaches.
- Make conscious connections between the big ideas from the content areas and what students will read and write during literacy instruction.

Prepare the Physical Environment to Tie Meaning to Text

- Use every inch of the classroom as a resource for students in their independent work.

- Make it apparent through words and pictures posted on the walls what students are learning about.

Collaborate with Professional Colleagues

- Take a schoolwide perspective on meeting students' needs.
- Work in grade-level or content-area teams.
- Find time to articulate across grade levels: topics and genres, enduring concepts, shared resources, expectations, and assessments.

WAYNE E. WRIGHT

There are a wide variety of program models for ELL students. The best, most appropriate, and most feasible program for a school is determined by such factors as the sociocultural context of the school and background of the students, and the unique needs of the ELL student population to be served. All effective program models, however, share the following characteristics.

- **Effective programs ensure that ELLs attain proficiency in English.**

ELLs have the right to acquire English language proficiency to the highest levels possible (Corson, 2001). Indeed, they need English to succeed in school and in life in the United States. ELL programs must therefore provide systematic and direct ESL instruction that is (a) tailored to the linguistic needs of the ELL students, (b) designed to help them improve their English language proficiency each year, and (c) designed to help them ultimately be redesignated as fluent English proficient. Language and literacy instruction goes beyond the cognitive processes of individual students and their acquisition of discrete skills (Street, 1984; Wiley, 2005). Effective teachers understand the crucial role they play in helping their students obtain communicative competence in English for a wide range of social and academic purposes. Effective programs recognize that attaining proficiency in English can take several years and thus are longitudinal, spanning several grade levels. Effective programs do not push ELL students into mainstream classrooms before they have the language skills necessary to succeed in them academically.

- **Effective programs ensure that ELLs are given equal access to the core curriculum.**

ELLs have the right to learn the same academic content as English-proficient students. But academic instruction must go beyond the memorization of facts and acquisition of knowledge and skills as outlined in state content standards. Critical pedagogy (Freire, 1993; Wink, 2000) emphasizes that teaching and learning amount to more than the simple transfer of knowledge and skills from teacher to student, deposited in their heads the way money is deposited in a bank. Rather, education must be transformative, enabling ELL students to learn and use relevant content knowledge to challenge the unequal power relations in society that have adversely impacted them, their families, and their communities. Effective programs empower students with the linguistic and cultural capital necessary to succeed in school and to pursue opportunities for higher education and careers that can lift them out of lives of poverty and oppression. Equal access to the core curriculum may be provided by teaching content areas in the native language or teaching content areas through the use of sheltered instruction or using a combination of the two. Avoiding one-size-fits-all approaches and curricular materials, effective programs provide differentiated instruction tailored to the linguistic and educational needs of each student.

- **Effective programs value students' native languages.**

Effective programs have a "language-as-resource" orientation (Ruiz, 1984) by using the native language of the ELL students as a resource for teaching and learning. Also, understanding the devastating consequences of primary language loss (Fillmore, 1991; Wright, 2004), effective programs promote additive bilingualism (Baker & Jones, 1999; Freeman, 2004). Emergent bilingual students are not expected to give up their native language as they develop proficiency in English. The highest quality programs help students become fully bilingual and biliterate in English and their home language. Where this goal is not feasible, effective programs make ample use of effective primary language support and find other ways to value, honor, and build on students' native language skills.

- **Effective programs value students' home cultures.**

ELLs should not be expected to give up their home cultures to become "Americanized." Schools should not be viewed as assimilation factories. Critical realism (Corson, 2001) recognizes that diversity is the reality of the United States. Critical pedagogy emphasizes the need to value students' home cultures as a strength upon which to build. Effective programs help ELL students become bicultural so they can function well in their home and community environments as well as in the wider American society. These programs help students to understand and appreciate America as the multicultural society it is, and prepare students to be effective citizens within this society and in the world.

- **Effective programs make use of multiple ongoing authentic assessments.**

Effective programs recognize the problems, limitations, and potential harm of high-stakes standardized testing for ELLs. They use authentic language and content-area assessments throughout the year to obtain valid measures of students' progress. The results of these assessments, combined with their understanding of linguistics and second language acquisition, help teachers make professional judgments as they plan instruction tailored to the unique language and educational needs of each student.

- **Effective programs have teachers who are fully credentialed and certified to work with ELLs.**

Many outstanding new and veteran teachers who are not certified to work with ELL students may nonetheless have ELLs placed in their classrooms. These teachers have a responsibility to do everything they can to meet the needs of their ELL students as they pursue appropriate training and additional certification.

- **Effective programs have teachers who are advocates for ELL students and their families.**

In effective programs, teachers go beyond just providing comprehensible instruction for their students. These teachers know their ELL students and understand the challenges they and their families face within the sociocultural contexts in which they live. They understand how imbalances in power relations in society may disadvantage students' families and silence their voices. Critical pedagogy requires teachers to take action when injustices occur. Teachers need to advocate for their students within their schools and districts to ensure that they receive the services and resources to which they are entitled. Teachers are often in the best position to judge the impact of various policies and programs on their ELL students and their families, and they have a responsibility to inform and work with parents and to speak out and fight for changes when such policies and programs are failing or having harmful effects.

- **Effective programs provide on-going professional development opportunities for teachers and administrators.**

Teachers and administrators are professionals. As professionals, it is imperative they keep current with their field, have opportunities to reflect on their practice, and network with others in their field. Thus, effective programs provide on-going opportunities for professional development for teachers and administrators of ELL students. In addition to school or district training, educators in effective programs join professional organizations, attend professional conferences, and read the professional literature. Through such activity, ELL educators are able to further develop the teaching and learning in their classrooms and schools, and are better able to advocate for their students.

- **Effective programs promote active parental involvement.**

Effective programs recognize and overcome linguistic, cultural, and other barriers preventing the full participation of ELL parents. As primary stakeholders, parents of ELL students must be included in decision-making processes that affect students and therefore must be provided with accommodations to facilitate their full participation.

Concrete ways that administrators and teachers can address each of these characteristics of effective programs are outlined in Wright (2010).

■ What kinds of programs are available for English language learners?

DONNA CHRISTIAN

As English language learners (ELLs) face the challenge of mastering English and acquiring academic skills and knowledge for success in school, schools are challenged with designing programs to help them achieve these goals. ELLs are not homogeneous; they vary in socioeconomic status, community background, the variety of English or other languages they speak, and in many other ways. Furthermore, they enter U.S. schools at every grade level and throughout the academic year. Although students who enter at the elementary level have more time to acquire language and academic skills than do ELLs who enter at the secondary level, all still need appropriate and challenging instruction from the very beginning, through the first or second language, or both.

A variety of program alternatives have been developed to meet the diverse and complex needs of ELLs. Some incorporate content instruction in the native language.

- *Two-way immersion* programs serve ELLs who speak a common native language along with native English speakers. For both groups of students, the goals are high levels of first and second language proficiency, academic development, and cross-cultural understanding. All students experience an environment in which both languages are valued and developed, and academic content is learned through two languages. These are typically full K–6 or K–12 instructional programs.[1]
- *Developmental bilingual* programs also aim for high levels of proficiency in English and the students' native language, with strong academic development, but the students served are

---

1. Two-way immersion programs are also sometimes referred to as *dual language programs*. This guide takes a broad view of dual language education as a bilingual program that promotes bilingualism and biliteracy (that is, additive or developmental bilingualism), academic achievement in two languages, and positive cross-cultural understanding for its target populations. Under this broad view, two-way immersion is one type of dual language education.

primarily ELLs. Students generally participate in these programs for five to six years and receive academic instruction in both languages. The model has also been referred to as "late-exit" or maintenance bilingual education.[2]

- In *transitional bilingual* programs (also known as "early-exit" bilingual education), academic instruction in the students' native language is provided (to varying extents and for varying lengths of time) while they learn English. As their English proficiency develops, students move to all-English, mainstream classes, typically after one to three years.

- *Newcomer* programs are specially designed programs for recent arrivals to the United States who have no or low English proficiency and often limited literacy in their native language. The goal is to accelerate their acquisition of language and academic skills and to orient them to the United States and U.S. schools. Students typically participate in such programs for one to one and a half years. Although newcomer programs exist in elementary schools, they are more prevalent at the secondary level. Some programs follow a bilingual approach; others focus on sheltered instruction in English.

Other program models offer primarily English instruction to ELLs. This choice is often made when ELLs in a school come from many different language backgrounds.

- In *English as a second language (ESL)* programs (also known as English language development [ELD] programs), ELLs may receive content instruction from other sources while they participate in the ESL program, or they may be in self-contained classrooms. They receive developmentally appropriate English language instruction tailored to their level of English proficiency. In some schools, students go to another classroom for ESL instruction, often with a group of students with similar English language proficiency (the "pull-out" model). In other cases, an ESL specialist works with the students in their classroom, either by co-teaching with the classroom teacher or by working with individual ELLs or small groups during independent or group work time to support their language and academic learning (often called a "push-in" approach). The "push-in" model is preferred by some because it promotes better integration of ELLs with fellow students, encourages more coordination of language and content instruction, and may be easier to schedule. It does, however, require close collaboration between teachers, which may be a challenge. Students generally participate in ESL programs for one to five years, depending on their initial level of proficiency and rate of progress.

2. Developmental bilingual programs are also sometimes referred to as *one-way developmental bilingual programs*. This guide considers one-way developmental bilingual programs to be a type of dual language education because they share the goals of additive or developmental bilingualism with other types of dual language programs. One-way developmental programs differ from two-way immersion programs in terms of target populations.

- Another ESL-oriented program model is *sheltered instruction*,[3] which offers ELLs grade-level, core content courses taught in English using instructional strategies that make the content concepts accessible to ELLs and that promote the development of academic English. Most sheltered instruction programs are designed to meet all the requirements for credit toward grade-level promotion or graduation. Students remain in them for two to three years. The term *sheltered instruction* may also be used to describe pedagogy rather than a program design. Sheltered instruction practices and individual sheltered instruction courses can be and often are implemented in conjunction with other program alternatives.

Program alternatives for ELLs differ on several dimensions. Some work toward bilingualism (two-way immersion, developmental bilingual), while others emphasize proficiency in English (ESL, sheltered instruction). The focal student populations vary, particularly in the homogeneity of their language backgrounds, and the length of participation also differs, with some programs short term or transitional (one to four years) and others longer in duration (six or more years). Finally, the necessary resources vary from model to model in features such as teacher qualifications (language skills and professional preparation) and the extent of bilingual curricula and materials needed.

■ What are the most effective kinds of programs for English language learners?

KATHRYN LINDHOLM-LEARY

The academic achievement of English language learners (ELLs) has received considerable attention, particularly with respect to underachievement. Most of the research in this area addresses policy issues relating to the best way to educate ELLs and consists primarily of evaluations of various program models. In a recent comprehensive synthesis of the empirically based research on the achievement of ELLs (Genesee et al., 2006; Lindholm-Leary & Genesee, 2010) there was strong convergent evidence that the educational success of ELLs is positively related to sustained instruction through the student's first language. Almost all evaluations of students at the end of elementary school and in middle and high school show that the educational outcomes of bilingually educated students, especially in late-exit and two-way programs, were at least comparable to, and usually higher than, their comparison peers. There was no study of middle school or high school students that found that bilingually educated students were less successful than comparison-group students. In addi-

3. Sheltered instruction is also sometimes referred to as *specially designed academic instruction in English (SDAIE)*.

tion, most long-term studies report that the longer the ELL students stayed in the program, the more positive were the outcomes. Students who participated in an assortment of different programs and those who received no educational intervention (that is, they were put into mainstream English classes with no additional assistance) performed at the lowest achievement levels and had the highest dropout rates. These results hold true whether one examines outcomes in reading or mathematics achievement, GPA, attendance, high school completion, or attitudes toward school and self.

The studies reviewed in various syntheses of research on the education of English language learners also indicates that students who achieved full oral and literate (reading and writing) proficiency in both languages had higher achievement scores, GPAs, and educational expectations than their monolingual English-speaking peers (Genesee et al., 2006; Lindholm-Leary & Genesee, 2010; Lindholm-Leary & Hernandez, 2009). In addition, there were significant positive correlations between subject matter in the two languages, so that students who scored high on measures of reading (or math) achievement in Spanish also performed at high levels on measures of reading (or math) achievement in English. These results suggest that educational programs for ELLs should seek to develop their full bilingual and biliterate competencies in order to take advantage of these interdependencies across languages.

Thus, the best models for ELL students are those that are specially designed to provide students with sustained and consistent instruction through the first language (at least through sixth grade), with the goals of full oral and literate bilingual proficiencies. Further, a program that is enriched and consistent, provides a challenging curriculum, and incorporates language development components and appropriate assessment approaches is also endorsed by research on factors associated with effective programs for ELLs.

■ What is the best way to promote the English language development and academic achievement in English of English language learners when we do not have a bilingual program?
FRED GENESEE

Success in oral language (including language for academic purposes) and literacy is more likely in structured programs such as English as a second language (ESL), sheltered instruction, or bilingual programs that are designed to meet English language learners' (ELLs') particular second language learning needs (Lindholm-Leary & Genesee, 2010; Saunders & Goldenberg, 2010). Simply mainstreaming ELLs in English-medium classes without making provisions for their particular linguistic and cultural needs is not likely to be successful for most students. Moreover, ELLs who participate in enriched, cognitively challenging programs that are consistent and coherent across grades achieve significantly higher literacy and academic results than ELLs who participate in a hodgepodge or incoherent set of programmatic interventions from grade to grade. School administrators must work with their teaching and curriculum personnel to develop programs that are sensitive to ELLs' particular linguistic and cultural backgrounds so that they are coherent across grade levels. This calls for team work and plenty of time for planning.

When it comes to academic achievement, instructional approaches that are most successful with ELLs are those that modify the use of English to ensure that academic content is comprehensible and, at the same time, develop the English language skills that ELLs need to succeed in academic domains. Sheltered instruction (SI) is one such approach. In SI, teachers teach the core curriculum in English but modify it to meet the language development needs of ELLs. Specific strategies are used to teach particular content areas so that the material is comprehensible while at the same time promoting English language development (see Echevarria, Vogt, & Short, 2010, for more details). While SI shares many features of high-quality instruction for native English speakers, it is characterized by careful attention to ELLs' distinctive second language development needs and aims to bridge the achievement gap between mainstream and ELLs.

When it comes to literacy development, interactive and direct instructional strategies work well (Genesee & Riches, 2006). Interactive instruction emphasizes learning through interaction with other learners and more competent readers and writers (e.g., the teacher, other students in the class, older students) and also engagement in using written language. The goals of interactive approaches include general literacy outcomes (e.g., enjoyment of reading/writing, autonomy as a reader/writer, familiarity with authentic written language) as well as the acquisition of specific reading and writing skills (decoding, paragraphing, punctuation) and strategies (using context to discover the meaning of unfamiliar words in text). Instructional conversation is an example of an effective interactive instructional approach (Saunders & Goldenberg, 1999). Direct instruction emphasizes explicit and focused instruction of specific reading/ writing skills and strategies, such as decoding, vocabulary, or comprehension skills. Instruction that combines interactive with direct approaches has much to recommend it since it involves teaching specific reading and writing skills within carefully designed, interactive contexts. Interaction between learners and between learners and their teachers creates a learning context in which adaptation to and accommodation of individual differences and preferences among ELLs can be accomplished. Carefully planned interactions in the classroom can be both the medium for delivering appropriate instruction about literacy and academic material and the message, insofar as the very language that is used during interactive instruction, if planned carefully, embodies many key features of language for literacy and broader academic purposes. Direct instruction of specific skills ensures student mastery of important reading and writing skills that are often embedded and even obscured in complex literacy or academic tasks. Presenting direct instruction in interactive learning environments ensures that it is meaningful, contextualized, and individualized. Research indicates that a focus on both specific reading/writing skills and meaningful use of reading/writing for communication, intellectual engagement, and personal enjoyment is important for the success of ELLs (August & Shanahan, 2010).

What are the essential components of a sheltered English immersion (SEI) program?

WAYNE E. WRIGHT

Sheltered English immersion (SEI), sometimes called structured English immersion, typically refers to self-contained classrooms for English language learners (ELLs) with teachers who are trained and certified to provide effective language and content instruction for ELL students. While bilingual education is the most effective approach for ensuring ELL students do not fall behind academically and master grade-level academic content as they are developing proficiency in English, a quality SEI program is the next best option for a school when a bilingual program is not viable for policy, ideological, or practical reasons.

Effective SEI classrooms have three essential components: (1) English as a second language (ESL) instruction, (2) sheltered content-area instruction, and (3) primary language support (Table 4.1).

The SEI classroom teacher provides ELL students with daily, focused, systematic ESL instruction. Each state has established English language proficiency (ELP) standards and has identified and described specific levels of English language proficiency. These standards and proficiency-level descriptors should provide the basis for high-quality ESL instruction. There are several advantages to having SEI teachers provide in-class ESL instruction in their own classrooms rather than having ELL students pulled-out for ESL instruction by an ESL specialist teacher. (1) The students are not pulled out and thus do not miss anything in class. (2) The ELL students avoid feelings of embarrassment that might occur if they were pulled out of class for instruction. (3) SEI teachers can coordinate their ESL instruction to prepare their ELL students for specific sheltered content instruction lessons. (4) Things SEI teachers learn about their ELLs through ESL instruction can help them tailor their sheltered content-area instruction to appropriate levels. Finally, (5) SEI teachers can coordinate interactions between English-proficient students and ELLs at different proficiency levels in the classroom in a manner that will further assist ELLs in their English

TABLE 4.1 Essential Components of Sheltered English Immersion

ESL Instruction	Sheltered Instruction	Primary Language Support
Focused, systematic instruction in the English language designed to help ELL students improve their English proficiency and ultimately be redesignated as fluent English proficient.	Grade-level academic content areas are taught in English, but in a specially designed manner that makes the instruction comprehensible for ELLs while supporting their English language development.	A variety of strategies and techniques involving the effective use of students' native languages to increase their comprehension of English during ESL and sheltered content instruction.

language development. Furthermore, the school saves money by not having to hire additional ESL teachers to provide pull-out instruction.

The SEI classroom teacher also provides ELL students with grade-level academic content-area instruction. However, such instruction is sheltered, meaning that it is specially designed in a manner that makes this instruction comprehensible for ELLs, while supporting their English language development. In some states this is called specially designed academic instruction in English (SDAIE). Sheltered instruction is based on each state's academic content standards and can be guided with tools such as the Sheltered Instruction Observation Protocol (SIOP).

In addition, even though English is the medium of instruction in SEI classrooms, effective teachers enable ample primary language support to help make ESL and sheltered content-area instruction more comprehensible.

SEI is the model mandated by the English for the Children initiatives in California, Arizona, and Massachusetts, and even these laws acknowledge the role of primary language support, stating that teachers "may use a minimal amount of the child's language when necessary."

It is helpful to think of effective SEI instruction according to the following formula:

SEI = ESL + Sheltered Instruction + Primary Language Support

In other words, a high-quality SEI program includes daily, direct, systematic ESL instruction, sheltered contentarea instruction, and ample primary language support.

The three English for the Children initiatives state that ELL students should be in SEI classrooms for a period not normally intended to exceed one year. However, there is no research that suggests that most ELLs can learn enough English in one year to be placed in a mainstream classroom.

Furthermore, Federal law makes it clear that ELL students are to receive ESL and sheltered instruction until they are redesignated as fluent English proficient and thus no longer in need of special services. Thus, ELL students should remain in effective SEI classrooms until they are truly ready for English-only instruction in mainstream classrooms.

■ What is the difference between English as a second language (ESL)/ English language development (ELD) and sheltered instruction/ specially designed academic instruction in English (SDAIE)?
WAYNE E. WRIGHT

English as a second language (ESL) and specially designed academic instruction in English (SDAIE) are both critical components of any program model for English language learners (ELLs). Federal law requires schools to help ELLs (1) develop English proficiency and (2) meet state academic content standards. ESL instruction focuses on the first of these requirements, while SDAIE focuses on the second. SDAIE is also referred to as sheltered instruction.

The purpose of ESL instruction is to help ELLs become proficient in English. Interactive listening, speaking, reading, and writing activities help students acquire the vocabulary and structure of the language and develop communicative competence for social and academic settings. ESL is sometimes referred to as English language development (ELD), particularly at the elementary level. ESL is a separate content area, just as math or science is a separate content area, and has its own standards and curriculum. The short-term goals of ESL instruction are to help students improve their level of English proficiency each year. The ultimate goal is redesignation as fluent English proficient, meaning students no longer require extra assistance and can succeed in a regular, mainstream classroom.

SDAIE instruction focuses on the teaching of content-area subjects— language arts, math, science, and so forth—in English using a wide range of strategies and techniques that help make the instruction comprehensible for ELLs. The ultimate goal of SDAIE is for ELLs to master the same content-area standards as all other students do.

Elementary ELLs, whether in bilingual or English-medium program models, need at least thirty minutes of focused ESL instruction each day. Some schools and districts create their own ESL curriculum, while others adopt a commercially produced ESL/ELD program. In English-medium program models, all other content areas are taught in English using SDAIE strategies. In bilingual programs, some content areas are taught in the students' first language and the others are taught in English using SDAIE strategies; as ELLs develop proficiency in English, the amount of SDAIE content-area instruction increases as students gradually transition to mainstream instruction in English. At the secondary level ELLs need SDAIE content-area courses and at least one period of ESL each day.

ESL instruction is for ELLs only. This is easily provided in classrooms in which all students are ELLs. In classes that include both ELLs and non-ELLs, teachers need to structure their classrooms in a manner that allows them some time to work separately with the ELLs each day to provide ESL instruction. Alternatively, a specialist ESL teacher may pull students out of the class for ESL instruction (pull-out ESL) or remain in the class to provide instruction there (push-in ESL). SDAIE instruction, however, includes many strategies and techniques that are appropriate and effective for all students.

While ESL focuses on teaching English and SDAIE focuses on teaching content, there is some overlap. Students will learn some content during ESL, and effective SDAIE instruction will help students gain greater proficiency in English. In fact, the Sheltered Instruction Observation Protocol (SIOP) model—a popular model for SDAIE instruction—emphasizes the need for content-area lessons to have both language and content-area objectives (Echevarria, Vogt, & Short, 2008a). Nonetheless, these language objectives should *supplement*, not *supplant*, daily ESL instruction. This overlap is advantageous for ELLs. For example, a SDAIE science lesson on the water cycle is made more comprehensible when preceded by an ESL lesson on talking about the weather.

Some assume that ELLs no longer need ESL instruction once they achieve a basic level of English, and that SDAIE instruction alone will help them become proficient. However, if schools stop providing dedicated ESL instruction, many ELLs may not progress beyond their current level for several years and will fall further behind as the content-area instruction demands increase each year. Many ELLs who sound fluent learn to decode print yet fail to comprehend what they read because they lack vocabulary and an understanding of complex sentence and discourse structures. Thus, ELL students need both ESL and SDAIE instruction each year until they are redesignated as fully English proficient. Administrators can ensure their ELLs learn English and meet state content standards by ensuring their teachers obtain proper training and provide effective instruction in both ESL and SDAIE.

■ What should the English-as-a-second-language (ESL)/English language development (ELD) component of a program look like?
NANCY L. COMMINS

It takes a comprehensive approach to adequately prepare second language learners to work on the ideas and understandings of the academic curriculum. English as a second language (ESL) or English language development (ELD) is a critical part of overall instructional planning designed to meet the needs of English language learners who, in order to become academically successful, have a tremendous task in front of them. They must learn about the content, be able to talk about it clearly, read for meaning, ask and answer questions, discuss ideas, and express themselves in writing. Eventually, they must be able to do all this within the conventions of standard English (Miramontes, Nadeau, & Commins, 2011). For this reason, second language learners must receive instruction and practice in how the English language works. English as a second language provides time for ELLs to work on language with peers at a similar level of language development in a stress-reduced environment.

In many places, second language learners suffer from either inattention or misguided policies, or both. In some states and districts highly scripted curriculums have been mandated. Others have instituted extremely long blocks of time dedicated to "learning English" but with no connection to the concepts and ideas students will need to learn to engage in the academic curriculum. These kinds of approaches do not serve students well. Ideally, ESL/ ELD instruction helps students make sense of and perfect what they will need to talk about and understand to be successful in the rest of their day. Planning for ESL instruction should begin with the language used to talk about the conceptual understandings students are to acquire within a culturally affirming context. Teachers can choose a variety of activities and texts to convey those ideas and practice the language.

An example of a district that has taken dramatic steps to improve instruction for its second language learners is Aurora Public Schools in Aurora, Colorado. Their Alternative Language Program Framework includes an *English Language Development (ELD) block* (typically 45–60 minutes)— a specific time allotted daily for students to work in proficiency level groups where students are taught the language necessary to help them become academically successful. When asked to describe the ELD block, two educators in APS[4] summed it up as follows:

ELD is time for students to practice, play with, and learn language at their proficiency level always with an eye to moving forward. It is a set time, a slice of the day, where students are grouped by proficiency level when language is the content. The aim is for students to 'get it right' (not memorize grammar), to focus on form, fluency, and application *tied to the grade-level curriculum*. ACE is a guiding construct: Instruction must be Age appropriate, Context rich, and Engaging. Students should always be able to see that what they are learning serves them in the rest of the day. ELD is not about word games, puzzles, phonics, or diagramming sentences. It is the time for students to be immersed in what it sounds like and looks like when they and others express their ideas about important concepts in English.

4. Thanks and gratitude to Jean Burke and Piper Hendricks for their input and extraordinary dedication.

In APS, the ELD block entails a gradual release of responsibility by the teacher and assumption of responsibility by the learner. Each lesson begins with teacher modeling followed by guided practice, where students practice together with the teacher's help. Every lesson then includes shared and independent practice, where students are actively engaged with each other and held individually accountable for producing the target language. Teachers monitor progress daily during lessons built around functional language tied to what students will read, write, and learn about the rest of the day. Their goal is to explicitly teach the nuances of language that they would not get otherwise.

Contrary to the notion that ESL is a time when students are "missing" something, students are in fact gaining a lot, but careful scheduling is necessary so that students do not miss core content. If proficiency level differentiation takes into consideration native English speakers, this block of time can be viewed as language enrichment time, when all students are engaged in meaningful interactions designed to increase their fluency in the academic register.

As important as an ESL/ELD block is, it is not sufficient to meet all the English language development needs of students. Every adult in every instructional setting has a responsibility to make instruction comprehensible and take into account the language demands of the curriculum. In Aurora this means that their Alternative Language Framework also includes *content instruction with all teachers using sheltering techniques, all day, every day*. In this way, they build grade-level appropriate content understandings by paying attention to both the content and language demands of the curriculum. Common components in all parts of the day include student interaction through listening, speaking, reading, and writing; use of English language proficiency standards to guide planning and assessment; visual representation of abstract concepts; and standards-based teaching and ongoing assessment of language development.

This comprehensive approach demands that all teachers be conscious of and address the needs of second language learners. The strongest outcomes occur when teachers collaborate to connect what students are working on in ESL/ELD with what they are reading and writing about during language arts and learning in other areas of the curriculum (social studies, math, science, and the arts).

■ What is the best bilingual model of instruction?
KATHRYN LINDHOLM-LEARY

Two-way bilingual immersion (TWBI) education is a program that has the potential to promote the multilingual and multicultural competencies necessary for the new global job market while eradicating the significant achievement gap between English speakers and English language learners (ELLs). The appeal of two-way programs is that they combine successful education models in an integrated classroom composed of both English proficient (EP) speakers and ELLs, with the goals of full bilingualism and biliteracy, grade-level academic achievement for both groups, and multicultural competencies.

TWBI programs provide ELLs and native EP speakers with academic instruction that is presented through two languages in an integrated environment. The major goals are the following: (1) Students will develop high levels of oral language and literacy in English and the non-English language. (2) Academic achievement will be at or above grade level as measured in both languages. (3) Students will have positive attitudes toward school and themselves and will exhibit positive cross-cultural attitudes and multicultural competencies.

The definition of TWBI programs (or dual language programs) encompasses four critical features: (1) The program involves instruction through two languages, where the non-English language is used for a significant portion (at least 50 percent) of the student's instructional day. (2) The program involves periods of instruction during which only one language is used (that is, there is no translation or language mixing). (3) Both ELLs and EPs are participants in a fairly balanced proportion. (4) The students are integrated for most content instruction. TWBI programs have surged in popularity over the past twenty years (from 37 programs in 1987 to over 350 programs in public schools in twenty-five states and the District of Columbia).

Several investigators have examined the reading and math achievement of students in TWBI at late elementary or secondary levels to determine the long-term impact of these programs. These studies are consistent in showing that overall, ELLs made significant progress in both languages: they scored at least to well above grade level measured in both languages by middle school, and they performed at comparable or superior levels compared to same-language comparison peers. On both norm-referenced and criterion-referenced standardized tests of reading and math achievement in English, previously designated ELL students scored not only significantly higher than ELLs in the state, but they also performed on a par with native English-speaking students in English-only classrooms (Collier & Thomas, 2009; Howard, Sugarman, & Christian, 2003; Lindholm-Leary, 2001, 2005; Lindholm-Leary & Howard, 2008). These positive results for dual language programs also hold true for other languages such as Mandarin, Cantonese, and Korean (Lindholm-Leary, 2001, in press).

Studies have also examined students' attitudes toward school and the TWBI program. In studies of secondary students who had been in a TWBI program in elementary school, results showed that students had very positive attitudes toward school and the TWBI program. Most students believed that learning through two languages helped them learn to think better, made them smarter, and helped them do better in school. Students also felt valued in the TWBI program, were glad they participated in it, and would recommend it to other students.

In sum, the TWBI program has been carefully developed according to the theoretical and empirically based literatures on effective schools and second language learning to more adequately address the cultural, ethnic, and linguistic diversity represented in today's classrooms. However, like mainstream classes, not all TWBI program classes are high quality; the quality and effectiveness of the TWBI model implementation can vary tremendously from school to school. Results demonstrate that well-implemented TWBI programs are successful in promoting high educational outcomes for both ELLs and EP students; that is, students demonstrate bilingual proficiency, biliteracy, achievement at or above grade level, and positive attitudes.

■ How do we decide what kind of program for English language learners is appropriate for our school?

ESTER J. DE JONG

If schools decide to design a special program to meet the needs of English language learners (ELLs), they need to make an informed decision that responds to the community's specific context. The tremendous variation within and among ELL populations makes it impossible to approach the schooling of ELLs with a "one-size-fits-all" approach. Instead, districts and schools should adopt a flexible approach to address the diversity that exists in their student population. Flexibility does not imply random decisions. The district and the schools should articulate their program choice according to a consistent program philosophy, grounded in principles of effective programs for ELLs.

ELLs are not a homogeneous group; rather, they have become increasingly more diverse. The number of students is one variable. For example, when a district has multiple language groups with few speakers of each language, it is difficult to implement a bilingual program. If, on the other hand, much of the ELL population comes from the same language background, bilingual education is a feasible option. Similarly, students with strong first language (L1) literacy skills and highly educated parents have significantly different needs from students with interrupted schooling or limited L1 literacy skills. When various student populations exist side by side in the district, different programs should be implemented in recognition of these different needs.

To avoid random or conflicting policies, it is important that district leaders make themselves familiar with common program options for ELLs (such as two-way immersion programs, developmental bilingual education, self-contained English as a second language [ESL] programs, and pull-out ESL classes) and their theoretical underpinnings, strengths, outcomes, and implementation challenges. Further, school and district leaders must find out about the needs of the ELLs in the school and the district. Once the ELL population has been identified (through a home language survey, language and literacy assessments, or academic skills assessment), schools and the district must develop a plan to address their needs. This plan should involve the whole school because the responsibility for ELLs lies with all staff. Schools must develop a shared vision for the education of all students that reflects the entire range of linguistic and cultural diversity in the school, not only the ELLs.

Regardless of the particular program model chosen, an effective whole-school plan for educating ELLs and fluent English speakers needs to be systemic and principled, i.e., grounded in what we know about bilingual learners and their learning processes. The following four core principles can frame effective programming for bilingual students (de Jong, 2011):

Principle 1: Striving for Educational Equity

The first principle is an overarching principle. Educators who strive for educational equity create school environments where each individual feels valued and respected. They work together to ensure that formal and informal language policies and practices at the school, program, and classroom level fairly represent the diversity in the school and do not discriminate systematically against certain groups of students.

Principle 2: Affirming Identities

The second draws our attention to how languages and cultural experiences are represented in schools. Educators who value this principle demonstrate respect for students' linguistic and cultural identities. These educators validate students' linguistic and cultural experiences in school policies and classroom practices and purposefully create spaces for diverse student voices.

Principle 3: Promoting Additive Bi/Multilingualism

The third principle highlights languages as resources to draw on and nurture. Educators who promote additive bi/multilingualism understand the role that students' existing linguistic repertoires play in language and literacy development and in content learning. They create opportunities for using, developing, displaying, and engaging in multiple languages by building on students' existing linguistic repertoires and extending these into new ones. They make knowing multiple languages an integral part of their curriculum and instructional decisions.

Principle 4: Structuring for Integration

The fourth principle recognizes schools as complex systems with diverse, interconnected parts that can work together to create an environment of mutual respect and equity. Educators who structure for integration promote representative involvement of constituents with diverse perspectives and expertise in decision making, including language policy, program structure, curriculum and materials, classroom structures, assessment practices, and extracurricular activities. These educators reject the notion that language minority groups (students, parents, teachers) must unilaterally assimilate to fit into the existing system. Instead, educators who structure for integration work to build a linguistically and culturally responsive system for all of their constituents.

These four principles transcend traditional English-medium, bilingual, and multilingual models and are applicable across a wide range of linguistically and culturally diverse contexts. Administrators and leadership team members at the district and school levels can use these principles to guide their decision making about appropriate programming for the bilingual learners their schools.

DIEP NGUYEN

Several factors should be considered in deciding on the best program for English language learners (ELLs) in your district.

1. The most important factor to consider is the profile of your students as a group. A complete group profile includes pertinent information about the ELLs' immigration; sociocultural, linguistic, and educational history, such as level of educational background; English as a second language (ESL) proficiency; native language proficiency; and ethnic background. For example, if you have large numbers of students from the same language background (such as Spanish or Chinese) and equally large numbers of English-speaking students who want to become bilingual, a two-way immersion program is a good option to consider. If the students are mostly immigrants from one language background, a one-way developmental or maintenance bilingual program may be appropriate. If there are substantial numbers of ELLs who speak different languages, a sheltered ESL program may be feasible, ideally with native language support. If there are only a few ELLs at the school, a pull-out or push-in ESL program may be the only option (in this case, the administrator must make sure that mainstream teachers who have ELLs in their classes understand how to use sheltered instructional strategies). The first principle of good programming is *know your students.*
2. The second factor to consider is the sociopolitical climate of your community. In other words, the community context in which you operate a program has great influence on its success or failure. Your program design and approaches need to meet the needs of your students and be accepted by the community. For example, while some communities may be ready to embrace dual language programs, in other communities a transitional bilingual program or ESL program may be a better first option. Review the political climate in your community constantly in order to gauge their

readiness for more innovative approaches. Spend time getting to know your community and educate parents and colleagues about different options for ELL students before launching a program. The second principle at work here is *know your community*.

3. Regardless of the program model chosen, the measure of true effectiveness of the program lies at the instructional (teacher-student) level in each classroom. Consider your resources (both human and material) carefully before adopting a model. Issues that need to be considered include staff expertise and competence, administrative buy-in, materials variety and availability, and evidence of the effectiveness of similar programs elsewhere. Visit school districts that have effective programs, spend time in the host classrooms to find evidence of their instructional program's effectiveness, and ask questions that will help you decide if a particular model is a match for your school district. It is important to be realistic about the resources you have. The third principle is *assess your resources*.

4. Basic research on teaching and learning, as well as evaluation studies conducted on existing programs, provides valuable information when it is time to make decisions about the core values and design of your own program. To ensure that instructional effectiveness is at the heart of your design, spend time with others reviewing research on program effectiveness and best practices. Seek out experts in the field who have either studied or implemented these models and ask them for advice on your choice. The fourth operating principle here is *be informed, be in the know*.

5. Finally, adopt a general approach based on sound research and best practices. However, tailor the design to meet the needs of your students using your local resources. Do not be afraid to differentiate your program options for your students. In other words, wherever appropriate, use different program options for different subgroups of students at your local school district. The fifth operating principle here is *differentiate your program*.

Most of all, be sure to create a flexible and student-focused system of instructional services for all your ELL students. In the end, it is less about the program than it is about the quality of instructional services that you can make available for your students. Think about the program as the frame or skeleton that supports instruction, which is the real meat of ELL education. Remember that it's all about quality education for all students.

■ How do we create a positive school environment for English language learners and their parents/members of their households?

REBECCA FREEMAN FIELD and ELSE HAMAYAN

Schools that see linguistic and cultural diversity as resources to develop rather than as problems to overcome offer more positive environments for

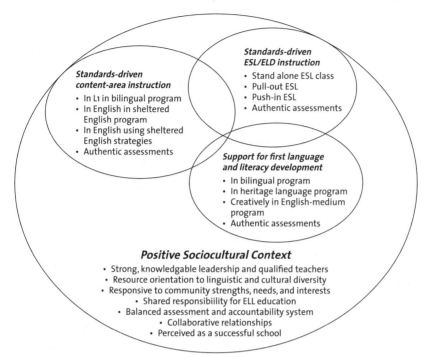

Standards-driven content-area instruction
- In L1 in bilingual program
- In English in sheltered English program
- In English using sheltered English strategies
- Authentic assessments

Standards-driven ESL/ELD instruction
- Stand alone ESL class
- Pull-out ESL
- Push-in ESL
- Authentic assessments

Support for first language and literacy development
- In bilingual program
- In heritage language program
- Creatively in English-medium program
- Authentic assessments

Positive Sociocultural Context
- Strong, knowledgable leadership and qualified teachers
- Resource orientation to linguistic and cultural diversity
- Responsive to community strengths, needs, and interests
- Shared responsibiility for ELL education
- Balanced assessment and accountability system
- Collaborative relationships
- Perceived as a successful school

FIGURE 4.1 Critical features of effective programs for ELLs/bilingual learners.

English language learners (ELLs)/bilingual learners and their families and household members. Schools with a positive sociocultural orientation make efforts to connect with and build on the linguistic and cultural expertise that ELLs and their families and communities bring with them to school. Although not all schools can develop programs that lead to bilingual and biliteracy development, every school can find creative ways to link the school with the community to support ELLs, welcome their families, and provide a more enriching educational experience for all students.

Administrators can lead this effort by encouraging their school leadership team (which should include parents and community members) to review the school's orientation toward linguistic and cultural diversity as reflected in their general school environment, policies, programs, curriculum, materials, instructional practices and assessments, and parental and community involvement (Figure 4.1). We focus here on the visibility of languages other than English in the general school environment and on the integration of culture into the curriculum.

An easy and obvious place to begin is to ask whether the languages that the ELLs/bilingual learners, their parents, and the local communities speak are readily observable and audible at school. The relative visibility or invisibility of linguistic and cultural diversity sends a strong message to bilingual learners, their families, and the rest of the student body about the value of those languages and cultures at school. The following kinds of questions can help guide the leadership team: Is there evidence of languages other than English at school, for example, in student work on the walls in the hallways and in the classroom? Are there books in languages other than English in the library, and are they displayed as prominently as books in English? Are students encouraged to use their home languages as resources in content-area instruction? Are materials and resources available in the languages that the students speak at home or in the community? Does the school partner in any way with community-based organizations? If so, what is the purpose and nature of these partnerships? When the leadership team identifies a problem, they can work together to address that problem given their resources and constraints. For example, if they see little to no representation of the more than thirty languages spoken by students in their school, they can brainstorm creative ways to bring those languages into the school, and they can reflect on what happens over time as a result of the changes they have made.

It is important for educators to think of a school's orientation toward linguistic and cultural diversity as an integral part of what they already do, rather than as one more thing that they have to do. For example, as educators review their curriculum (as part of the regular curriculum review process or in preparation for teaching), they can ask themselves how culture is conceptualized within their curriculum. There are different perspectives on integrating culture into school life. Culture may be thought of as (1) a lesson to be taught and studied, (2) a subject to be integrated into the curriculum, (3) a human-relations issue to be dealt with at school, (4) a school reform movement in education, or (5) a multilayered, multifaceted social framework within which schooling takes place (Banks & McGee Banks, 2009). During the curriculum review, educators can look into the representation and evaluation of different linguistic and cultural groups and take steps to ensure that the curriculum they teach fully integrates the cultural contributions and perspectives of the diverse groups represented at their school and in society.

Integrating a resource orientation toward linguistic and cultural diversity into the curriculum does not mean a lack of attention to standards and accountability requirements. For example, schools can draw on what González, Moll, & Amanti (2005) call "cultural funds of knowledge" from the home or the community as a link between ELLs' prior knowledge and the concepts and skills they need to develop at school. Students might use their family and community histories as a thematic center of an integrated unit. In social studies they might learn to conduct qualitative research into the community, and then write expository texts to share what they learned. In math, they might conduct quantitative studies of language use first among students in their class, and then throughout the school and larger community. In language arts, they might draw on their inquiry-based math and social studies projects as a foundation for writing persuasive texts that argue for solutions to problems that they identify in their homes, school, and community, and as a basis for social action.

An integrated multicultural curriculum can help link the school and the community. This approach can bring the languages and literacies used in students' homes and throughout the community into the school as resources to build on, to help ELLs make connections between their prior knowledge and skills and the new abstract content-area knowledge and skills that they need to develop at school, connect children with their families and other community members, enrich the lives of the English-speaking students as they explore the rich linguistic and cultural diversity in their neighborhood, and address challenging state standards and accountability requirements. Perhaps most important, linking the school and the community in this way prepares students to think critically about the world in which they live and to develop the tools they need to change that world.

■ How do we plan for language development?
JOHN HILLIARD and ELSE HAMAYAN

Decisions regarding the use of English and the students' native language must be made carefully and with great deliberation. These decisions must focus on how the students' two languages or, at a minimum, how supported forms of English are to be used in instruction. Language allocation decisions must be considered at three levels (Figure 4.2).

1. The programmatic level: How much instruction over the course of the entire program will be delivered in which language?
2. The curricular level: Who, where, when, and what will be delivered in the two languages or in a sheltered English versus a mainstream environment?
3. The instructional level: What actually happens linguistically between teacher and students during instruction?

These decisions must be planned over the long term that the student is in a particular school rather than year by year or, worse, randomly. In fact, the language development plan in one school should connect with the next level of schooling that the student will attend.

At the programmatic level, the allocation of languages for instruction in a bilingual program has to be determined in terms of the proportion of time spent in each language during each year of participation. In a dual language program, students receive either 50 percent of their instruction

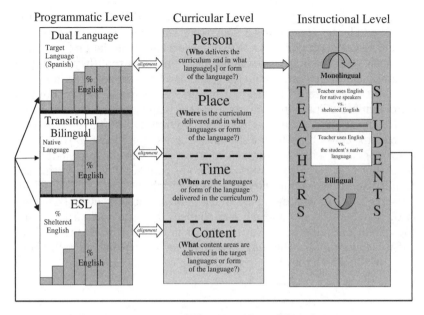

FIGURE 4.2 Language allocation and use in programs
for second language learners.

in English and 50 percent in the other language, or they start out with a larger percentage in the language other than English and gradually receive more instruction through English until the proportion is 50:50. In a transitional bilingual program, students receive a higher proportion of their instruction initially in their native language, which is gradually phased out for an all-English education. In the case of an English-medium program, the decision has to focus on the amount of time spent in a sheltered English environment versus a mainstream setting. If possible, as much of the instruction should be delivered initially through sheltered strategies until the students are proficient enough to survive in the mainstream classroom without special support. At a minimum, the more abstract the content area, the more important it is for that teacher to shelter the instruction.

At the curricular level, in a dual language or transitional bilingual program, you need to determine which language is used for what. In an English-medium program where not all teachers are skilled in sheltering instruction, the decision has to do with which content areas are taught through a sheltered format and which components of the school day are spent in the mainstream classroom (taught by teachers who use sheltered instructional strategies). It is natural for these decisions to be influenced by contextual factors such as the availability of resources, both human and material, as well as scheduling issues. However, it is critical that these decisions be made from the learner's perspective and that they make developmental and pedagogical sense. In dual language programs, the program design dictates that support for the minority student's language be maintained at a level of no less than 50 percent. In transitional bilingual programs where there are no such programmatic constants, it is important to maintain support in the native language for as long as the students need it. Instruction in the native language must be diminished gradually rather than being offered haphazardly from year to year. Similarly, for students who are receiving instruction only in English, those content areas that are more cognitively demanding must be taught through sheltered strategies, and that support must be reduced gradually, based on student need, rather than be dropped abruptly.

At the instructional level, teachers must adhere to the language of instruction (or, if it is an English-medium program, to the sheltering of English) very carefully. Otherwise, the long-term language development plan will be altered and may not follow a path that makes sense for the learner.

It is only through careful long-term planning that ELLs' development of English language proficiency, acquisition of academic content-area knowledge, and, ideally, maintenance of their native language can continue to evolve through the students' entire experience in school, from kindergarten until graduation from high school.

■ How do we plan for biliteracy development?
KATHY ESCAMILLA

In terms of planning for biliteracy development, it is important to remember a simple axiom—biliteracy means two! As simplistic as it sounds, it is often the case that biliteracy privileges one language over another, delays the introduction of one language until a different language is 'learned well,' and/or attempts to develop two language and literacy systems without connecting the languages one to another. It is also quite frequently the case that literacy instruction is reduced to reading instruction with little attention to oracy, writing, and the development of metalinguistic skills. Planning for biliteracy must first consider a broadened attention to the development of language skills writ large that includes a focus on reading but that also pays equal attention to writing, oracy, and metalinguistic skills teaching. Given the short school day, planning a comprehensive literacy program in one language is a challenge, thereby making the planning of a comprehensive biliteracy program a double challenge. However, educators and parents dedicated to raising and nurturing biliterate children believe it is a challenge worth pursuing.

In planning for biliteracy instruction, it is important that educators plan for (1) literacy development in students' native language; (2) language

Planning for Biliteracy
Understand the similarities and differences between the two languages and teach this knowledge explicitly to your students.
Allow students enough time to develop literacy in two languages.
Plan for explicit teaching to transfer. Teach students how to bridge between the two languages.
Respect the construction of the non-English language: use materials and methodologies authentic to that language.

FIGURE 4.3 Key considerations in planning for biliteracy.

and literacy development in students' second language; and (3) explicit opportunities to help students make cross-language connections. It is also critical that this biliteracy program be articulated across grade levels and that equal status and value be given to both of the languages that are part of the biliteracy program (Figure 4.3).

In an on-going longitudinal study of biliteracy development titled Literacy Squared® (Escamilla & Hopewell, 2010), researchers have developed a biliteracy intervention for grades K–5 that has incorporated the three components listed previously. This particular intervention was developed for Spanish-speaking children; however, it is possible that other researchers could replicate it with other languages. Components of the Literacy Squared® intervention include the following:

- **Research.** There is a dearth of research about biliteracy development—most biliteracy programs are based on monolingual English approaches to teaching literacy. Ongoing research in this area is critical.
- **Assessment.** Children's developing literacy skills in both languages should not be viewed separately but need to be measured and evaluated in terms of a trajectory toward biliteracy. Trajectories toward biliteracy should see achievement in one language paralleling achievement in a second language.
- **Professional Development.** Teachers and school leaders must learn the fundamental concepts about trajectories toward biliteracy and the instructional components and techniques that need to be used with fidelity and consistency across grade levels to achieve biliteracy.
- **Instructional Components**
  - Spanish literacy. Daily, explicit, and direct Spanish literacy development using techniques that are authentic to Spanish and not adaptations from English with a focus on oracy, writing, and metalinguistic development as well as reading.

- Literacy based ESL. Daily, explicit, and direct instruction in English as a second language with a focus on book-based English literacy development that may complement but is not duplicative of Spanish literacy instruction.
- Cross-language connections. Frequent opportunities to compare and contrast language and literacy features between English and Spanish with a focus on discussion and dialogue.

To conclude, there are no doubt many ways to plan for biliteracy development; however, if the development of biliteracy is to be achieved, the program must include a robust view of literacy development, and it must be planned and implemented with fidelity and consistency across grade levels by teachers who are themselves biliterate and have excellent preparation in the field and the support of the school leadership.

KAREN BEEMAN AND CHERYL UROW

As programs plan for biliteracy it is important to consider the current demographic profile of English language learners (ELLs). Bilingual education is based on the research that demonstrates that when children are provided a solid base in content and literacy in their dominant language, they will be able to transfer these skills to English (Cummins, 1981; Ramirez, et al, 1991, Thomas & Collier, 1997). This theory has led educators to look at bilingual education as a set of either/or questions: students are dominant in either English or another language (not both); initial literacy should be taught in English or another language (not both). But with the majority of ELLs being born in the United States (Swanson, 2009) and growing up in a bilingual world, it has become increasingly difficult to look at our students as either/or.

We need to remember that ELLs are bilingual learners. They are exposed to English literacy on a daily basis: on television, in stores, on street signs. They are also exposed to language and literacy in their home language at home and in their community. Given this context, the need for sequential literacy—where literacy instruction is conducted wholly in the dominant language until students have developed a solid base—is a fallacy. Providing bilingual learners with literacy instruction in only one language is looking at these students through the old either/or paradigm. Simultaneous literacy instruction allows these bilingual learners to use all their linguistic resources, and it reflects the bilingual world in which they live.

Simultaneous literacy instruction as a path to biliteracy does not mean teaching two monolingual literacy classes every day. It is not the adoption of literacy programs, strategies, or methods designed for literacy in a single language. Rather, simultaneous literacy instruction is the implementation of a purposeful path towards biliteracy beginning with developing oracy skills in each language by planning for the development of oral language skills in both languages, and then matching the literacy skills to these oracy skills. In addition, time should be allocated for bridging between the home language and English. The bridge is that time during the lesson or unit that is focused on promoting and taking advantage of the transfer of concepts and skills between languages by explicitly teaching metalinguistic awareness and skills. (Beeman & Urow, in press)

Time must be dedicated to literacy instruction in each language, with special care taken not to allow the use of English during literacy instruction in the non-English language. Because the United States is an English-dominant society and because students are aware that English is the language of power, allowing English during the non-English language time can erode learning in and the prestige of the non-English language. The strategies, materials, and methods used to teach literacy in the non-English language must be authentic to that language. For example, while the names of letters are taught in English, beginning with the consonants, letter names are not as crucial in developing literacy in Spanish. Rather, the sounds of the vowels are taught first, and then these vowels are matched with consonants to make syllables.

If simultaneous literacy instruction more closely matches the reality of the experiences of ELLs today, it makes sense that the simultaneous path to biliteracy be given more consideration. Implementation of the simultaneous path toward biliteracy, however, depends on a clear and thorough understanding of how the two languages work together and on developing a clear and well-established plan for the bridging between languages.

MONICA MACCERA FILPPU

Until recently (see for example, Escamilla & Hopewell, 2010) the majority of the research on the literacy development of English language learners (ELLs) has focused on students who are sequential bilinguals—that is, they have developed language competence in their native language *before* they are significantly exposed to a second language. In these cases, literacy skills that are acquired in one language transfer to the other language as long as there is continued development of the other language. There has been significant study of which features of language and literacy tend to transfer more readily and which tend to require more explicit instruction.

My challenge as a bilingual educator has been that most of my students do not fit into the sequential bilingualism model. Most of the ELLs I have worked with in Washington, D.C., are simultaneous bilinguals. That is, they are exposed to both languages at home with multigenerational families, by watching television, and in the community. In trying to design a literacy instruction program for these students (in the context of a two-way immersion program), I was hard-pressed to determine which language was their "native" language. In which language should I introduce literacy? What research could I use to explain their struggles and successes? The most valuable lesson I have learned, therefore, is that for our students, first and second language literacy development are inextricably linked. They are happening at the same time, whether formally or informally, and they need to be addressed by the instructional program.

How do we do this at Oyster Bilingual School? We promote a dual language curriculum with simultaneous biliteracy instruction for all students and an emphasis on metacognition and metalinguistic awareness. All students receive literacy instruction in English and the target language (Spanish, in our case). Typically, students are not divided by language dominance for this instruction. In most cases, such a division would be impossible, as most children do not fall neatly into Spanish-dominant or English-dominant classifications. Usually, students have one teacher who is responsible for literacy instruction in Spanish and one who is responsible for literacy instruction in English. Some students have two teachers in the classroom at all times, and some students rotate between two classrooms, spending half of their day with each of two teachers. In both situations, however, teacher collaboration is of the utmost importance because it is important that both teachers see themselves as equally responsible for the students' literacy development in both languages. By working closely together, teachers are in a better position to talk with students about the fact that they are learning in two languages and to help them make the connections between what is learned in each language.

We promote a workshop format for literacy instruction in which each child is reading and writing at his or her level and developing the skills he or she most needs for meaningful communication through reading and writing. Along with the types of strategy lessons recommended for such an approach (Taberski, 2000), we include lessons specifically designed to help students understand how their bilingualism affects their literacy development process. For example, I have done mini-lessons, such as *Finding a "just-right" book in my second language* and *What do I do when I don't know the word for what I want to say in Spanish/English?*, as well as skill-specific lessons that focus on contrastive analysis of Spanish and English. One of my favorites for first grade begins with showing examples of how different students in the class have formed the possessive in Spanish and English and talking about why some students say "Pedro's casa" instead of "la casa de Pedro." Using reflective practices such as these we are able to develop literacy skills in two languages for all students.

🗨 ■ How do we promote first/home language literacy development when we cannot have a bilingual program?
DIEP NGUYEN

Depending on the community that you serve, efforts to support native/home language literacy can range from informal classroom efforts to formal programs of family literacy to provide the opportunities for parents and other community members to use what they know to teach the students to read and write in their respective native languages. Some efforts that have been fruitful in districts across the country include the following:

- The simplest way of supporting native language literacy is to inform parents of the importance of these skills for their children and ask them to invest their time in teaching their children to read and write in their native language. Many parents of English language learners (ELLs) look to educators to guide them in making language choices for their children. Parents need to know that we, as educators, believe in and encourage the use of native language literacy at home.
- The most informal way of supporting home language literacy is to allow and encourage students to express themselves in their native language in writing when appropriate. To accomplish this task, the teacher may have to solicit a parent volunteer who can respond to the students' writing and assist the teacher in the translation/interpretation of the students' work into English when necessary.
- Another informal way of supporting native language literacy in an English-medium program environment is to sponsor before- or after-school clubs or groups where students can practice native language literacy through reading clubs or writing clubs supervised and led by a bilingual adult (staff or parent volunteers).
- Many immigrant communities, while believing that native language maintenance is not a required responsibility of the public schools, have an earnest desire to teach their own language to their children. Many communities have after-school classes or weekend schools to teach their native language to children. We can support these efforts by offering classroom space for these programs during after-school hours gratis or for a nominal fee.
- A more proactive approach is to sponsor family literacy programs after school at which parents can work with teachers in activities that enrich and teach native language literacy skills for students. Successful family literacy programs always include three educational components: (1) the parents learn to become reading and writing instructors with their children; (2) parents and children have ample opportunities to read and write together; and (3) there is a direct link between the literacy practices in the program and the instructional goals for reading and writing for the students during the school day. However, it is important to be sensitive to the

cultural "ways with words" (Heath, 1983) of the students you serve so that you can establish family literacy programs that are culturally responsive to the language traditions of families. We try to involve key parent leaders and community members who can help use the "funds of knowledge" (González, Moll, & Amanti, 2005) within the community to create a family literacy that truly belongs to and serves the intended students and their families.

■ What is a heritage language program?
REBECCA FREEMAN FIELD

Although research demonstrates the effectiveness of additive bilingual programs, or programs that support the development of English language learners' (ELLs') first language while they add English, not all schools can implement dual language programs. Unfortunately, most programs for ELLs lead to subtractive bilingualism, or the loss of the ELLs' first language as they acquire English. Although subtractive bilingualism is the typical outcome for students in English-medium programs and transitional bilingual programs, this does not have to be the case. Schools can work to promote additive or developmental bilingualism for their ELLs even when they cannot offer a dual language program (de Jong, 2011).

When schools have a substantial population of ELLs or English speakers who come from the same home language background, a heritage language program may be feasible (Freeman, 2004). According to Guadalupe Valdés (2000), the term "heritage language speaker" is used to refer to students who are raised in a home where a language other than English is spoken, who understand and/or speak the heritage language, and who are to some degree bilingual in English and in the heritage language.

Heritage language programs target heritage language speakers (who may or may not be designated as ELLs), and they offer the heritage language as a core subject area such as language arts or a world language class. A primary goal of these enrichment programs is to enable heritage language speakers to broaden their linguistic repertoires in their heritage language. Heritage language teachers need to be specially trained so that they know how to build on the linguistic and cultural resources that heritage language speakers bring with them from home, and so that they can provide opportunities for these students to learn to use their heritage language for a wider range of oral and written purposes. Because these students collectively have such a wide range of expertise in their heritage languages, teachers must know how to differentiate their instruction.

Spanish for Spanish/Native Speaker (SNS) programs are the most common heritage language programs in U.S. schools today. Most of these programs are offered at the high school level. We can also find some examples of programs that support the maintenance and development of other heritage languages (such as native American languages and other immigrant/community languages), and some of these programs begin in the early elementary grades. Community-based heritage language programs are often found in churches, Saturday schools, or other community institutions. Schools can make efforts to link with existing community-based programs to strengthen possibilities for heritage language development for students, their families, and the community overall (Peyton, Ranard, & McGinnis, 2001).

Schools that offer transitional bilingual programs are well positioned to offer heritage language programs to their former ELLs. That is, when former ELLs meet the exit criteria to be redesignated as fully English proficient and are transitioned into the all-English academic mainstream, they can be offered classes that promote the maintenance and development of their oral and written expertise in their home language. In this way, the subtractive effects of transitional bilingual programs, the most common type of bilingual program in the United States today, can be attenuated. By offering a heritage language program, perhaps as a world language or as part of the language arts curriculum, schools can provide their former ELLs with structured opportunities to maintain and develop their home language after they enter the all-English academic mainstream.

SURVEY FOR REFLECTION AND ACTION

This survey is organized around critical features for planning effective instructional programs for ELLs. Read the following statements with your program for ELLs in mind, and indicate the degree to which you agree or disagree: DK—don't know; 1—strongly disagree; 2—disagree; 3—agree; 4—strongly agree. Identify your current program strengths and future possibilities that you can see. Then identify one to three concrete action steps that you can take to build on those strengths and realize those possibilities.

We understand that English language learners are everyone's responsibility.
Everyone who has ELLs in their classes/schools understands that they are an integral part of the instructional program for ELLs and that they must be equipped with the expertise and practices they need to educate these learners.

- General education teachers (elementary and secondary) DK 1 2 3 4

- Resource teachers (literacy, special education) DK 1 2 3 4

- Specialist teachers (art, physical education, music, health) DK 1 2 3 4

- Support staff (instructional assistants, secretaries, counselors) DK 1 2 3 4

- Administrators (central and school-based) DK 1 2 3 4

We assess the strengths and needs of our English language learners/bilingual learners.

Everyone at the school who comes into contact with ELLs (administrators, ESL and/or bilingual teachers, general education teachers, support staff) has a clear understanding of the following:

- Number of ELLs at the school (attention to language(s) represented)   DK 1 2 3 4

- ELLs' proficiency in English (listening, speaking, reading, and writing)   DK 1 2 3 4

- ELLs' proficiency in their home language(s) (listening, speaking, reading, and writing)   DK 1 2 3 4

- ELLs' educational history/academic background   DK 1 2 3 4

- ELLs' cultural background   DK 1 2 3 4

- Number of English speakers who speak a language other than English at home (i.e., heritage language speakers)   DK 1 2 3 4

- Heritage language speakers' proficiency in the heritage language (listening, speaking, reading, and writing)   DK 1 2 3 4

We clearly articulate our goals for ELLs/bilingual learners and our means of assessing student performance relative to those goals (*italicized statements may or may not be goals*).

Each of the relevant constituents (students, teachers, administrators, support staff, parents, community members) has a clear understanding of our goals for ELLs/bilingual learners and the means of assessing student performance and development relative to those goals.

- English language development for ELLs (social and academic language).   DK 1 2 3 4

- Academic achievement for ELLs (in instructional language[s]).   DK 1 2 3 4

- Cross-cultural competence for all students.   DK 1 2 3 4

- *Home language and literacy development for ELLs.*   DK 1 2 3 4

- *Heritage language/literacy development for heritage language speakers.*   DK 1 2 3 4

- *Second language/literacy development for English speakers.*　　DK 1 2 3 4

- Each of the relevant constituents understands and supports　　DK 1 2 3 4
  the goals of the program.

- Each of the relevant constituents understands and supports the　DK 1 2 3 4
  means of assessing student performance and development
  relative to the goals of the program.

**Our instructional program for ELLs/bilingual learners is aligned with state
content and language standards, and based on sound educational and language
proficiency standards.**
Specifically, the program includes the following critical components:

- ELLs have access to comprehensible, standards- based　　DK 1 2 3 4
  instruction in all content areas (in their L1 or using sheltered
  English strategies) so they can achieve academically while they
  learn English.

- ELLs have access to regularly scheduled, standards-driven,　　DK 1 2 3 4
  content-based ESL instruction so that they can acquire the oral
  and written academic English they need to achieve in all
  content areas.

- The program allows ELLs the time they need to reach all goals.　DK 1 2 3 4

- The program for ELLs/bilingual learners is an enrichment　　DK 1 2 3 4
  program, not a remedial program; that is, the home languages
  and cultures of our ELLs/bilingual learners are seen as resources
  to be developed, not as problems to overcome.

- All of the constituents (students, educators, parents, community　DK 1 2 3 4
  members) have a clear and coherent understanding of how the
  program is structured so that the target populations can reach
  their goals.

- There is a clearly articulated language plan that specifies how　DK 1 2 3 4
  languages are to be used for instructional purposes. This
  language plan is aligned with research on the instructional
  education model implemented in that context (i.e., TWI, DBE,
  TBE, SEI).

We ensure that our instructional program for English language learners/ bilingual learners has adequate resources for implementation.
The instructional program for ELLs/bilingual learners has the resources necessary for effective implementation, including:

- Appropriate curriculum in the language(s) used for instruction   DK 1 2 3 4

- Appropriate materials in the language(s) used for instruction   DK 1 2 3 4

- Qualified personnel with appropriate professional development;   DK 1 2 3 4
  i.e., all educators (including administrators and general
  education teachers, literacy and special education specialists,
  counselors, staff) have developed the expertise and practices
  they need to educate their ELLs/bilingual learners.

- Valid and reliable formative and summative assessments of   DK 1 2 3 4
  student performance and development relative to the goals of
  the program in the language(s) used for instruction.

We develop an authentic assessment and accountability system that will yield the range of data we need to inform all of our decision-making regarding the ELLs/bilingual learners in our schools.
Specifically, our assessment and accountability system includes policies and procedures outlining:

- The data/information we need to collect about ELLs' English   DK 1 2 3 4
  language proficiency, prior schooling, L1 literacy, and other
  important background factors so that we can make appropriate
  placement decisions.

- The different measures of student performance we need to   DK 1 2 3 4
  guide and differentiate our content-area instruction.

- The different measures of student performance we need to   DK 1 2 3 4
  monitor student growth and achievement relative to state
  content and language proficiency standards as well as all of our
  program goals.

- The different measures of student performance and teacher   DK 1 2 3 4
  practices that we need to make decisions about program and
  professional development.

- The different measures of student performance and teacher   DK 1 2 3 4
  practices that we need to demonstrate program effectiveness.

Program Strengths

1. _____

2. _____

3. _____

Future Possibilities

1. _____

2. _____

3. _____

Action Steps

1. _____

2. _____

3. _____

5

IMPLEMENTATING AND EVALUATING INSTRUCTIONAL PROGRAMS FOR ENGLISH LANGUAGE LEARNERS

GUIDING PRINCIPLES

- All our staff members share responsibility for the education of English language learners (ELLs).
- Our programs build on the linguistic and cultural resources that students and their families bring to the school and community.
- Parents of ELLs/bilingual learners are well integrated into the school community.
- Our program for ELLs/bilingual learners is well articulated horizontally across content areas and vertically across grade levels.
- We use valid and reliable evidence of students' performance and development from placement to achievement to inform instruction and to guide program development.

INTRODUCTION

Programs for English language learners (ELLs) must be well implemented in order for ELLs to reach all program goals. Research demonstrates that it takes time for ELLs to develop academic English and to achieve academically in all content areas. Furthermore, everyone who works with ELLs in the school must share responsibility for these students. These educators must also ensure that their programs and practices build on the linguistic and cultural resources that diverse student and community populations bring with them to school. Each professional at the school must understand how his or her part fits into the larger system, and each must be afforded opportunities to collaborate with other professionals in the school community so that ELLs have access to the educational opportunities to which they are legally entitled.

Knowledgeable administrators are key. They provide the leadership and the structure to ensure that the professionals working together in their school develop the expertise, practices, and opportunities to effectively implement their program for ELLs. Administrators set the tone for collaboration in the school district or school and can ensure that the program created for ELLs is an integral part of the daily working of the rest of the school or district. Once a theoretically sound educational program has been developed and an administrator has ensured that all the necessary human and material resources are available, he or she must ensure that the program for ELLs is well implemented and that it delivers results. This requires a coherent instructional approach across classes, a shared language among educators, close collaboration with the community, an authentic assessment plan, and the ongoing use of data to drive all decisions concerning the education of ELLs, from placement to achievement.

This chapter is organized around questions that administrators are asking about program implementation and evaluation. The answers that experts provide offer insight into effective implementation of programs for ELLs in a wide range of contexts. The chapter concludes with a Survey for Reflection and Action that administrators can use to review how well their program for ELLs is implemented, and to identify action steps they may need to take to improve their program.

■ How do we ensure that everyone in the school shares the responsibility for educating English language learners, not just those who are specialists in the field?
CYNTHIA MOSCA

A crucial responsibility of administrators is ensuring that everyone in a school and in a school district, regardless of the person's position or specialization, shares the responsibility of educating English language learners (ELLs). In our school district, we have tried to get everyone on board by committing to three major strategies that have become part of the school culture. The first strategy has to do with the school improvement plan (SIP), the second revolves around the provision of support in the mainstream classroom, and the third strategy concerns professional development.

Each of our schools has a SIP written by the staff and community of the school. We require each SIP to have one goal that specifically addresses the academic achievement of ELLs within the school community. That section of the SIP includes activities that help attain the goals and a method for measuring the success of the goal. Requiring each school to pay special attention to the needs of their ELL population within the SIP has proved to be quite effective. It brings those students into the foreground and promotes shared responsibility by all staff.

The second way that we obtain shared responsibility is by providing specialized support in the mainstream classroom. In grades four through six, English as a second language (ESL) teachers push into all English classrooms during reading to give extra support to students who are particularly struggling with reading. This is made possible by offering reading throughout the day so that ESL and reading specialists can be scheduled into every room on a regular basis. When the ESL teacher goes into that reading class, he or she serves reading groups that include ELLs and that also may include students who are not ELLs. Giving ESL teachers the more general role of support for all students leads to the perception that an ESL teacher can help all students. More important, it leads to the perception among reading teachers that they also have equal responsibility for all the students in the classroom, including those who are ELLs.

The third way in which all teachers come to develop a sense of responsibility for ELL students is through professional development. We offer opportunities for specialized course work to all of our teachers, and we especially encourage mainstream classroom teachers to take the courses. These courses lead to an ESL (or bilingual, for those teachers who have proficiency in another language) approval. We make it as easy as possible for these teachers to complete the course work by having cohorts go through the requirements right in their own schools. Whenever possible, we offer partial financial support for tuition.

With these strategies, we attempt to draw all school staff into the responsibility of educating ELLs so that they begin to see themselves as primarily accountable for these students. Without this shared responsibility, ELLs would be relegated to the remote corners of the school community, which does not help build the best learning environment for them.

How do we integrate parents of English language learners and community members into our program/school?
MARITZA MEYERS and R. C. RODRIGUEZ

Involving parents of English language learners (ELLs) and helping them become active members of the school community is an evolving process (Epstein et al., 2002). Remember that the most valuable tool we have in getting ELL parents involved is other ELL parents who have already formed a partnership with the school or district. Parents who have the knowledge that their children are learning English and growing in all academic areas will become educators of other parents.

Here are some suggestions for getting parents involved, first within the school community and then in the larger society.

Make Sure Parents Understand the Goals, Objectives, and Theoretical Basis for the Program Set Up for Their Children

- Organize at least one meeting for parents for this purpose. Use the KWL strategy, which allows misconceptions to be aired and addressed, and it helps parents form a true picture of their child's learning environment.
- Plan a bilingual/ESL classroom observation and allow time for processing afterwards.
- Focus on academics in addition to English language learning.
- Explain the research that stands behind the program.

Encourage Teachers to Make Home Visits
A visit to the home by a teacher provides great insight into how ELLs use their home language and English in their everyday lives. These visits also

lead parents to feel more comfortable with school staff and thus to be more likely to venture into school.

Let the Native Language Play a Significant Role within the School

- Increase resources in the native language by hiring, whenever possible, bilingual teachers, psychologists, counselors, social workers, secretaries, and community liaisons.
- Have postings throughout the school in the native language.
- When offering workshops for parents of ELLs, make sure they are in the native language (with the exception of ESL classes, of course).

Make it Easier for Parents to Attend Events at School

- Provide transportation for parents. Designated stops at various locations throughout the community will facilitate transportation to and from school functions.
- Offer child care services during parent workshops and meetings.
- Provide meals at the meetings that are appropriate to the time of the meetings.
- Dedicate a room in the school to parents where informal meetings, or *cafesitos,* can be held in this "parents' homeroom."

Offer Classes for Parents

Survey parents as to their need for various types of classes and workshops, including the following:

- ESL, literacy, technology, GED, using community resources (such as library and clinics), and citizenship classes.
- Make-and-take or craft workshops that can be done in coordination with the children.
- Cross-cultural communication. Do not shy away from cross-cultural issues; instead, deal with them in an open and positive way.
- Classes on how to help children with school work at home. When parents become closely involved in their children's learning process, they can provide valuable feedback to the teacher, and this in turn helps to integrate them into the school mainstream.

Encourage Participation in School Governance

- Parent Advisory Committees. Encourage ELL parents to join not only the advisory committee that focuses on ELL issues but other committees as well.
- Board of Education (BOE) meetings. A facilitator can act as translator during the meeting and can then provide a brief summary of what transpired during the meeting.

Recruit Parents as Volunteers or Paid Assistants

It is important to note that not all ELL parents can fulfill these roles, as many are working parents or have other children at home. When parents begin to participate in the functioning of the school they feel ownership and shared responsibility in their child's education and will encourage other parents to participate as well. It is also a great way for them to get to know the workings of a school intimately. The following are ways that ELL parents can work or volunteer at school:

- Translators. When ELL parents are bilingual and have received a formal education in their native country, they can assist you with translating instructional materials, documents, parent letters, newsletters, and brochures. When ELL parents assume the role of translator, one must be cautious of the following:
  1. Allow enough time for translation. Translating is time-consuming. However, with proper time and planning, your translator can be a valuable resource.
  2. Always have other native speakers review and edit the translation.
  3. Be aware of regional dialects or language differences that could result in an ineffective translation.
- Tutors. We have found this type of parental involvement to be the most beneficial for both the school and the parent. Training and supervision are key to the success of this strategy. ELL parents can work one on one or with small groups of students under the direction of the teacher. Many tutorial resources and materials can be purchased today to help you focus on academic or linguistic goals and objectives. However, make sure that these materials are parent friendly.
- Monitors on school trips or other special events, in the lunchroom or library, or school clubs.

Hold Activities that Integrate the English-speaking and ELL Community

The child is the common element that creates the opportunity for gatherings such as the following:

- Workshops where children and parents come together to participate in activities.
- School shows at which all children perform. Showcase a performance in the native language.
- Cultural activities and exhibits.
- Story-telling nights where stories from different cultures are shared.

ROBERT FUGATE

At Greenfield Elementary School, parents of English language learners (ELLs) participate in an after-school English as a second language (ESL) class once a week. The class is designed to teach the parents writing and computer skills as well as basic English language skills. During the class, the parents write cookbooks of their own recipes in their first languages and then translate them into English. While the parents are working in the computer lab, their children are participating in a homework/study skills workshop led by high school students volunteering their time. Each week after the parent class a potluck dinner is held, and the parents participate in a drawing for door prizes. The door prizes and the dinner are necessary incentives to attract as much parent participation as possible. During the dinner, the parents talk with one another. This helps them feel less isolated in their community and more comfortable in coming to the school.

As most of the parents participating in the class are Spanish speakers, some bilingual instruction is necessary to meet their individual language needs. The parents' educational levels also vary from those who do not read and write in their first language to those with much education and first language literacy. Because the parents have varying levels of education and English language proficiency, the parents with the most proficient English language skills act as interpreters for the parents with lower proficiency. This allows all parents appropriate comfort levels to participate actively in the class and not to feel intimidated by the language barrier. It also fosters a sense of camaraderie among the parents; they know they are not alone.

Additional benefits of the class are the parents' comfort in coming to the school for programs, teacher conferences, and visiting their children at lunch. They know that the staff members at Greenfield Elementary School are sensitive to their needs and to the language barriers. The ESL teachers serve as liaisons between the classroom teachers and the parents. They also do some interpreting, as needed. Another benefit for the parents is their children seeing their own parents as language learners in their own school. This has led to building a language learning community at the school where children and parents are stakeholders. During the time the class has met, the parents' comfort with the English language has grown, along with their proficiency and literacy levels.

The parent ESL class is possible as the result of a grant that provides funds for all materials and people necessary to make it work. The program is sponsored by the Chesterfield Public Education Foundation and administered by the Chesterfield County Public Schools Department of Business and Government Relations in collaboration with the Instruction Division.

■ How can teachers build on the linguistic and cultural resources that their students bring with them to school?
JIM CUMMINS

The issue raised in the question implies a more fundamental question: *Why should teachers build on the linguistic and cultural resources that their students bring with them to school?* The rationale and relevant research related to why teachers should build on students' linguistic and cultural resources are considered initially and then a core set of instructional strategies for realizing this goal are outlined.

RATIONALE

Students' linguistic and cultural resources contribute to the teaching and learning process in three fundamental ways.

- Activation of students' cultural and linguistic knowledge constitutes a form of scaffolding that helps make conceptual input more comprehensible and enables students to use their existing home language (L1) skills and conceptual knowledge as stepping stones to more accomplished performance in English (L2).
- Considerable research points to the centrality of teacher-student identity negotiation in mediating students' engagement in learning. When students' cultural and linguistic knowledge is expressed, shared, and affirmed within the classroom, they are likely to invest themselves more fully in the learning process.
- When students' L1 is encouraged as a cognitive tool within the classroom, it becomes a resource for cross-language comparison and transfer, thereby enabling students to increase their awareness of the vocabulary and structure of English.

Scaffolding. There is universal agreement among cognitive psychologists about the significance of students' background knowledge for learning. We learn by integrating new input into our existing cognitive structures or schemata. Our prior experience provides the foundation for interpreting new information. No learner is a blank slate. In reading, for example, we construct meaning by bringing our knowledge of language and of the world to the text. As Fielding and Pearson (1994) point out, research conducted in the late 1970s and early 1980s consistently revealed a strong reciprocal relationship between prior knowledge and reading comprehension ability: "The more one already knows, the more one comprehends; and the more one comprehends, the more one learns new knowledge to enable comprehension of an even greater array of topics and texts" (p. 62). Snow, Burns, and Griffin (1998) express the instructional implications of this point as follows:

> Every opportunity should be taken to extend and enrich children's background knowledge and understanding in every way possible, for the ultimate significance and memorability of any word or text depends on whether children possess the background knowledge and conceptual sophistication to understand its meaning (p. 219).

In the case of ELL students, and particularly those who are in the early stages of learning English, much of their background knowledge is likely to be encoded in their L1. Thus, their L1 is directly relevant to the learning of L2. This implies that students should be encouraged to use their Lɪ to activate and extend their conceptual knowledge (e.g., by brainstorming in groups, writing in Lɪ as a stepping stone to writing in L2, carrying out Internet research in their Lɪ, etc.).

Affirming identities. Extensive research from the fields of anthropology and sociology have documented the role of societal power relations in explaining patterns of minority group achievement (see Cummins, 2001, for a review). Groups that experience long-term educational underachievement (e.g., African Americans, Latino/Latina students, Native Americans) tend to have experienced material and symbolic violence at the hands of the dominant societal group over generations. A direct implication is that in order to reverse this pattern of underachievement, educators, both individually and collectively, must challenge the operation of coercive power relations in the classroom interactions they orchestrate with minority group students.

Within the classroom, societal power relations are expressed in the negotiation of identities between teachers and students. The ways in which teachers negotiate identities with students can exert a significant impact on the extent to which students will engage academically or withdraw from academic effort. The influence of broader societal power relations on classroom interactions was documented many years ago by research in the American southwest which reported that Euro-American students were praised or encouraged 36% more often than Mexican-American students and their classroom contributions were used or built upon 40% more frequently than those of Mexican-American students (U.S. Commission on Civil Rights, 1973). Classroom instruction that acknowledges and builds on students' cultural and linguistic knowledge is not only scaffolding more accomplished performance; it is also communicating to students that their cultural knowledge and linguistic talents are valued within the school community. This process challenges the frequent devaluation of students' language and culture in the society at large.

Extending language awareness. Researchers have frequently observed that bilingual students transfer concepts and linguistic features across their two languages in contexts where both languages are valued and encouraged by the school. Unfortunately, however, many classrooms become "English-only zones" because teachers are unaware of the potentially positive connections between languages and unsure of how to manage multiple languages in their classrooms. Some of these cross-language connections are obvious, as in the case of connections between the academic lexicon of English (derived primarily from Latin) and the lexicon of Romance languages (e.g., Spanish) where the vast bulk of the vocabulary (both everyday and academic) derives from Latin (e.g., English *encounter*– Spanish *encontrar*). In the case of noncognate languages, the creation of dual language stories or other textual forms can draw students' attention to differences and similarities in their languages. For example, a Grade 7 student (Kanta), who wrote a 20-page Urdu-English story with two of her classmates (Madiha, Sulmana) based on their collective immigration experiences, commented:

> It helped me a lot to be able to write it in two languages and especially for Madiha who was just beginning to learn English because the structure of the two languages is so different. So if you want to say something in Urdu it might take just three words but in English to say the same thing you'd have to use more words. So for Madiha it helped the differences between the two languages become clear.

In short, in actual classroom practice, instruction that builds on students' cultural and linguistic knowledge will often simultaneously scaffold input and output, affirm students' identities, and deepen their knowledge of how languages work.

CLASSROOM STRATEGIES: THE ROLE OF IDENTITY TEXTS

The initial step in creating a classroom space where students' linguistic and cultural resources are valued and built upon is to ask ourselves collectively as educators (a) what image of the student is currently being enacted in our classrooms, and (b) what image of the student would we aspire to promote through our instruction. Thus, we can ask, to what extent is our instruction promoting an image of the student as:

- Capable of becoming bilingual and biliterate?
- Capable of higher-order thinking and intellectual accomplishments?
- Capable of creative and imaginative thinking?
- Capable of creating literature and art?
- Capable of generating new knowledge?
- Capable of thinking about and finding solutions to social issues?

As a school community, if we aspire to move in these directions, we will explore instructional strategies that enable students to showcase their cultural knowledge and linguistic talents as well as to demonstrate their intellectual and imaginative thinking skills. The construct of *identity texts* attempts to capture the kinds of cross-curricular projects that will enable and support students in expressing and expanding their sense of self in association with literate endeavours.

Identity texts describe the products of students' creative work or performances carried out within the pedagogical space orchestrated by the classroom teacher. Students invest their identities in the creation of texts which can be written, spoken, signed, visual, musical, dramatic, or multimodal. The identity text then holds a mirror up to students in which their identities are reflected back in a positive light. When students share identity texts with multiple audiences (peers, teachers, parents, grandparents, sister classes, the media, etc.) they are likely to receive positive feedback and affirmation of self in interaction with these audiences. Although not always an essential component, technology acts as an amplifier to enhance the process of identity text production and dissemination. Family involvement is typically an integral component of identity text construction (see Cummins & Early, 2011; Marshall & Toohey, 2010). For examples of dual language identity texts see http://thornwoodps.dyndns.org/dual/index.htm and www.multiliteracies.ca.

It is clear that if schools are to build on students' linguistic and cultural knowledge, instruction must go beyond simply transmitting the curriculum to students in a one-size-fits-all manner. Students must be given opportunities to co-construct knowledge in interaction with the teacher, building on the funds of knowledge that exist in their communities (Moll, Amanti, Neff, & González, 1992). For bilingual/ELL students, dual language identity text creation represents a key concept in planning instruction that (a) scaffolds students' literacy accomplishments in English to levels that they would have been unable to produce without use of L1 as a cognitive tool, (b) affirms their bilingual and biliterate identities as well as their intellectual and creative potential, and (c) deepens their awareness of language in general and, more specifically, the connections between their L1 and English.

ESTER J. DE JONG

One could respond to the question *How can teachers build on the linguistic and cultural resources that their students bring with them to school?* with a long list of activities or strategies. This would not provide a framework for decision making, however, that teachers and administrators need on a daily basis to reflect on their practices. The latter needs a more principled approach because this supports consistency in practices and a coherent vision at the classroom and school level.

What might such a framework for decision making entail? Based on research on effective programs for bilingual students, key principles can be identified that can function as useful tools to create and reflect on high-quality learning environments for all students, including ELLs (de Jong, 2011). These key principles are built on one basic, foundational principle, namely the *Principle of Educational Equity*. This principle is grounded in a fundamental respect for individuals for who they are and in the importance for schools to engage in nondiscriminatory practices. The following three principles support this overarching goal specifically for linguistically and culturally diverse students.

The *Principle of Affirming Identities* stresses the importance of validating diverse cultural experiences and of creating spaces for diverse student voices. Teachers find out what knowledge students have developed at home and in the community ('funds of knowledge'; Gonzalez, Moll, & Amanti, 2005) and incorporate this knowledge into their curriculum content to make meaningful connections to their students' lives. Teachers use different media to allow students to explore their identities. One elementary teacher used critical autobiographies (Brisk, Burgos, & Hamerla, 2004) to create opportunities for her students to give voice to their bilingual experiences and think critically about issues of language and culture. Examining their own bilingual lives, the students read, talked, and wrote about social, political, economic, cultural, and linguistic aspects of bilingualism and schooling.

The *Principle of Promoting Additive Bi/Multilingualism* stresses respect for multilingualism, by providing opportunities for the development of bilingual students' native languages to the maximum extent possible in addition to providing access to effective instruction in the second language. This can imply the implementation of an additive bilingual education program, such as a two-way immersion or one-way developmental program. When a bilingual program is not feasible, teachers can still strategically use the native language for concept development or clarification (e.g., by previewing in the native language); they can use and create bilingual materials and group students in ways that support students' use of the native language.

The third principle considers how a school's various components (students, parents, teachers, programs) relate to each other and how these relations reflect equal status among those involved. *The Principle of Structuring for Integration* includes ELLs and other students from diverse backgrounds in decision making from the very beginning, not as an added-on afterthought. It acknowledges that engaging in linguistically and culturally responsive practice asks that all participants in a school be involved in creating an environment of respect and a sense of social justice. It is not only the responsibility of minority language speakers to adjust and fit into the existing system; the system also has to change. Educators promote representative involvement of different constituents in decision making at all levels, including parents and community members. They advocate for a strong, broad expert base related to linguistic and cultural diversity throughout the school, valuing the expertise of specialist bilingual and English as a second language teachers.

In summary, quality schools for bilingual learners treat ELLs as emergent bilingual and bicultural and complete individuals (Principle of Educational Equity). Educators in these schools formulate and implement policies and engage in practices that reflect respect for linguistic and cultural diversity (Principle of Affirming Identities) and that accept, develop, and extend existing linguistic repertoires within and across languages (Principle of Promoting Bi/Multilingualism). They carefully consider how diverse linguistic and cultural resources are equally reflected and valued in all aspects of the school (Principle of Structuring for Integration). These principles can guide decision making in any linguistically and culturally diverse school context, including bilingual, multilingual, and English-medium programs.

■ **How do we articulate our program so that it provides the intensity, continuity, and length of time that English language learners need to acquire academic English?**
MARITZA MEYERS and CYNTHIA MOSCA

It is crucial for an effective program for English language learners (ELLs) to be well coordinated and for all staff to be on the same page. To achieve that goal, formal and informal articulation strategies must be in place so that the various services that ELLs receive remain well coordinated. Formal articulation strategies are typically part of the textual history and culture of the school or school district: they are usually written down and are adhered to rather formally. Informal articulation strategies, on the other hand, happen more on the spur of the moment and may change slightly from year to year, depending on current needs and conditions.

FORMAL ARTICULATION STRATEGIES

- Monthly meetings with district and school administrators to provide updates for program issues, state mandates, personnel, and certification issues.
- Scheduled meetings at a district or school level for institute days, early release days, or building curriculum meetings on particular issues regarding ELLs.
- New teacher orientation about ELLs who are served in the district for all new teachers.
- ELL-focused mentoring program for all new teachers who will have ELLs in their classrooms.
- A formal document focusing on ELL education distributed to all individuals who come into contact with ELLs. The document can include the following:
    1. A language development plan. This plan specifies how ELLs are to reach the goals and objectives set for them. It also describes the allocation of language of instruction in the various programs available to ELLs.
    2. Long- and short-term goals that ensure acquisition of academic language. This part of the document specifies the best ways to assess these students, how to provide the best opportunities for

them to experience enriched academic language and content learning, and how to ensure standards-based learning.
3. Guidelines for hiring practices, which include a forum of teachers and parents working together. A collaborative hiring process leads to increased levels of commitment and knowledge regarding school and programs goals.

INFORMAL ARTICULATION STRATEGIES

- Professional development on ELL issues and strategies for all staff members that includes:
  1. On-site training and coaching in the classroom as well as visits to successful schools.
  2. Courses with partial scholarships leading to ESL or bilingual endorsement as specified by the state.
  3. Opportunities for all staff members to attend local and state bilingual and ESL conferences.
- Creating a school culture where open communication is the norm and all staff members are free to ask questions through face-to-face conversation, telephone, or email.
- After-school meetings on specific issues that any staff member can request. Any major issue should be discussed collaboratively, and opportunities must be provided, especially to teachers, to discuss practices, student progress, effective lessons, and program goals.

With these strategies in place, we ensure that ELLs are seen as the responsibility of all teachers, administrators, and departments. Without this shared responsibility, ELLs would be less likely to receive quality support in an integrated way and for as long as they need it.

■ How do we ensure that the general education teachers and English as a second language teachers collaborate to address the content and language needs of the English language learners?
JANA ECHEVARRIA

In our extensive work developing the Sheltered Instruction Observation Protocol (SIOP) Model with teachers who have English language learners (ELLs) in their classrooms (Echevarria, Vogt, & Short, 2008a, 2010a, 2010b), one thing has become clear: English as a second language (ESL) specialists alone cannot adequately meet the needs of the ever-growing numbers of ELL students (Echevarria, Short, & Vogt, 2008b). All school personnel share in the responsibility of educating ELLs. While the ESL teacher offers valuable expertise in language development, the general education teacher also must understand the importance of tending to the second language acquisition needs of ELLs while delivering content to these students. The best way to accomplish this goal is to have a good, collaborative relationship between the ESL teacher and the general education teacher.

From our work, we have found that there are essentially three overarching factors that contribute to productive collaboration: training, time, and relationships. First, many administrators have reported that when their staff have all been trained in the same approach for teaching ELLs, the school "speaks the same language," which contributes greatly to good collaboration. Too often, teachers are compartmentalized into areas such as special education, language arts, general education, ESL, and so forth, and each area receives different kinds of professional development experiences. Fragmented professional development can be an impediment to collaboration and can contribute to feelings of territoriality.

Once teachers, specialists, and administrators approach the education of ELLs in a coherent way, the next factor for making sure collaboration takes place is to provide time in which to collaborate. This sounds easy. However, extra time is sorely lacking in a school day. While recognizing the limitations on time, let me mention a couple of ways that administrators have found to allow teachers time for collaboration. In elementary schools, there may be an ELL team that meets to discuss issues and then takes the information back to their grade-level meetings. Many of those issues also are discussed during monthly staff meetings. If the collaboration is as specific as lesson planning and coordination of instruction, some schools find funds to provide substitutes for planning days or extra pay for after-school planning sessions. In secondary schools, conference periods are coordinated so that the ESL and general education teacher share planning time. In other cases, coverage is provided during a given period to free up time to collaborate. Again, collaboration takes less time when staff members share the same approach to instruction and the same terminology.

Finally, collaboration is a voluntary process, since one really cannot be forced to collaborate, even if mandated by the administration. An issue that impedes effective collaboration is territoriality. Administrators serve an important role in helping to defuse such situations by valuing each teacher and clearly communicating that a team approach is called for. The ESL teacher needs to understand that he or she brings a wealth of knowledge to the setting and will continue to have an important role as a leader on ELL issues. The general education teacher likewise needs to understand that each student is as important as the next and that utilizing all available resources is in everyone's best interest. The ESL teacher may start by developing a strong relationship with several teachers who are willing to collaborate. Then, at staff meetings, these teachers may be invited to talk about the benefits of their collaboration for students and general education teachers alike.

Collaboration has become a buzzword in education. It is much easier to talk about than to implement. However, we have seen that over time the relationships necessary for effective collaboration can develop, as long as the administration is committed to making it happen.

LYNNE DÍAZ-RICO

Educating English language learners (ELLs) requires the collaborative effort of classroom teachers and English as a second language (ESL) specialists. In this process, it is essential that site administrators be strong leaders who keep the staff's vision focused on the goal of providing high-quality education for ELLs, in part by helping staff members develop the skills and practices needed to implement this goal (Díaz-Rico, 2004; Díaz-Rico & Week, 2006).

To provide high-quality instruction, educators face four key challenges: sustaining high academic expectations, tracking success in English proficiency while monitoring fair grading practices, ensuring a high level of teamwork, and promoting a supportive environment for students' primary language and culture. A description of each challenge follows, along with recommended solutions.

Research has shown that students take at least three to five years to acquire the academic language needed to master the elementary curriculum. While they are acquiring this academic English, ELLs must also keep pace with native English speakers' academic performance. Educators walk a tightrope: How does one make content understandable to a non-English speaker without the language-support activities themselves slowing the curricular pace? How can ELLs maintain access to the same level of information and produce the same quality of performance that is expected of high achievers? Techniques of specially designed academic instruction in English (SDAIE) or sheltered instruction include the use of modified teacher speech (clear enunciation, simple sentence structures, reduced use of slang and idioms, increased use of gestures), modified instructional delivery (use of primary language resource materials, peer coaches, visuals), and modified texts (teacher-created text outlines, simplified text, and audio recordings of text available in learning centers). Each lesson in a content domain should have both language development objectives and content goals. The site administrator monitors instruction closely so that language development takes place while academic standards are met.

An integrated connection between placement scores in English proficiency and subsequent instruction ensures that the ELL is properly placed according to language skills. A tracking folder that follows the ELL from placement to achievement and includes a checklist of proficiency goals level by level provides a structured means for accountability in English language acquisition. As part of sustaining high academic expectations, the site administrator bears the responsibility of monitoring the report card grades received by ELLs so that these grades are neither artificially inflated because of lower expectations nor deflated owing to unfair competition with native English speakers.

A high level of collaborative teamwork is needed to ensure that ELLs succeed to the same degree as do their native-English-speaking peers. If the school has an ESL coordinator, the role of this specialist is to model SDAIE/ sheltered techniques for mainstream teachers, to administer proficiency tests and maintain records, to help create materials for SDAIE-enhanced content delivery, and to educate parents in their role of instructional support. (In a high-quality program, there is no expectation for the ESL coordinator to "pull out" ELLs for instruction away from the mainstream classroom.) A mutually respectful, collaborative relationship between classroom teachers and the ESL specialist has several key elements: The collaboration should be based on shared goals, parity of status, shared responsibility for key decisions, shared resources, shared accountability for outcomes, and a sense of emergent trust (Friend & Cook, 2000). These elements are best fostered when the administrator also models these elements. If problems arise, the administrator's role is to facilitate open lines of communication and problem solving.

In a school setting that promotes inclusion, much support is evident for maintaining students' primary language and affirming the culture in which that language lives. School staff who are bilingual, welcome signs and announcements in the primary languages, time set aside within the curriculum for instruction in a foreign or heritage language, financial support for translators or community liaison workers, and a full range of primary language resource materials in a central library or classroom resource centers. These efforts send the community the message that English language instruction is an additive rather than subtractive influence on students' native language skills. A commitment to linguistic multicompetence ("everyone is bilingual") is a vote for collaboration not only between teachers and specialists but also between the school and community. The administrator sets the tone by actively and enthusiastically embracing diversity and making it possible for collaboration to flourish.

■ How should English language learners be grouped for instruction?
ESTER DE JONG

As a general rule, districts should strive to group English language learners (ELLs) age appropriately by grade level and organize their services in such a way that ELLs will have access to grade-appropriate content and language instruction. Grouping ELLs becomes a complex issue as practical issues such as the number of ELLs, available resources, and the desired program model interact with program philosophy and good intentions. Some issues are outlined below.

Prioritizing services around *language proficiency levels* helps ESL/bilingual teachers develop targeted lessons for a particular proficiency level. Handling a wide range of proficiency levels can be challenging, particularly if the teacher cannot communicate in the students' native language. Grouping ELLs by proficiency level must take age differences into consideration, avoiding too large an age gap within one class (for example, a first grader and a second grader can be placed together but a first grader and a third grader should not be placed together). If grouping by language proficiency level involves multiple grades, content learning tends to be sacrificed. Depending on the program type, language proficiency grouping may also isolate students at the same level by not exposing them to more proficient students.

The choice to group students by *language background* is also influenced by program type. Bilingual services require a certain amount of clustering by language background to create optimal opportunities for the use of the native language for content and literacy instruction. It is important that within the context of bilingual programs, schools create systematic and frequent opportunities to interact with native English speakers. English as a second language (ESL) programs, on the other hand, can be organized either for one-language groups or for mixed-language groups. In this context, grouping students from the same language group together is sometimes considered disadvantageous because it may discourage use of the target language. Some argue that heterogeneous language grouping facilitates English language learning because it creates a communicative need to use English. While the latter is often the case, the issue is more complex. First, whether students exclusively use their first language during second language classes is not only a function of the ELLs. It also depends on the language environment created by the teacher and the larger school culture. Second, grouping students by language background can be advantageous in the ESL classroom if the teacher knows how to capitalize on the bilingual resources available for both content and language learning. Using the native language as a scaffold can accelerate ELLs' academic language development. Regardless of the grouping chosen, schools should consider native/non-native speaker interactions in addition to groupings that involve only ELLs.

Grade-level placement is often the most appropriate grouping practice. It is important that ELLs be placed with students who are academically and socially their peers. ELLs should never be placed in a lower grade simply because their English is limited. At the same time, the diverse backgrounds of ELLs require districts and schools to develop policies regarding the placement of overage students (older students with academic and literacy skills that are well below grade level, students whose schooling has been interrupted or limited) as well as students who enter the school district during the school year. However, grade-level placement must also be considered in connection to available services. A multi-age or combination-grade classroom can be an appropriate placement if this arrangement allows the school to provide bilingual/ESL services.

Regardless of their grouping practices, districts should be aware of the advantages and disadvantages of different grouping options, take steps to counter the potential negative effects of certain grouping practices, articulate their grouping practices clearly as part of their school plan, and demonstrate how grouping practices promote excellence and meet academic, language, and sociocultural goals for all students, including ELLs.

NANCY L. COMMINS[1]

Sound instructional programs in linguistically diverse schools purposefully plan for differentiation along multiple dimensions. One is the language background of the learners in the group (Commins & Miramontes, 2005). Three groupings are possible: *heterogeneous groups*, where teachers work with students who are native speakers and students who are second language speakers of the language of instruction; *second language groups*, where all the students in front of the teacher are working in their second language; and *primary language groups*, where every student in front of the teacher is a native speaker of the language of instruction. Each setting offers opportunities for linguistic and academic development not necessarily available in the others. Together they can provide the full range of instruction that students need to become academically proficient in English.

Heterogeneous groups. English language learners typically spend the most time in heterogeneous groups. They benefit in these settings when they can experience "authentic" communication with fluent English-speaking models and are exposed to a rigorous academic program. Because of the presence of native English speakers, teachers usually adhere more closely to grade-level or subject-area curriculum and expectations.

Heterogeneous groups, however, can be quite stressful for second language learners. When teachers plan with native speakers in mind, it is easy to overlook the language demands of instructional activities and texts, making the pace and content of the lessons beyond the grasp of many. Having to compete with more proficient native speakers can inhibit second language learners' attempts to express themselves in English.

Second language groups. Second language groups allow ELLs to work on both the structure of English and the academic content side by side with

---

1. This response is based on ongoing work with Silvia Latimer and Sheila Shannon.

students with similar language needs. When teachers focus on making information understandable and allow for language practice, students usually feel more comfortable and tend to participate more actively in these groups than in heterogeneous groups.

However, it is not wise to segregate students into special classes all day. If their teachers are trained only as language teachers, students' access to the concepts of the academic curriculum may be limited. If their teachers are content teachers, they may not be familiar with strategies appropriate to a second language setting. In any case, their opportunities to hear and use English with native models in an academic setting will be limited.

Primary language groups. This third setting, available in programs that incorporate students' primary language into instruction, can allow students to go deeper into concepts, work on higher-order thinking skills, and make use of a full range of text materials. Although there are great benefits to primary language instruction, if students spend their day learning only in their first language, they will effectively be denied the opportunity to learn a second language. Grouping solely by first language may also contribute to a segregation of students along racial and ethnic lines.

Why is this planning with language background in mind important? This kind of planning allows teachers to utilize the instructional strategies most appropriate for the learners in front of them. These understandings also shed light on how students experience instruction across their day. Ideally, second language learners should have opportunities to work in each kind of group each day. In all-English programs, at a minimum both homogeneous second language and heterogeneous groupings should be part of daily instruction.

Accomplishing these goals necessitates schoolwide planning to organize the adult human resources and allow the grouping and regrouping of students both within and across classrooms. This kind of planning also allows schools to maximize limited resources, such as primary language speakers or second language specialists.

■ How can we effectively use instructional assistants in English language learner education?
JOBI LAWRENCE

As an educational community and as stakeholders in our educational systems, we all bear a responsibility to engage in conversations that seek to challenge our assumptions and our beliefs about the school organizational culture and the impact those beliefs and/or assumptions have on our schools. Administrators have a tremendous opportunity and professional obligation to set the tone for the organizational culture of the schools to which they are accountable. This overarching principle guides the response to this question through a brief discussion of titles, job descriptions and duties, professional development, and leveled/tiered system of employment.

TITLES

Many interchangeable titles are utilized for instructional support staff: *paraeducator, paraprofessional, instructional assistant,* and teacher associate just to name a few. At first glance these titles might all seem equally appropriate, with the decision to select one term or the other equally unimportant. While we would not be satisfied if our employee was only partially professional or minimally engaged in the educational setting, we use terms such as paraeducator and paraprofessional and inadvertently set the tone to imply a second-class citizenship for many of our English language learner (ELL) support staff. Utilizing titles such as instructional assistant, teacher associate, and other references that promote high expectations and a positive image for support staff can serve as the first step in ensuring that such important members of our ELL educational team are valued and respected by their colleagues and educational stakeholders.

JOB DESCRIPTIONS/DUTIES

The law related to the requirement for instructional assistants/noncertified staff members to serve under direct supervision of certified staff is very clearly delineated. However, there are many interpretations of the law in daily practice that do not provide appropriate instructional settings for our students. ELL instructional assistants should never replace the teacher/certified staff member in the classroom, and they should not be delivering direct instruction or re-teaching material that the student did not master during direct instruction. It is important that ELLs receive supplemental instruction, repetition of content and concepts, and native language translation when available and appropriate. These are the types of services that can be provided by ELL instructional assistants to enhance ELL success.

PROFESSIONAL DEVELOPMENT

Providing professional development for instructional assistants has become more important as these positions have increased both in numbers and as a proportion of all instructional staff over the past two decades (Schmidt, Greenough, & Nelson, 2002). If we want to realize the full potential of ELL instructional assistants, it is critical that administrators seek out and provide professional development opportunities to maximize the potential of support staff members. There are many professional development opportunities offered through institutions of higher education and Area Education Associations/Regional Assistance Centers that would not require district financial support. ELL support staff should also be invited to district sponsored professional development events even if the district cannot reimburse staff members for their time. Many ELL instructional assistants would attend professional development opportunities if invited to participate, regardless of compensation.

LEVELED/TIERED ASSIGNMENTS

One approach to matching the skill set of the ELL instructional assistant to the requirements for their position includes a thorough assessment of the background, skills, and dispositions of each individual employee. While many ELL instructional assistants are hired to provide translation services and native language support to ELL students and their families, few districts formally evaluate the native language proficiency (including academic language proficiency) of the support staff. While many ELL instructional assistants are required to provide content-area support (many times in the form of re-teaching or supplanting direct instruction by the content teacher), very few districts formally evaluate the content knowledge and formal educational background of the support staff. A systematic approach to assessing the skills, background, and dispositions of support staff members would allow for the assignment of a level/tier that would then be utilized to determine appropriate placement of each employee and help to ensure that the ELL instructional assistants are hired into positions that are a good match for their skill set. When considering how to utilize ELL support staff in the educational setting, educational leaders need to consider how to build and sustain an organizational culture that values and respects the contributions of the support staff and takes into account factors such as those discussed in this section.

■ How should we assess the language proficiency of English language learners?

MARGO GOTTLIEB

Language proficiency assessment of English language learners (ELLs) should include measures of both English (L2) and the native language (L1) regardless of the of the students' instructional program. An assessment in English language proficiency is necessary because it forms the basis of programmatic and instructional decisions. An initial assessment of the native language is necessary so that teachers and administrators have baseline data on the students for placement purposes and for planning differentiated instruction, whether in one language or two. One reason for assessment in two languages is that ELLs' language proficiency, in both L1 and L2, runs along a continuum. Some ELLs come with very little or no proficiency in English and others have language and literacy skills that allow them to survive in the mainstream classroom with some support. L1 proficiency can be even more varied for ELLs. Some ELLs have fully developed L1 across the language domains. Others may be strong in their L1 oral language but may not have had prior experiences with literacy. Thus, assessment of both languages yields the most complete picture of the students' total language proficiency.

ENGLISH LANGUAGE PROFICIENCY

Federal and state laws define, in large extent, how English language proficiency is to be assessed. Since 2001, the Elementary and Secondary Education Act has set general parameters for the development and implementation of English language proficiency assessment for ELLs. Among its required features, these measures must:

- Represent the four language domains: listening, speaking, reading, and writing (that also generate a derived comprehension score from listening and reading).
- Be anchored in academic content standards, whether from individual states or common core state standards.
- Reflect the language of language arts and mathematics.
- Define descriptive performance levels.

States or consortia have had to develop or adopt English language proficiency standards and to use an assessment tool that reflects those standards.

NATIVE LANGUAGE PROFICIENCY

To date, standardized measures of native language (L1) proficiency that parallel the new generation of standards-referenced tools of English language (L2) proficiency are in the development phase. Therefore, school districts with dual language or developmental bilingual students must continue to design strong classroom assessments in L1. In that way, ELLs' L1 proficiency can be initially determined and monitored side by side with their L2 proficiency.

The overall design of classroom assessment for L1 proficiency and the collection of data need to be structured in a fashion similar to L2 proficiency in order to yield meaningful results that can be reported and used in comparable ways. Because there are variations among classrooms, L1 proficiency assessment must be systematic, reliable, and agreed upon by the teachers who are implementing it. If results are to be generalized to a program level, standard ways of interpreting and reporting data need to be in place. Therefore, administrators, working with teachers, have to select, modify, or develop rubrics or scoring guides that capture the language performance of students. In addition, an assessment schedule should be devised so that data collection on specific tasks (such as oral or writing samples) occurs within a designated time frame. Table 5.1 illustrates how to track the relative language proficiency of students in dual

TABLE 5.1 **Mapping language proficiency assessment in L1 and L2 to form student profiles of language development.**

Levels of Language Proficiency	Oral Language Development				Literacy Development			
	Listening		Speaking		Reading		Writing	
	L1	L2	L1	L2	L1	L2	L1	L2
5								
4								
3								
2								
1								

language settings by using the same performance definitions for both L1 and L2 levels of language proficiency.

Defensible data are the cornerstone to establishing the effectiveness of any program for ELLs. For this group of students, L1 and L2 proficiency assessment data help document student progress toward and attainment of language proficiency standards. And because language proficiency works in tandem with academic achievement, reliable and valid assessment allows administrators to gain insight into the viability of their program at a school or district level.

▪ How should we assess the academic achievement of English language learners?
MARGO GOTTLIEB

The academic achievement of English language learners (ELLs) needs to be assessed in both the classroom and a large-scale context. At the classroom level, it is important for teachers to gather data on an ongoing basis to ascertain student achievement for each content area. When teachers assess the academic achievement of ELLs in English, they must keep in mind that the students' English language proficiency often confounds what we can learn about their performance. As a general rule, assessment should be done in the language of instruction. In fact, it should be embedded in instruction, motivating, and performance based rather than being a separate activity or test at the end of an instructional unit. Children can be assessed while they are engaged in hands-on activities and working on long-term projects, perhaps ones that integrate technology, so that they can use multiple grade-level resources to access content and create meaning.

The classroom is one source of information that tells teachers and other stakeholders, such as parents, how ELLs are achieving academically. To make the information consistent from student to student, classroom assessment must be standards based. Teachers can use the common core state standards or state academic content-area standards to help them gauge where the students are (keeping in mind that the standards are designed for native speakers of English) and as a starting place for developing rubrics to interpret students' original work. Instruction in English always needs to be differentiated by language for ELLs, and since assessment is bound to instruction, the rubrics must take into consideration the language proficiency that is necessary for completing the assessment tasks.

Looking at large-scale measures, most states and districts are administering tests in English as stipulated by the 2001 reauthorization of the Elementary and Secondary Education Act. Although this Federal mandate clearly states that students' achievement in mathematics and language arts can indeed be measured in a language other than English, at this time there are few, if any, national, standards-referenced tests that are available in Spanish or other native languages. Some states have translated their individual assessments or produced versions in plain English, but no state has designed an academic achievement test that accounts for the unique characteristics of ELLs. Even when academic achievement tests allow for accommodations, such as longer time to complete the assessment, the use of dictionaries, and directions given orally, students generally are unable to show what they know and can do until they reach a certain threshold level of English language proficiency. Thus, the data from academic achievement testing of ELLs are not very valid or meaningful. As a result, many students will appear not to be attaining the required criteria or standards, and consequently, their schools and districts are likely to be penalized.

For this reason, the assessment information that comes from teachers is critical. In some states there are attempts to develop more classroom-relevant, alternative assessments for ELL academic achievement. These alternative assessments ideally should be based on English language development standards, Spanish language development standards, state academic content standards, and Spanish language arts standards (for the 75 percent of ELLs in the United States who are Spanish speaking). Currently, there is a national push for computer-driven technology to deliver assessments that utilize various formats that yield more reliable and valid results than multiple-choice responses.

In conclusion, we need to drastically improve the ways in which we assess the academic achievement of ELLs because that is their key to school success. As long as ELLs' academic achievement is viewed as an absolute rather than as growth over time, the success stories will be few. We must strive to seek innovative means, both at the classroom level and at large-scale levels, to collect and report what our students can do in the core content areas.

When should English language learners exit their bilingual/English as a second language program?
ESTER J. DE JONG

The mere existence of an exit process as an integral part of a bilingual/ English as a second language (ESL) program often sends a powerful (negative) message to English language learners (ELLs) and their teachers that their program is "less than" the standard curriculum classroom. If schools fail to value and count ELLs' learning through their native language or in ESL classes until ELLs have left the bilingual/ESL program, the school overlooks the educational value of these programs and their important role in reaching academic, language, and sociocultural goals for their students. Administrators must purposefully work with their staff to avoid such perceptions and counter the potential marginalization that results from those perceptions. They can show that the bilingual/ESL program plays a positive role in the school, treat the program with equal status to the standard curriculum program, and promote high-quality, grade-appropriate instruction.

The purpose of exit policies is to develop guidelines for exiting ELLs that will ensure the success of ELLs in a standard curriculum classroom after ELLs no longer receive specialized services. It is inappropriate to set guidelines that merely aim at bare linguistic and social survival in the standard curriculum. After all, ELLs must master sufficient English not only to socialize with their peers and to participate in English language arts classes but also to succeed in math, science, social studies, and other content area classes. This implies that schools and districts must set exit guidelines that reflect high expectations. The following are some key considerations for developing exit guidelines:

1. Exit policies should reflect our understanding of second language learning as a complex and nonlinear process that takes time. Therefore,
   - Exit policies should be flexible, accommodating individual students' needs and histories and allowing for a gradual transitioning from bilingual/ESL programs to standard curriculum programs.
   - Exit policies should not be based on time factors (such as an arbitrary mandate that after one year, students should exit the program) but on the actual proficiency levels attained by ELLs.
   - Exit policies should make clear that the academic language development of ELLs will need continued support in the standard curriculum classroom after they exit.
2. Exit policies should reflect ELLs' age-appropriate social and academic language proficiency levels. Therefore,
   - Exit policies should include an assessment of oral as well as literacy skills.

- Exit policies should include assessment of the language skills necessary for content area learning (math, science, social studies, and other subjects).
- Exit criteria should reflect the demands of the grade level and should therefore vary from grade to grade (or from grade cluster to grade cluster).

3. Exit policies should use appropriate language and content assessments for ELLs, including authentic, classroom-based assessments that provide meaningful information about how the ELL is able to function socially and academically in the classroom at age-appropriate levels.
4. Exit policies need to take the level of preparedness of the standard curriculum classroom staff into consideration. Standard curriculum staff must have the skills to provide appropriate support for ELLs who have exited from the program to promote academic success. Therefore,
   - Professional development with respect to teaching ELLs must be offered to all staff.
   - Exit policies must be sensitive to the standard curriculum teaching expertise.
5. Exit policies should be developed collaboratively between bilingual/ ESL and standard curriculum teachers so that expectations for proficiency levels and academic preparedness are clear and consistent.
6. Exit policies and the decision-making process should be articulated clearly to all staff, students, and parents.

Finally, administrators must realize that the exit process affects class size and hence student assignment. They must plan ahead to ensure that the standard curriculum classrooms that receive the students do not become overcrowded classrooms. Some grade levels will be more heavily affected than others because of the large number of incoming students. Receiving classrooms should be given sufficient space to include the ELLs who have exited from bilingual/ESL programs. This requires making the exit process an expected, integral part of the school culture.

■ What should happen to English language learners after they leave the bilingual/English as a second language program designed for them?
ESTER J. DE JONG

For many years, the responsibility of teaching English language learners (ELLs) was placed squarely at the feet of the bilingual or English as a second language (ESL) program. Once the bilingual student left the program, he or she became invisible. The expectation was that once the ELL left the bilingual/ESL program, that student's problems were "fixed," and the student could be treated just like a native English speaker without any further accommodations to the curriculum or instructional practices. This practice is harmful for several reasons. First, it may take five to seven years (or more) for ELLs to catch up academically to their fluent English-speaking peers. Even with the support of a bilingual/ESL program, it is likely that they will need continued support after they have exited. Second, treating ELLs as native English speakers denies the bilingual and bicultural realities that continue to exist after ELLs leave their bilingual/ESL program. Third, the responsibility of educating ELLs should be that of the entire school, so that policies and practices will benefit all students in the school, including ELLs. One implication is that after ELLs exit their program, standard curriculum teachers must have the skills to provide the necessary continuing support ELLs need to meet the academic, language, and sociocultural goals of the school. Another implication is that accountability for ELLs cannot stop after the students exit the bilingual/ESL program.

Many districts consider the length of time that students remain in a bilingual/ESL program (exit rates) as a major indicator of program effectiveness. However, there is little evidence that an early exit guarantees subsequent academic success for the student. Rather, data from states such as California and Florida suggest that while former ELLs may perform quite well in earlier grades, the gap between their scores and that of English-fluent speakers may increase over time, particularly in the content areas, such as math and science. Once ELLs leave the bilingual/ESL program, therefore, it is important that schools and districts continue monitoring their academic achievement.

First, a process can be set up whereby the standard curriculum teacher reports on a regular basis on how the exited ELLs are performing in their classroom to parents and school leadership. Any issues that arise in the course of the transition from the bilingual/ESL classroom to the standard curriculum classroom can be immediately addressed by the standard curriculum teacher, the former ESL/bilingual teacher, and support personnel. Second, the school and the district should systematically collect specific information regarding the achievement of exited (or former) ELLs. There are two general ways of doing so.

1. Districts can administer follow-up surveys or use other assessments that are administered in the school/district. A follow-up survey can examine social integration, academic performance, and the extent to which the ELLs are able to demonstrate grade-appropriate academic English skills.
2. Districts can disaggregate academic achievement data for exited ELLs as a special subgroup. This procedure requires that districts be able to track ELLs after they have exited the program. Tracking can be done by assigning an exit code to the individual student. For

example, the Florida Department of Education uses the code LF for students who exited within the last two years and LZ for students who exited more than two years ago. Such an exit code could also include program-type data, if districts are interested in documenting programmatic outcomes. Districts may also elect to include the nature of the exit process as part of the exit code. For example, parents sometimes take their child out of the bilingual/ESL program before the teachers considered the student ready. This situation differs from an exit process in which the staff agrees that bilingual/ESL services can end. Collecting these data allows the district to examine whether there exists a gap between former ELLs and fluent English speakers. If a gap exists, it may point to inequalities within the system that should be addressed by the school staff as part of whole-school reform efforts.

■ How do we use data on student performance to make decisions about the implementation of our program for English language learners?
DIEP NGUYEN

Student performance data should be used for both short-term and long-term program implementation decisions. Different sets of data, both formal and informal, when combined appropriately, can guide daily program decisions as well as long-term changes.

USING DATA TO MAKE DAILY PROGRAM OPERATIONAL DECISIONS
Patterns that emerge from classroom assessment data, when disaggregated, can help determine whether individual students or groups of students are meeting learning goals and expectations. Using data to make daily program operational decisions prevents educators from making sweeping overgeneralizations about the success and needs of ELLs. Yearly results from a language measure such as the Idea Proficiency Test (IPT) or the Language Assessment Scale (LAS) can be analyzed to gauge the yearly progress of ELL students in particular classrooms, schools, and second-language programs. This analysis will guide program decisions for the following year in terms of classroom instruction, staff development needs, and the needs for targeted assistance for a specific group of students. In our school district, each January, ELL students' IPT results and their overall ESL levels are incorporated to construct the staffing plan and program adjustments for the next school year at each school.

Students' portfolios are extremely helpful because they provide evidence of progress and learning that helps to transition a student out of a transitional bilingual program or ESL program or identify additional assistance that a student may need. Exit criteria that are based on student's performances, as evidenced in a comprehensive student assessment portfolio, are essential in order to ensure that (1) the student meets standards required for transition, (2) the student will be successful in an all-English mainstream classroom environment once exited, and (3) there is a consistency in a student's evaluation from teacher to teacher and from school to school.

Student performance data are also useful in identifying subgroups of students who may need additional targeted assistance in a particular content subject. In School District 54, for example, to recommend particular students for the Reading and Math Targeted Assistance Program, teachers use the student's IPT results, his or her profile as indicated by the Qualitative Reading Inventory (QRI), and other classroom assessments. With these data submitted by the teachers, the targeted assistance program can be designed for each student's specific areas of weaknesses in reading or math. The data gathered on each student's reading performance are used to construct groups of students for instruction as well as to make decisions about the targeted assistance program design and evaluation.

USING LARGE-SCALE, LONGITUDINAL DATA TO MAKE LONG-TERM CHANGES, PUBLICLY REPORT ON PROGRAM UPDATES, AND VALIDATE A PROGRAM

While making small program adjustments can be based on yearly data of students' performances, school districts also need to collect multiyear data to study patterns of growth and the long-term effects of second language programs. The types of data currently used for this purpose are often large-scale tests that are tied to accountability and standards of instruction. However, triangulating large-scale quantitative analysis with qualitative data collected from classroom assessments will yield richer evidence of learning by students. Furthermore, results from quantitative analysis, when compared to qualitative evidence, can be used to create internal validity for the study.

Another helpful strategy when collecting and analyzing longitudinal data is to involve an outside evaluator or researcher as a partner in the study. This person can bring his or her expertise in assessment to the task and provides a valuable outsider's point of view when it is time for data analysis and interpretation. The combination of emic (insider) and etic (outsider) perspectives not only protects the "contextualized objectivity and thus defensibility" of the results but, more important, contributes to the overall quality and depth of the study (see Gottlieb & Nguyen, 2007, for further discussion).

Since large-scale assessments are often required by the state and Federal government, the choice and purposes of each assessment are guided by political agendas as much as by educational goals. Each assessment must be re-examined at the local school level before investing in its results to construct the local school's longitudinal data pool. For example, if a state assessment is due to sunset in a year or two, it is best not to include that data set in the longitudinal study. The integrity of each data subset is extremely important in order to ensure the reliability and validity of the longitudinal study. It is also appropriate to note here that not all data need to be included in the study. The inclusion of particular data sets must be guided by the goals of each program and the questions that drive each longitudinal study.

▣ ■ What should an evaluation of a program for English language learners include?
KAREN SAKASH

A program evaluation is used to determine to what degree a program is achieving its intended outcomes. If a program is on track, with English language learners (ELLs) achieving academic and English proficiency and all program components flourishing, then such evidence can be used to rally support, including funding, for an ELL program. Alternatively, evidence-based decisions for program modifications are often recommended through evaluations.

Program evaluation planning often prevents difficulties that might arise later. A good program evaluation is driven by clear goals for each program component and is continual throughout the duration of a program, always leading to thoughtful improvements and often leading to further definition of goals and objectives. Clear goals can be turned into relevant questions regarding the efficacy of program components, and these questions can be explored and answered through a variety of valid and reliable evaluation techniques, including assessment instruments, participant surveys, questionnaires, interviews, focus groups, and observation tools. These techniques provide both qualitative and quantitative data. Data are gathered using multiple measures on both student achievement and other program components such as parent participation, professional development for ELL and mainstream teachers, program management, and resource acquisition and allocation.

Evaluation data should be relevant, important, credible, and timely. Some examples of key questions that lead to the selection of evaluation measures are: What effect is the program having on its participants? Are ELLs making progress toward achieving state standards? Are ELLs learning in the core subject areas? Are mainstream and ELL teachers developing new knowledge and skills to better serve ELLs in the classroom? To what degree are parents involved in the education of their children?

Persons who design and implement program evaluations can be internal, if the expertise exists in a school district, or they can be external to the district if a program is grant funded and it is stipulated that an external review is required by the funding agency. In either case a program director must work very closely with the evaluator to communicate clearly about the program, oversee data collection efforts, and make sure the administrative tasks of the program evaluation are handled professionally and efficiently. Sophisticated research designs are not necessary for effective evaluation studies that are oriented toward program improvement, but interpretable feedback is. A program evaluator often works with the program director to understand the audience for the evaluation, which may include parents, teachers, other administrators, members of the school board, the media, or state and Federal program officers.

Usually a comprehensive written report is submitted to the program director and sometimes an oral report is provided to representatives from the district prior to the written report. The report typically includes a one- to three-page executive summary that can be used for briefing others about the successes of the program and the areas that need further refinement. A written report should minimally consist of the following sections:

- An overview of the program, its context, goals, and objectives.
- The evaluation design and methodology used, including a description of instruments used for gathering data, and data collection and analysis procedures (attachments of actual surveys and instruments used are usually included).
- A description and analysis of the findings/outcomes of each program component.
- Recommendations to continue or revise program components.

A useful evaluation highlights the successes of the program and provides direction in planning for the future. Challenges are sometimes identified, and suggestions for meeting these challenges are offered. Communication is key between a program evaluator and an administrator, and an effective evaluation includes input from all major constituencies in the program.

SURVEY FOR REFLECTION AND ACTION

This survey is based on the guiding principles about program implementation and evaluation that were articulated in the Introduction to the chapter. Read the following statements about your ELL program implementation and evaluation. Indicate the extent to which each of the following applies to your school: DK— don't know; 1—strongly disagree; 2—disagree; 3—agree; 4—strongly agree. At the end of the survey, write down one to three strengths and future possibilities you identified through your school-based ELL program implementation and evaluation assessment. Then identify one to three concrete actions that you can take to improve the services that you provide for ELLs at your school.

All our staff members share responsibility for the education of ELLs.

- Everyone who works with ELLs in our school (general education   DK 1 2 3 4
  teachers, administrators, support staff, bilingual and ESL
  teachers, parents) understands their responsibility to the ELLs
  at our school and shares in that responsibility.

- Teachers have opportunities to plan together and collaborate with each other on a regular basis so that they can effectively address their ELLs' language, literacy, and learning needs over time.   DK 1 2 3 4

Our programs build on the linguistic and cultural resources that students and their families bring to the school and community.

- There is observable and audible evidence of the linguistic and cultural diversity of our students and surrounding community in our general school environment.   DK 1 2 3 4

- There is evidence of the linguistic and cultural diversity of our students and surrounding community in our policies.   DK 1 2 3 4

- There is evidence of the linguistic and cultural diversity of our students and surrounding community in our programs.   DK 1 2 3 4

- Teachers regularly draw on the linguistic and cultural diversity of the students in their classes in order to make the curriculum meaningful and relevant to students' lives.   DK 1 2 3 4

- School staff members draw on and work with the linguistic and cultural resources of community-based organizations to enrich the lives of all students.   DK 1 2 3 4

Parents of ELLs/bilingual learners are well integrated into the school community.

- Parents of ELLs understand and support the educational initiatives at our school (e.g., they support their children's home language and literacy development, provide a supportive environment for homework, come to parent-teacher conferences, and help with school activities).   DK 1 2 3 4

- ELL parents are involved in the decision making at our school (e.g., they participate in the home-school association, serve on school leadership teams, and act as community liaisons).   DK 1 2 3 4

Our program for ELLs/bilingual learners is well articulated horizontally across content areas and vertically across grade levels.

- ELLs have access to comprehensible, standards-based instruction in all content areas so they can achieve academically while they learn English.   DK 1 2 3 4

- ELLs have access to regularly scheduled, standards-driven,   DK 1 2 3 4
  content-based ESL instruction so that they can acquire the oral
  and written academic English they need to achieve in all
  content areas.

- The program allows ELLs the time they need to reach all   DK 1 2 3 4
  program goals.

We use valid and reliable evidence of ELLs' performance and development from placement to achievement to inform instruction and to guide program development.

- ELLs are immediately identified and placed into appropriate   DK 1 2 3 4
  programs based on valid and reliable assessment of their
  language, literacy, and learning strengths and needs.

- Valid and reliable data on ELL performance and development   DK 1 2 3 4
  relative to all program goals are regularly collected.

- ELL performance data are used to inform instruction.   DK 1 2 3 4

- ELLs' performance and development are monitored after they   DK 1 2 3 4
  are designated as proficient in English.

- The program is regularly monitored and evaluated.   DK 1 2 3 4

- Appropriate data are used to guide program development.   DK 1 2 3 4

Strengths of our ELL program implementation

1. _____

2. _____

3. _____

Future Possibilities

1. _____

2. _____

3. _____

Action steps

1. _____

2. _____

3. _____

CLASSROOM INSTRUCTION
AND ASSESSMENT

GUIDING PRINCIPLES

- All of our instruction takes into account that English language learners (ELLs) are learning abstract concepts in a language in which they are still developing proficiencies and within a cultural context that may be new to them.
- We create language-rich learning opportunities for all students that draw on the linguistic and cultural resources of our ELLs/bilingual learners, their families, and the local community.
- We address the varied needs of our ELLs by differentiating and scaffolding instruction.
- We use classroom-based assessments of the performance and development of ELLs/bilingual learners to guide our instruction.

INTRODUCTION

Good classroom instruction and authentic assessment of students' performance and development are critical to help English language learners (ELLs)/bilingual learners develop proficiency in English, learn what they need to learn in school, and reach their potential as bilingual/bicultural individuals. Although administrators do not need to have an in-depth knowledge of how to teach and assess ELLs themselves, they do need to have a basic understanding of best practices in the field. Effective leaders must be prepared to make informed observations of classes that serve ELLs and to have grounded conversations with all of their constituents (students, parents, teachers, administrators, district officials, community members) about classroom practices in their schools. When conversations about the education of ELLs are based on observations of actual classroom practice and evidenced by valid and reliable assessments of student performance data, administrators can focus and sustain their professional and program development efforts.

When monolingual general education administrators and teachers are introduced to sheltered instructional strategies to address the diverse language and learning needs of their ELLs/bilingual learners, many say, "these are just best practices" (in other words, practices like those they have learned for monolingual English-speaking students). However, experts in the field agree that effective instructional strategies for ELLs/bilingual learners involve more than best practices for monolingual English speakers. Effective instructional strategies for linguistically and culturally diverse learners are informed by an understanding of the following:

- how students learn content area concepts through two languages.
- how students develop social and instructional oral and written language in English and their home language(s).
- how culture influences language education at school.

Teachers of ELLs/bilingual learners, regardless of the program they are offering, must have a good understanding of bilingualism and the development of students' native language while they are acquiring a second language. Equipped with a theoretical understanding of how children learn in two languages at school, teachers and administrators can make informed decisions about instructional strategies for ELLs in their classes.

Effective teachers assess the particular language, literacy, and learning strengths and needs of their ELLs/bilingual learners in relation to all of the students in their classes. They plan instruction to build on the linguistic and cultural resources that ELLs/bilingual learners bring with them to school, including their knowledge of their home language and their literacies in that language. These educators clearly articulate content, language, and literacy objectives that are appropriate for the particular learners in their classes, and they organize language-rich, print-rich, highly interactive classroom practices that use a repertoire of strategies to reach their instructional goals. Effective educators of ELLs, whether they work in ESL, bilingual, or general education classes, use classroom-based assessments of their ELLs' academic learning and achievement as well as of their language and literacy development to guide them in making decisions about instruction, the curriculum, and the program.

Effective instruction of ELLs/bilingual learners also means going one step further and turning what many educators (and many other people in general) would think of as a disadvantage—ELLs' diversity—to a possibility for enriching the education of all students, including students from monolingual English-speaking homes. ELLs bring an extraordinary richness to school that can add splendor to the fabric of the educational community.

This chapter addresses administrators' and leadership team members' questions about these aspects of the instruction of ELLs/bilingual learners and concludes with a Survey for Reflection and Action. This survey focuses attention on areas of effective classroom practices that are emphasized by the experts in this chapter and provides a common language that all of the school staff can use to discuss practice. Administrators can use this survey to begin their classroom observations and subsequent instructional conversations with teachers. As educators identify particular strengths and challenges in their classroom practice, we encourage them to revise the survey as necessary to focus and sustain their observations and actions.

■ What are the best instructional approaches for English language learners?

YVONNE S. FREEMAN and DAVID FREEMAN

English language learners (ELLs) are expected to learn English, and they are expected to keep up with native English-speaking classmates in the content areas, including language arts, social studies, science, and math. Teachers can best meet these challenges by teaching English through content and organizing curriculum around themes (Freeman & Freeman, 2011).

REASONS TO TEACH LANGUAGE THROUGH CONTENT

1. Students get both language and content. Research in second language acquisition shows that students develop proficiency in a second language when they receive comprehensible input— messages they understand (Krashen, 2000). If the input is a science or a social studies lesson, then the students acquire both English and academic content knowledge at the same time.
2. Language is kept in its natural context. When language is taught through content, the language is kept in its natural context. Each content area has its own vocabulary and its own way of presenting information, so that, for example, students learn the language of science as they study lessons about weather patterns and temperatures.
3. Students have reasons to use language for real purposes. When teachers teach language through content, students use English words and structures as they write, read, and talk in the course of investigating interesting content area topics.
4. Students develop the academic vocabulary of the content areas. As students study the different content areas, they naturally learn the technical academic vocabulary of each area. Rather than studying isolated lists of words, students learn vocabulary in context.

REASONS TO ORGANIZE CURRICULUM AROUND UNITS OF INQUIRY

At the elementary level, teachers often organize instruction around units of inquiry or themes. At the secondary level, teams of teachers can coordinate curriculum to provide thematic instruction (García, 2002). These units should center on essential questions taken from the content standards. Organizing curriculum around meaningful units of inquiry provides several benefits for ELLs.

1. When units of inquiry are based on big questions, students see the big picture, so they can make sense of English language instruction. Teaching through units makes it easier for ELLs to follow the lessons. The students know the general topic, so they can better connect activities to key concepts. Knowing the theme also makes it easier to understand the details of each lesson.

2. Content areas are interrelated, so that teachers connect the different content areas during the day. The math lesson can reinforce and expand the concepts and language introduced in the science lesson, and the story a teacher reads can further unify and develop academic content and vocabulary. Students also become familiar with the structure of texts in different academic subjects.

3. Vocabulary is repeated naturally as it appears in different content-area studies. Students acquire English as the result of hearing and seeing the same words in different contexts. The same terms come up in the discussion of a story, in a social studies discussion, and in a science chapter when the whole curriculum is centered on a unit of inquiry.

4. Through units of inquiry based on big questions, teachers can connect curriculum to students' lives. In fact, ELLs, with their varied backgrounds, often serve as a rich resource for the class. When curriculum touches students' lives, they become more involved and they learn more.

5. Because the curriculum makes sense, ELLs are more fully engaged and experience more success. Because students know the topic and are becoming familiar with the vocabulary, they invest more energy in trying to follow the lessons. As they more fully engage with lessons, they acquire more English and develop higher levels of content area knowledge and skills.

6. Since units of inquiry based on big questions deal with universal human topics, all students can be involved, and lessons and activities can be adjusted to different levels of English language proficiency. All the students are studying the same topics, but the kinds of activities they do and their responses differ depending on their level of English proficiency.

■ **What can the general education classroom teacher do to teach English language learners effectively while they are in the general education class?**

DEBORAH J. SHORT

General education teachers who have English language learners (ELLs) in their classrooms need to plan their lessons and deliver instruction in such a way that the students receive high-level content material in a sheltered context. The SIOP (Sheltered Instruction Observation Protocol) model (Echevarria, Vogt, & Short, 2008a) is a proven, research-based approach for sheltered instruction that helps ELLs develop oral language proficiency while building academic English literacy skills and content-area knowledge. To implement the SIOP model appropriately, teachers need to understand how academic English is used in their subject area. The SIOP model consists of eight components.

Preparation: Teachers need to develop language and content objectives linked to standards. They also need to plan for meaningful activities that spark purposeful communication about the subject's academic concepts with oral and written language practice. Use of supplementary or adapted materials can help students who struggle with textbooks.

Building Background: Lessons need to connect new concepts with the students' personal experiences, cultural backgrounds, and past learning. Teachers must teach key vocabulary and concepts directly and provide opportunities for students to use this vocabulary orally and in writing throughout the lesson and unit.

Comprehensible Input: Teachers must become skilled in using the following sheltered techniques to make language and content more meaningful:

- Gestures, pantomime, demonstrations, and role-playing
- Pictures, real objects, and other visual aids
- Graphic organizers, manipulatives, and the chunking of text
- Restating, repeating, speaking at a speed appropriate to the proficiency level of the students, reducing use of idioms, and simplifying sentence structures

Teachers also need to explain academic tasks clearly, both orally and in writing, while modeling or providing examples so that students know the steps they should take and can envision the desired result.

Strategies: Teachers must provide students with explicit instruction and practice in learning strategies. They must scaffold instruction, beginning at a level that encourages student success and providing support to move students to a higher level of understanding. They may scaffold information with techniques such as anticipation guides and graphic organizers as well as with systematic questioning and verbal cues.

Interaction: Teachers must provide frequent opportunities for interaction so that students can practice important skills such as elaborating, negotiating meaning, clarifying information, persuading, and evaluating. Students should interact with each other and with the teacher. Cooperative learning groups offer effective ways for students to share information, solve problems, and prepare products that integrate their English and content knowledge.

Practice/Application: Teachers must include a variety of activities that encourage students to practice and apply the content they are learning and practice and apply their developing academic language skills as well. Over several days, all four language skills (reading, writing, listening, and speaking) should receive attention and practice.

Lesson Delivery: A teacher knows that a lesson has been delivered effectively when the content and language objectives have been met, the pacing was appropriate, and the students had a high level of engagement. Classroom management skills play a role in effective lesson delivery.

Review/Assessment: At the end of each lesson, teachers should spend time reviewing key vocabulary and content concepts with the students, who have received considerable input through a new language. Throughout each lesson, teachers need to use frequent comprehension checks and other informal assessments to measure how well students retain information. Teachers must also offer multiple pathways for students to demonstrate their understanding of the content.

By following the SIOP model and the suggested strategies, it is likely that mainstream teachers will be more effective in helping their ELLs attain content standards and develop academic oral language and literacy skills at the same time. (More information and resources on the SIOP model are available at www.cal.org/siop.)

■ How can teachers differentiate content-area instruction and assessment for English language learners at different levels of English language proficiency?

STEPHANEY JONES-VO and SHELLEY FAIRBAIRN

The first step in effectively differentiating instruction and assessment for English language learners (ELLs) is to know one's students, with specific attention to the following:

- Their English language proficiency (ELP) levels in listening, speaking, reading, and writing
- Their background knowledge/experience (including details about their prior schooling and literacy in their first languages)
- Individual factors such as immigrant/refugee status, cultural factors, prior difficult experiences, age, language distance, social distance, and psychological distance
- "Special" needs related to giftedness/disabilities
- Student interests

Once teachers know their students, they can identify "essential learning" goals (Wiggins & McTighe, 2006) grounded in standards. These goals must be the foundation of the content objectives of each lesson and should be based on the same content for all students. The language objectives, describing how students use listening, speaking, reading, and writing to achieve the content objectives, provide the locus for language-based differentiation to occur. As such, these language objectives must target the linguistic proficiency of students in the classroom.

In the spirit of backward lesson design (Wiggins & McTighe, 2006), we recommend that assignments/assessments be developed prior to the creation of lesson plans. Figure 6.1 represents the interdependent elements

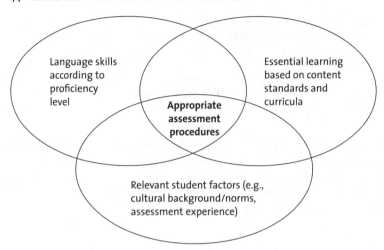

FIGURE 6.1 Factors that must inform appropriate ELL assessment.

that must inform the development of assignments/assessments appropriate for ELLs (Fairbairn & Jones-Vo, 2010, p. 55).

Having developed standards-based objectives and assignments/assessments aligned with those objectives, students' backgrounds, and students' English language proficiency levels, teachers move into lesson planning and delivery. Based on a clear understanding of student needs, they are able to provide differentiated instruction that empowers ELLs to meet content objectives.

To illustrate this differentiation process, consider the following scenario:

Juan Carlos, a 13-year-old migrant student with limited literacy in his native language, Spanish, has recently moved from another state and entered a sixth grade science classroom. English language proficiency test results reveal that he is performing at the following levels in English: listening = Level 4, speaking = Level 4, reading = Level 2, writing = Level 2 (Composite Level = 3). In addition to the variability in his oral and written English language proficiency, he has gaps in his education.

APPROACH TO ASSESSMENT

Using descriptors of what Juan Carlos can do with listening, speaking, reading, and writing, educators can understand why it is unreasonable to expect Juan Carlos to perform at grade level without appropriate scaffolds and support, and why it is important to design level-appropriate assignments/assessments for him.

Administrators and teachers must recognize and embrace the fact that, by definition (and based on test data), assessments for ELLs at various levels should look different from those designed for native speakers of English. Administrators can take the lead in ensuring that ELLs are assessed in appropriate ways that provide meaningful and useful data. In particular, multi-page timed tests are contraindicated for a Level 3 student, particularly when her/his proficiency level in reading is 3 or below, due to the unreasonably heavy linguistic demands of such tests. Instead, administrators need to encourage teachers to innovate ways to ascertain ELLs' levels of content knowledge, skills, and abilities that are not dependent upon language mastery. For instance, if a teacher were to expect a written assignment from Juan Carlos (currently Level 2 writing), s/he might consider using visually supported graphic organizers that students complete with phrases and simple sentences and/or require students to supplement writing with visual support to enhance meaning (e.g., drawing, magazine pictures, clip art).

APPROACH TO INSTRUCTION

In keeping with the differentiated assignment/assessment expectations set according to Juan Carlos' English proficiency levels, administrators must urge the student's teachers to focus writing instruction for him at a level that enables him to engage with the curriculum. For instance, since Juan Carlos is at Level 2 in writing, it would be appropriate for teachers to prompt and scaffold written language production by modeling content/academic language and providing sentence examples and models.

Teachers need ELL-focused professional development so that they can appropriately tailor their expectations, instruction, and assessment to align with ELLs' current knowledge and performance levels (see Fairbairn & Jones-Vo, 2010, for a step-by-step guide to differentiating instruction and assessment for ELLs). As a result, teachers will be empowered to integrate ELLs into all content-area classes, expecting them to participate to the full extent of their current linguistic capability. In so doing, classroom/content teachers, with the support of administrators and in collaboration with ESL teachers, can assume responsibility for effectively teaching all of the students in their classrooms.

■ **How do we ensure that English language learners develop English language proficiency?**
YVONNE S. FREEMAN and DAVID FREEMAN

According to Krashen (1992), there are two ways of developing a new language: through acquisition or through learning. Acquisition of language occurs subconsciously when we receive messages we understand, what Krashen calls comprehensible input. Acquisition occurs in classrooms when teachers engage students in authentic communicative experiences and teach language through content. We also acquire language through reading. Reading is a rich source, better for acquiring academic vocabulary than oral language.

Learning, in contrast, is a conscious process in which we focus on various aspects of the language itself. It is what generally occurs in classrooms when we study grammar, vocabulary, and isolated facts. Learning may help students succeed on tests of isolated bits of information, but learning does not lead to higher levels of language proficiency.

Acquisition, rather than learning, results in competent language users. Students acquire language when they receive messages they understand. Teachers, then, must learn how to make the input comprehensible. There are a variety of strategies teachers can use to ensure that they provide comprehensible input (Freeman & Freeman, 2009).

STRATEGIES TO MAKE THE INPUT AND CONTENT COMPREHENSIBLE
If at all possible, teachers should *preview* and *review* the content in the student's first language.

1. Use visuals, including graphic organizers, multimedia, and realia (real things). Try always to move from the concrete to the abstract.
2. Use gestures and body language.
3. Speak clearly and pause often.
4. Say the same thing in different ways (paraphrase).
5. Write down key words and ideas. (This slows down the language for English language learners (ELLs).
6. Give students strategies to draw on cognates.
7. Make frequent comprehension checks.
8. Have students explain main concepts to one another working in pairs or small groups. They could do this in their first language.
9. Above all, keep oral presentations or reading assignments short. Cooperative activities are more effective than lectures or assigned readings.

READING PROVIDES COMPREHENSIBLE INPUT
When students understand the language and content that is being taught, they acquire language. They also acquire language when they read. When ELLs read frequently from content texts, they acquire the vocabulary and the structures of academic content subjects. Krashen (2004) claims that reading "is one of the best things a second language acquirer can do to bridge the gap from the beginning level to truly advanced levels of second language proficiency." Teachers of ELLs, then, must provide their students with opportunities to read a large variety of high-interest, comprehensible books to build general vocabulary, and teach them strategies to comprehend content area texts to build academic vocabulary.

When teachers engage ELLs in extensive reading and provide strategies for making both oral and written input comprehensible, their students will acquire high levels of English language proficiency.

GISELA ERNST-SLAVIT and MICHELE R. MASON

All teachers in U.S. public schools now have access to specific information about their English language learners' (ELLs') English language proficiency level across all four language domains—listening, speaking, reading, writing (TESOL, 2006). This information is available from results of the state-mandated English language proficiency assessment administered to every ELL either at the beginning of the school year, upon arrival at the school, or in the spring. ELL teachers and paraprofessionals often are responsible for keeping track of this data. ELL personnel may also have additional evidence of ELLs' developing language proficiency in English and students' home languages that can inform instructional and placement decisions.

We must embrace the idea that *all* educators with ELLs in their classrooms are *de facto language teachers*. This includes mainstream teachers, content-area specialist teachers (i.e., biology, algebra, literature, music, physical education), and others (i.e., literacy support, special education). Given the amount of time it takes to develop academic language proficiency in another language and the variability that exists from one individual to another, the few minutes or hours each day that ELLs spend with ELL teachers and paraprofessionals are insufficient for learning all the language skills needed to achieve academic success. English language proficiency and academic success cannot be left to what ELLs "pick up" by chance in mainstream classroom settings. Instead, ELL students need explicit, systematic, and deliberate instruction in English, emphasizing knowledge and skills in using the linguistic components while, at the same time, fostering the use of language for meaningful purposes.

It is necessary, therefore, that all educators regardless of specialty teach basic knowledge about the English language, including vocabulary, grammatical features, and discourse structures (e.g., Egbert & Ernst-Slavit, 2010; Gottlieb, Katz, & Ernst-Slavit, 2009). For example, let's think about mathematics, often considered to be a universal language. While there are many similarities among number systems across the world, many differences exist. More specifically, ELLs have to learn new words (denominator), concepts (exponents), and expressions ($3x + 8x = 90 + 3y$) and, in some cases, relearn different procedures (long division) and ways of communicating mathematical thinking (discourse). In addition, many ELLs are familiar with the metric system but are new to pints, pounds, feet, quarts, and ounces. Yet other students come from countries where decimal numbers are represented with commas instead of periods, or where large numbers are written using periods instead of commas (2,000.00 vs. 2.000,00). Therefore, in order to succeed in the mathematics classroom, ELLs will need to become proficient in the language of mathematics. Thus, student success in each content area will depend on having teachers who can model the kind of language students will need to access the different texts and materials, complete diverse learning tasks, and pass high-stake assessments.

✎ ■ When and how should an English language learner begin to read and write in English?
ERMINDA GARCÍA

We must first shatter the myth that English language learners (ELLs) are not capable of engaging in literacy in English, at least not until they are proficient speakers of the language. Rather than sheltering these students from literacy, we need to immerse them in rich and appropriate literacy experiences (García, 2004). To attain this goal, the language of reading and writing must be meaningful to the learners. Literacy must be based on the knowledge and skills that students bring with them, including linguistic awareness of the alphabet or written symbols from their first language. For students who come from a native language that uses the Roman alphabet, the transfer of knowledge from the first language to English is significant. For students coming from a non-Roman alphabet, the transfer is broader and usually happens at the comprehension strategy level. Regardless of the specificity of the transfer from first to second language, we cannot ignore the power of the knowledge base that children bring to the task of learning English (Hudelson, 1989).

Literacy in English must also be based on the knowledge and skills that students bring with them from their proficiency in oral English. In other words, students can read and write what they can say more easily than they can read and write text they cannot comprehend orally. Then, if we provide appropriate learning supports in a meaningful context and many opportunities and reasons to practice, we can help ELLs become literate in English, their second language. They can, in turn, reap the benefits in accelerated language development that results from reading and writing in that language.

To place ELLs on the path to literacy from the beginning, we need to give them frequent and varied opportunities for reading and writing. A beginning ELL needs to do more than to read controlled pattern sentences and complete sentence starters. Although these types of limited reading and writing activities are helpful, too much reliance on them restricts their written language development. Additionally, it is very hard to expose students to real-life, authentic, meaningful language when we restrict the choice of words in reading or writing material. We need to include the following kinds of reading and writing instruction for beginning level ELLs:

- Daily reading and writing, where students are free to express feelings and opinions.
- Writing in response to literature, where students write about a topic springing from the literature they just read.

- Literacy projects, where students become immersed and invested in first reading and then in developing their own writing.

Simply put, to become a reader, you must read; to become a writer, you must read and write. Effective literacy instruction for ELLs begins with a recognition of the assets all students bring with them and with the realization that literacy helps further the development of language proficiency. In this way we can raise not only our own expectations but our students' expectations about what they can accomplish as readers and writers.

LYNNE DUFFY

There is no formula to follow or any magic time to teach reading in English to an English language learner (ELL). Teachers of ELLs must consider the concepts and skills they want to teach to their students and the types of reading instruction and the strategies they will use. Furthermore, teachers must consider the individual student they are teaching. Once we understand these factors, we can decide when we should have an ELL begin to read in English.

Many bilingual teachers will say they do not teach reading in English for several months or even years, yet these teachers are in fact teaching English reading almost from day one. A teacher can immerse learners in different kinds of text. The classroom environment, for example, is covered with print. Teachers use written directions to turn in homework, list jobs for the students, label objects, and so on. Often the walls in a bilingual classroom are covered with text written in the native language and English. In an English as a second language (ESL) classroom, the text may be in English with pictures or symbols. Instructional language can be taught using print in the classroom environment as long as it is meaningful and comprehensible to the student.

Reading instruction can be used as a way to develop oral language. Specifically, reading quality literature and nonfiction books to students using comprehensible input will accelerate oral (academic) language skills. It develops vocabulary, promotes fluency, and allows ELLs to hear language in a natural and meaningful context. Building background knowledge and providing comprehensible input, a teacher can use text to help facilitate comprehension skills and knowledge that apply to both (all) languages. Bilingual teachers have a bigger advantage because they can use the native language to help clarify meaning and enhance comprehension. Furthermore, they can help facilitate discussion about literacy and language by pointing out similarities and differences that are specific to each language.

The types of reading instruction and strategies we use with students determine how much English reading a student can handle. We teach word knowledge (phonemic awareness, phonics, and vocabulary), comprehension, and fluency, using guided reading, shared reading, read aloud, and silent reading to individuals, small groups, heterogeneous groups, ability groups, and whole groups. Some of these strategies we can begin in English right away; for others we need to wait.

After we determine what aspects of reading we are trying to teach, we then determine if they are appropriate for the individual student. Let us take an example of a student who is literate in her own language but does not have oral language skills in English. This student understands the concepts of decoding, sentence structure, vocabulary, and different text structures of different genres. She simply needs to learn the specifics of the new language, English. However, this student first needs to develop oral language skills before she is ready to learn how to read in English. She cannot learn sight word vocabulary if she does not understand the words or know how the words fit into a sentence. She cannot learn letter-sound correspondence without first having some experiences with the written symbols and sounds in English, particularly if the native language does not use the Roman alphabet or if a particular sound is not present in her native language.

Other students may not be literate in any language. These students would benefit from being taught how to read in their first language, a language they have oral proficiency in, before they are taught how to read in English. These students are learning many new concepts involved in reading (decoding, text structures, and so on). This task is even more difficult for the student if done in a language that is still being acquired. With policies varying in different states and low-incidence languages found throughout the school system, bilingual instruction is not always possible. Teachers need to consider the following factors when deciding appropriate literacy instruction: the students' educational history (length of time in school, consistency, and so on), the level of proficiency in their native language, their level of proficiency in English, learning concerns they may have, their age, and their attitudes toward literacy and language. It is only after we consider our students' strengths and needs that we can determine when and how to teach different concepts and skills of English reading.

■ **How do we promote English language learners' oral language development, and use that as a foundation for academic language and literacy development?**
NANCY CLOUD, FRED GENESEE, and ELSE HAMAYAN

Teachers can promote English language learners' (ELL's) oral language development in many ways to support their performance in reading and writing across the curriculum. Even though teachers know the importance of oral language development to reading and writing, they often do not give it the time and attention that is necessary to support reading comprehension or writing. In the process of learning English, ELLs are learning far more than isolated words. They are learning how to put words together into phrases, how to communicate meaningfully by using precise terms and descriptive details, and how to keep thoughts flowing with transition words.

One way to give oral language development the time and attention it needs is through thematic teaching. Here it is possible to build student's oral language across books and activities, giving them plentiful practice opportunities to use language that has been targeted (words, word families, phrases, and sentence patterns) both orally and in writing.

Fundamental to this process is the linguistic analysis of texts to identify language learning opportunities. What nouns, verbs, adverbs and adjectives, prepositional phrases, transitions words, sentence patterns, and discourse structures are possible to teach within a lesson or a unit? What can students learn about English while they are learning about interesting subject matter? For ELLs, it is not just about school-related academic vocabulary, although of course this is very important. They may also need to learn everyday words. When teaching about insects, for example, in addition to teaching *larvae, thorax*, and *antenna*, teachers may also want to teach everyday language like *bug* (and idioms like *stop bugging me*), *fly* (noun and verb; how the plural and past tense are formed), adjectives like *creepy*, and verbs like *buzz* (and idioms like *buzz off*). Teachers may want to teach descriptive words about size, color, texture, and appearance. This language will not be highlighted in the text because it is written for native speakers of English. Resources (see for example, Graves, 2006, and Carlisle & Katz, 2005) are available that can help teachers determine what words or phrases to teach. The following are some of the suggestions for teachers:

- Select words and phrases that are important for understanding the selection.
- Do not exceed the number of words that a student can remember (say around six to ten per lesson, depending on the learner's age and stage of proficiency).
- Select words that can advance student's word learning skills (words with particular prefixes or suffixes, for example).
- Teach words and phrases that are frequent, useful, and likely to be encountered in the content area.
- Build on what students already know in their home language.

So the teacher's job is to make his/her own decisions about what language can and should be taught and not just take cues from the text (see Cloud, Genesee, & Hamayan, 2009, for more ideas). Since language will have to be taught in addition to teaching grade-level concepts, it may take more time to get through the unit.

In short, oral language and authentic communication should always be part of the main lesson objectives when teaching any content area. For this reason it is crucial for all teachers who have ELLs in their classroom to have clear language as well as content objectives. Teachers can use many tools to make language learning a clear objective, such as word notebooks, semantic webs, and children's thesauruses. They can show interest and enthusiasm in word and phrase learning and encourage students to ask questions and to be curious.

What the administrator can do to encourage teachers to use oral language as a building block for literacy and academic language includes the following:

- Establish a well-planned thematic teaching structure in your school.
- Make it possible for teachers (by giving them time and training) to do linguistic analyses of content area texts.
- Create a culture where all teachers attend to language objectives in addition to content objectives.
- Give teachers the extra time they need to really teach language while they teach a content lesson or unit with ELLs.

■ How do we teach for transfer?
JILL KERPER MORA

The construct of transfer of learning is fundamental to effective teaching and program design for second language learners. Teachers in any type of program for these students can set the conditions to facilitate transfer, especially in literacy instruction. First, teachers must consider whether the literacy skills and concepts they are teaching are language and literacy universals or language specific. Universals are principles and skills that apply to every language and, in particular, to reading and writing alphabetic languages, such as Spanish or English. An example is that text written in any alphabetic language maps sounds onto print in systematic and regular ways. Language-specific concepts and skills, on the other hand, are those that are particular to the sound and spelling systems of a specific language. Teachers can be more effective and efficient by learning about and teaching those features of English that are unfamiliar to their English learners because those features do not exist or are used differently in the linguistic system of students' first language (L1). Teaching for transfer is not double teaching, since many literacy skills do not have to be relearned in English if the student has already mastered the concept or skill in his/her L1.

Teachers can facilitate cross-linguistic transfer through explicit teaching of similarities and differences between students' L1 and English. In many bilingual and dual language classrooms, specific time is dedicated to teaching for transfer, with language features and transferable skills selected as teaching points to enhance students' awareness of how the languages work systematically and/or differently. In English-medium settings, monolingual teachers can ask students for translations or examples from their native languages to compare and contrast with "the way it is said or written" in English. An example is the use of cognates to teach vocabulary. Cognates are words that have similar spelling and meaning but with variations according to the phonology of the two languages, such as *university/universidad* in English and Spanish. Many cognates are derived from Latin or Greek roots and are useful in focusing students on the way words are formed to convey meaning. This type of teaching for transfer provides students the opportunity to observe and apply principles of word structure and parts of speech. Knowledge of English/Spanish cognates can give Spanish-speaking students access to over 10,000 vocabulary words with relative ease, as they discover how the words compare and contrast in their two languages.

Teaching for transfer in the content areas requires a focus on what is called the Language-Concept Connection (Mora, 2008; see also http://moramodules.com/Lng-Concept/Default.htm). Teachers can determine whether students are unfamiliar with a new content-related concept or whether they know the concept but do not know the L2 (second language) labels for the concept. The Language-Concept Connection teaching model provides teachers with a framework for deciding when the concept itself needs to be the focus of teaching or descriptive and explanatory language in L2 is needed for students to be able to discuss, read, and write about the content.

In general, teaching for transfer requires flexibility and openness to L1 and L2 language use that takes advantage of "teachable moments" as well as planned explicit instruction focusing on such knowledge areas as the phonological system and linguistic structures of L1 and/or L2. Visuals on the classroom walls that illustrate principles of transfer and language-specific knowledge are also helpful in promoting cross-linguistic and content transfer. Teachers can also use discrete-point grammar checklists or language-focused writing rubrics to show students evidence of transfer as well as to identify teaching points.

■ How do we ensure that English language learners can read and write in all content areas?
MARÍA PAULA GHISO

Reading and writing are inseparable from learning content—from reading and writing about real issues for real purposes. This interconnectedness is evident as we witness students' engagement when they are given opportunities to learn about the world and use the processes of reading and writing to delve into topics of interest. How, then, do we include English language learners (ELLs) in this process of inquiry, when at times it appears as if they do not have the language skills to take part in the critical thinking required in content areas?

PROVIDE RICH CONTENT ACTIVITIES

In an effort to help students achieve, many teachers end up watering down the content to which they expose students or providing students with activities that focus on rote skills. ELLs *can* engage in critical inquiries about content-area knowledge. In fact, using reading and writing to learn about the world is interesting work and often provides the motivation students need to overcome challenges posed by language. For example, students might learn geography through their own migration patterns and even critically investigate the interconnected histories of different regions, such as that between Puerto Rico and the Philippines. A student with a beginning proficiency in English might label photographs or sort words and visuals to compare regions and look for geographical patterns.

FOCUS ON ACADEMIC LANGUAGE

Although many ELLs may appear to be fluent in English, it takes much longer to acquire academic language than social language. Students may be able to interact in a social setting but may encounter difficulties when dealing with academic texts and tasks because these do not provide the same types of context support and feedback as a face-to-face interaction. Once we realize that a student may be proficient in social language but still be developing academic language, we can consider how to scaffold the student's experiences and interactions with reading and writing so that he or she may better engage with content-area concepts and texts. In a geography inquiry, students might create visual models of land forms and manipulate natural forces (water, wind) to observe and record their effects, and use graphic organizers as a platform for writing. Visuals, timelines, and drama activities are just a few strategies that provide students with additional cues to the content.

GET TO KNOW TEXTS

Recognizing the difference between academic and social language means that teachers must look closely at content-area texts to unpack the implicit language skills needed to access them for particular purposes. A text that at first glance appears easy may in fact pose many challenges to an ELL who is still acquiring academic language. We need to examine the language of the text, identifying potentially difficult vocabulary, sentence structure, genre, rhetorical style, and other features. We need to ask the following questions: What do students need to know to access a particular text? Do they have this background knowledge? What type of language is used in a particular text and in the activities we ask students to engage in? What is challenging about this language for ELLs? Understanding the content-area text from a language perspective is the first step toward figuring out how to scaffold a student's interaction with it. For instance, we might consider the vocabulary of a content area—terms such as longitude and latitude—or the ways that an informational text is organized, in order to tailor instruction so that students are introduced to essential concepts and to ways of reading nonfiction text features such as diagrams, headings, and labels.

GET TO KNOW STUDENTS

A student's background, such as prior educational experiences, level and characteristics of oral and written first and second language acquisition, area of origin, culture, and exposure to particular concepts, influences how he or she interacts with the content-area material and the reading and writing processes used to engage with such concepts. Different facets of a lesson might be more or less difficult for different ELLs. For instance, the extent of prior knowledge about any particular topic differs widely, and it is necessary to figure out how to connect students with concepts and experiences that are unfamiliar to them. This can seem overwhelming; however, the English as a second language (ESL) teacher can be a valuable resource for providing information about particular students and suggesting ways of adapting lessons to meet their needs. It is also important to remember that ELLs bring valuable knowledge about the world to class that would benefit their native English-speaking peers. For example, students from different countries have varied experiences with a range of forms of government, such as democracies, totalitarian states, and theocracies. Connecting to these histories can be a means to make an abstract social studies concept more concrete. It is also a way to draw on the expertise of ELLs and help cultivate more global understandings for all students.

COLLABORATE WITH OTHER TEACHERS

Ensuring that ELLs read and write in all content areas becomes a less daunting task when teachers work together to form nuanced portraits of students, to understand student interactions in different classroom settings, and to align their strategies and expectations of particular students. For this joint work to be most fruitful, it is necessary to break down assumptions about divisions of labor. ELLs are not solely the responsibility of the ESL teacher. Reading and writing are not solely the responsibility of the language arts teacher. However, both the ESL and the language arts teachers can work in conjunction with the content-area teachers to ensure that ELLs read and write in the content areas. When the education of ELLs becomes the priority of the school as a whole, we can more successfully foster the engagement and continued growth of students who are often forgotten by the system.

■ What materials can we use with English language learners?
JEANETTE GORDON and LUCÍA MORALES

Many factors need to be considered when selecting materials for English language learners (ELLs). The most important are the students' ages, their level of language proficiency in English, the amount of schooling they have had in their native language, and the amount of native language support they are receiving in school.

It is critical that the materials selected be age-appropriate and that they support grade-level curriculum. Regardless of the students' English language proficiency, materials must focus on concepts being taught at that particular grade level. You may be asking yourself, "How am I supposed to do that when I have students who don't even read a word of English? Wouldn't it be best to give these students materials from a lower grade level, such as kindergarten or first grade?" While this might seem like a logical solution, giving students texts that do not focus on age-appropriate, grade-appropriate concepts could cause students to lose interest in reading and feel embarrassed (especially if the texts are babyish-looking for their age/grade) as well as cause them to fall further behind in academics.

What do we do? One possible solution would be to provide students with materials in their native language. The second would be to find materials at a lower readability level that support an age- and grade-appropriate curriculum. A combination of these two types of materials is the most effective for ELLs.

Research shows that the stronger the native language of the child is, the easier it will be for the child to transfer concepts and skills to the second language. Although not all schools are capable of providing native language instruction to their students, this does not mean that the school cannot provide access to native language materials to support the child's learning, both in school and at home. There are many great multilingual resources available online for no cost. Some sites have text in as many as 32 different languages. Multilingual books, world news, and content-area graphics and word banks are just a few of the materials that can be found on the Internet to support instruction for ELLs. Students provided with these types of resources will have access to academic content in their native language even as they are in the process of acquiring the second language.

When considering what materials to purchase in English for ELLs, one needs to consider which would best lead to high academic achievement. Since students are to master grade-level curriculum, it is best to purchase materials that target those concepts. Fortunately, many publishers have created high-interest books at a variety of readability levels that would be appropriate to use with ELLs. Some publishers have gone so far as to build reading strategies into content-area texts and to highlight key terms. (An annotated bibliography of recommended materials, as well as a list of publishers, is available at http://tools.thecenterweb.org/cwis/.)

But what do these high-interest books look like? What should the teacher or administrator be looking for? The best kinds of books to look for are those that are nonfiction and relate to the themes being studied at the various grade levels in your facility. The books should be highly visual (even for older students). Ones with realistic photography are always great because they can be used at any grade level and tend to appeal to students of any age. When selecting the texts to purchase, it is much better to find four or five books at different readability levels related to the same topic and purchase a few copies of each rather than buying the same book in sufficient copies for every student in the class to have one. By having a variety, teachers will be much better able to differentiate instruction for their students, and students will be more likely to find a book they like and feel comfortable with. Such resources provide options for narrow readings, where students read progressively more complex text related to the same content. The simpler books help provide the background knowledge and vocabulary needed to read more complex books about the same topic.

Another variable that is important when selecting materials is to choose the resources that match the program's needs. Rather than buying an English as a second language (ESL) program and having your teachers proceed through it in order, you can purchase the programs and materials that meet the school curriculum. For ELLs who are not receiving bilingual or dual language instruction, you should choose materials that preview the content instruction in general education classes. In bilingual programs, you need to find content-area materials in the students' home language(s) that would bridge to related information in English. In dual language and sheltered classes, multilevel and multilingual resources are paramount. In secondary classes, it is often not possible to preview grade-level content since students are often in many different classes across the grade levels. However, the goal is not to just teach ESL aligned with language arts standards because ELLs are often mainstreamed in specials and content classes before they take general education language arts classes. In schools that do not offer sheltered content classes, incorporating content area materials into ESL classes would be particularly important. ESL materials should ideally include content, explicit reading and writing instruction, as well as specific guidance on learning English as a new language within the context of the content and literacy skills being taught. If students are provided with materials to access to the curriculum via the native language and if they are given high-interest materials in English at easier readability levels with graphic and visual support, there is a great chance that they will find academic success. The following is a partial list of multilingual resources:

http://thornwood.peelschools.org/Dual/index.htm (online dual language literacy project).

http://www.bbc.co.uk/worldservice/languages/index.shtml (world news headlines in 32 languages/dialects).

http://www.childrenslibrary.org/icdl/SearchWorld?ilang=English (International Children's Digital Library: multilingual books online in 16 languages).

www.EnchantedLearning.com (great resource for content area graphics and word banks, downloadable books in various languages and much more).

http://onlinebooks.library.upenn.edu/archives.html#foreign (resources in 34 languages).

http://www.google.com/language_tools?html (use to search any topic in students' primary languages).

http://www.alanwood.net/unicode/#links (serves as a guide to use different language fonts/scripts on your computer; free access to these downloadable fonts/scripts online).

http://www.childrensbooksonline.org/library.htm

 ■ **How can we use technology to support the academic, language, and learning needs of our English language learners?**
JOHN HILLIARD

Technology changes so quickly that a list of appropriate software, hardware, Internet resources, or Web-based communicative options for use with English language learners (ELLs) would be outdated almost as soon as it was set in print. Even within the somewhat limited category of hardware, there is a dizzying array of items, such as personal computers, laptops, tablets, e-readers, handheld digital assistants, digital cameras, LCD projectors and smart boards, that have become an integral part of classroom instruction over the past few years. Furthermore, these items represent only that portion of technology specifically sanctioned for classroom use. When we take into account the additional hardware that enters the classroom illicitly, such as smart phones and gaming units, the result is an unpredictable mix of technology. The implication of this technology mix for the instruction as well as the assessment of ELLs is hard to gauge. Because of the ever-changing technology landscape, administrators might best limit themselves to identifying general guidelines for evaluating the applicability of technology to the instruction of ELLs. These guidelines must reflect the developmental needs of this specific group of learners.

LANGUAGE LEARNING AND TECHNOLOGY

To make an informed decision about the efficacy of commercially available language software, it is necessary to understand the distinction between *language acquisition* and *language learning*. Young children develop their first language through language acquisition. This developmental process is initiated by natural interaction with the primary caretakers, where the emphasis is on communication and the content of speech. When parents speak to their children, for example, they do not point out grammatical structures or rules that govern the sound system of the language. Older students who *learn* a second language, on the other hand, usually bring a more formal awareness of their first language to bear. For these students, there may or may not be a focus on the grammatical distinctions between the first language and the second. The *language learning* process tends to be less naturalistic and more structured, with the emphasis on the form rather than the content of the message. This approach is readily apparent in the decontextualized types of drills designed for language learners (*Hola, Paco.¿ Que tal?* Who is Paco and why am I saying "hi" to him?). These premeditated phrases are in direct contrast to the original production that is the hallmark of acquisition process.

We can never expect young children to use technology to acquire language, even with the best technology available. There are strong indications that younger learners are not able to distinguish among even the most basic aspects of language through technology. For example, children who are exposed to different versions of target speakers on DVD are unable to develop the necessary auditory discrimination to hear the difference between important phonetic elements of that language (Kuhl, 2004), whereas children who are exposed to the same linguistic input from live speakers easily develop and preserve this discriminatory ability. This has real implications for ELLs who are exposed to English not through interaction with native speakers but primarily through computer-assisted language learning (CALL).

Many of us who have used language learning technology with ELLs have bought into the computer-as-tutor model (Taylor, 1980). This model was based on the intrinsic strengths of the computer, which allow uninterrupted, repetitive drill and practice scenarios with objective feedback. The earlier limitations of CALL software made it much more of a medium for the *learning* of a second language than an environment for *acquisition*; therefore, it was less appropriate for younger learners, who were still acquiring skills in the first language. As CALL software/hardware advances and voice recognition and other interactive technologies become more reliable, it may be possible to incorporate more acquisition types of activities into the software that offer the young second language learner a more natural type of linguistic environment.

THE ROLE OF PRODUCTIVITY SOFTWARE IN THE INSTRUCTION OF ELLS

The main challenges to integrating technology into the instruction of ELLs are logistical and economic. The cost of many comprehensive software packages specifically designed for ELLs is beyond the means of many districts with small numbers of these students. For this reason, alternatives need to be considered. The productivity software that is generally found on most PCs or that can be bought at a reasonable cost (such as word-processing, presentation, spreadsheet, and database applications) has a valid role in the ELL classroom. One could even argue that if properly integrated into content-area curriculum, this kind of software can develop language skills without losing the content-area focus. The skills developed in using these types of applications are also relevant beyond the educational setting and prepare students for the workplace. An ELL student with the ability to collaboratively create and use a PowerPoint presentation that contrasts his family with the family of a fellow student, in English, is engaged at high levels with both language and content. This engagement is in contrast to the same student sitting alone and passively progressing through a CALL program that exposes him to the vocabulary and grammatical structures used to talk about one's family. Although the CALL software could have a valid use in previewing some of the language associated with this content, by itself it does not allow students to be active users of the language for instructional purposes, and so it should play only a supplementary role.

THE WORLD WIDE WEB

The last important category of technology that has direct relevance to the instruction of ELLs is the World Wide Web. The Web is the single largest repository of text-based and visual information in existence. This resource is multilingual and searchable, open to any user. These characteristics alone make it both a valuable and an intimidating resource for the instruction of ELLs. In addition to being a repository for vast amounts of shared information, the Web has become an important mode for social communication in the form of email, SMS (otherwise known as texting), Skype, Twitter, and social networks such as Facebook. As recent world events have shown, Web-based communication protocols can be powerful instruments of social change. The educational system, as closed-off as it seems to the classroom-bound practitioner, will not remain immune to the interconnective power of these forms of communication. Whether these communicative modes are directly harnessed for learning or act as unwanted and disruptive intrusions, they will nevertheless affect educational outcomes. All these forms of communication have important language-learning implications. In contrast to face-to-face communication, most of this Web-based communication exists in a decontextualized cyberspace. This environment begs for human cues, hence the development of emoticons [e.g.,;)] in text messaging and hashtags (#) in tweets which are used to ameliorate communicative miscues and supply pragmatic information for the user.

The potential of these new Web-based modes of communication for classroom use with ELLs can be broadly evaluated by taking into account the English language proficiency of the user and how the mode of communication can match and amplify their development. In the early stages of proficiency, students need to be exposed to language input that is contextualized through sensory, graphic, and interactive supports; in the later stages of proficiency those supports can be reduced or removed (Gottlieb, 2007). Web-based communication can run the gamut from highly contextualized and interactive with few literacy demands, as in a face-to-face Skype session with a pen pal in another country, to a decontextualized text message using abbreviated and unconventional written forms of language, such as "i plj alejns 2 th flg, of th untd sts of amrca." Understanding how technology can support the needs of ELLs at any stage in their development is the first step to integrating it into a successful program for ELLs (Figure 6.2).

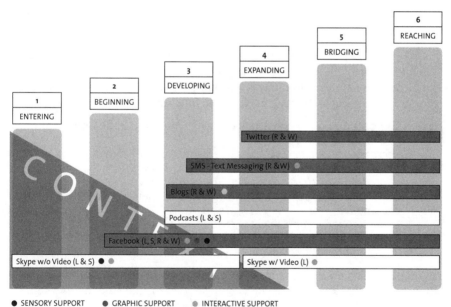

● SENSORY SUPPORT   ● GRAPHIC SUPPORT   ● INTERACTIVE SUPPORT

L = listening,   S = speaking,   R = reading,   W = writing

FIGURE 6.2 Aligning Web-based communicative modes as supports to English language proficiency levels. (Adapted by John Hilliard with permission from the work of Margo Gottlieb, Elizabeth Cranley & Andrea Cammilieri, WIDA.)

Here are some general principles for integrating technology into curriculum for ELLs that follow directly from the points just made:

- ELLs need to be active users of technology to access, evaluate, organize and synthesize, and disseminate information.
- ELLs need to use technology that encourages and assists them in interacting with native speakers in both instructional and social contexts.
- One way to understand the limitations of any commercially available piece of software is to try to identify which language domains (listening, speaking, listening, writing) it is targeting, and whether it relies on language learning or language acquisition activities.
- Computer software should never be used as the primary source for the learning of a second language. This is especially true for younger learners, who do not have access to extrinsic grammatical references in their first language.
- An understanding of the types of supports (sensory, graphic, and interactive) needed by ELLs at different levels of language proficiency can be used to match the learner to the appropriate technology.

WAYNE E. WRIGHT

Technology holds great promise for supporting the language and academic needs of English language learner (ELL) students. However, just as a piece of chalk, the technology is only effective as the teacher who uses it. Ineffective uses of technology include the following:

- *Using technology to keep students busy.* "You can use the Internet if you finish your work."
- *Recreating poor teaching techniques.* Drill-and-kill computer programs may be no better than drill-and-kill worksheets.
- *Supplanting teacher instruction.* Students should never spend more time on the computer than they spend with their teacher and classmates.
- *Using computers for a single software application.* Like buying a new car just to listen to the radio, this is a colossal waste of money and of the computer's power.

Computer-assisted language learning pioneer Carole Chapelle (2001) urges teachers to consider what value is being added for the students through the use of technology. By focusing on the value-added, teachers can implement technology in ways that benefit ELLs.

A wide range of English as a second language (ESL) software applications promise to help students improve their English. These can be effective if teachers are familiar with them and use them to complement and support their own ESL instruction. The best programs facilitate differentiated instruction by allowing students to progress at their own rate. Value added by other software or technology devices include benefits such as access to English or bilingual dictionaries, read-aloud of text, and embedded multimedia such as sounds, images, and videos which facilitate comprehension. Besides software, teachers can structure students' time online through WebQuests, which guide students to prescreened websites with specific tasks to complete related to topics being studied in class.

Despite these value-added benefits, in real life, ELLs need to interact with actual English-speaking human beings, not just with a computer. Research shows that a key to learning English is meaningful interaction with other speakers (VanPatten, 2003). Thus, the most effective uses of technology for ELLs entail tasks involving interaction surrounding or through the computer (Wright, 2010).

Students can work on projects in small groups that require the computer to locate information and/or to create a final project for presentation. For example, groups could research and create travel brochures and posters for different countries. ELLs must engage in authentic communication in order complete the task.

In addition to interacting *around* the computer, students can interact *through* the computer, engaging in meaningful conversations and collaborating with students in their own class or even others around the world. Here are just a few potential ways computers and other technology devices such as handhelds, smartphones and tablets can be used.

- *KeyPals*. ELLs can exchange written messages in English with partners through email or text chat. Oral language can also be practiced through audio and video chat. Text or recordings of interactions can used to guide instruction.
- *Blogs*. A blog provides interactive space for students to post their thoughts, writing projects, or multimedia presentations, and share them with the world. Online publishing elevates a class assignment for a grade to authentic communication with a real audience. Viewers can make comments and give helpful feedback.
- *Wikis*. A wiki provides collaborative space where students can create text-based or multimedia projects to show what they have learned and share them with the world.
- *Podcasts*. Students can collaborate to produce audio programs or videos that can be shared online, thus facilitating excellent oral language practice. They can easily be posted on video-sharing sites and embedded in their blogs, wikis, or other websites.

Effective uses of technology not only help facilitate ELLs' language and academic development, but also empower them with authentic 21st century communication skills.

■ How can classroom assessment of English language learners be used in a climate of high-stakes testing?
ELSE HAMAYAN

As high-stakes standardized testing becomes more prevalent in schools throughout North America, the value of classroom assessment increases dramatically. Two aspects of classroom assessment are so valuable that they make this type of assessment an essential component of every classroom for all students, particularly English language learners (ELLs). First, classroom assessment provides essential information that is sorely lacking from standardized testing to students, their parents, teachers, and administrators, including empirical evidence of what students can do relative to the content and language objectives of classroom instruction as well as of student learning over time. This is especially crucial for students receiving content instruction in their home language, when all standardized testing takes place in English. Second, classroom assessment can happen without taking precious learning time away from students because it is integrated with instruction. It follows that for classroom assessment to become accepted in the culture of a school district, it must yield information that is actually useful to different people and it must be fully integrated into the everyday routine of classrooms.

To make classroom assessment useful, results must be obtained and recorded in a way that makes sense to a large number of people: the students themselves, their parents, the teachers, and the administrators. The following guidelines can make classroom assessment more useful (Genesee & Hamayan, 1994):

- Plan assessment by answering the following questions: Who will use the results of assessment, and for what purpose? What will be assessed? When will it be assessed? How will it be assessed? How will the results of assessment be recorded?
- Identify common assessments that all teachers can use to organize comparable evidence of student learning within and across classes, grade levels, and instructional programs.
- Gather information through a variety of ways and classroom activities, including observation, conferences, student journals, and instruction-based tests.
- Keep good records by keeping track of important information about each student in the form of narrative records and checklists. Narrative records, qualitative in nature, yield information that is particularly meaningful to students and parents, whereas checklists allow information about each student to be quantified.

Quantified results of common classroom assessments are particularly appealing to administrators who need to show growth and attainment of standards. Checklists, rating scales, and rubrics that describe different levels of language proficiency are readily available (see Gottlieb, 2006; O'Malley & Valdez Pierce, 1996, for a comprehensive discussion of effective strategies for assessing and recording information about ELLs).

To integrate classroom assessment into the everyday working of the classroom, teachers must embed assessment in instruction. When this is done successfully, the result appears to the students and to an outside observer as nothing more than just another instructional activity (Gottlieb, 2006; O'Malley & Valdez Pierce, 1996). To integrate common classroom-based assessments into the everyday working of instructional programs, teams of teachers and administrators must select and use common assessments of student learning relative to state standards and program goals. When this is done effectively, we find teachers who ground their conversations about classroom instruction and student achievement on comparable evidence of student learning within and across classes.

The use of classroom assessment strategies does place greater demands on teachers. Futhermore, the inclusion of information obtained from common assessments in school and district assessment and accountability systems does require advocacy by those teachers and their administrators. However, without common classroom-based assessments of student learning over time, we find a continued overreliance on the results of standardized academic achievement test scores that are not valid for ELLs, and the continued labeling of schools with large populations of ELLs as failing.

SURVEY FOR REFLECTION AND ACTION

Use this survey to focus your observations of classes that serve ELLs (general education, ESL, bilingual). Use a plus sign (+) when you have observed exemplary practice in this area, a check mark (✓) when you have observed evidence of this practice, and a minus sign (–) when you have found no evidence of this practice. Be sure to jot down evidence of the practice that you observed. Use the data you collect on this survey to focus conversations with teachers and to guide decisions about professional development. Review your observations and evidence to identify strengths of classroom instruction and assessment at your school, future possibilities you can see, and concrete action steps you can take. Feel free to revise the survey as necessary to focus your observations on area of concern (such as particular strategies teachers are targeting in professional development).

All of our instruction takes into account that ELLs are learning abstract new concepts in a language in which they are still developing proficiencies and within a cultural context that may be new to them.	
Observation	Evidence
___ Clear articulation of big ideas and content objectives.	

Observation	Evidence
___ Lessons are divided into three phases: BEFORE, DURING, AFTER ___ BEFORE: Teachers use strategies to activate students' prior knowledge (i.e., past learning, personal experiences, cultural background) or create shared experiences as a springboard for learning new concepts. ___ DURING: Teachers use strategies to connect new learning to prior knowledge. ___ AFTER: Teachers use strategies to extend students' learning beyond the classroom in meaningful ways.	
___ Complex abstract academic concepts that are removed in time and space (*e.g., population growth*) are introduced in concrete here and now experiential activities/contexts (*growing number of students in a group; plants growing in height*) in print-reduced terms.	
___ Concrete experiential activities are saturated with oral language and embedded in print-rich, culturally relevant learning environments, enabling ELLs to connect new language to big ideas.	
___ Focus on content-obligatory and content-compatible vocabulary orally and in writing throughout stages of instructional unit.	
___ Strategic use of L1 to increase comprehensibility of complex content (*e.g., preview, view, review*).	

Observation	Evidence
___ Use of sheltered instruction strategies in English to make instruction comprehensible.	

We create language-rich learning opportunities for all students that draw on the linguistic and cultural resources of our ELLs/bilingual learners, their families, and the local community.

Observation	Evidence
___ Classroom/school is rich in oral and written language (English and other languages), including commercial and teacher-made materials and student work.	
___ Clear articulation of academic language and literacy objectives.	
___ A wide range of authentic and appropriate materials are available (in English and/or in the ELLs' home language) and materials are tied to big ideas explored in content area instruction.	
___ The instructional units are multicultural and include contributions and perspectives of the diverse cultural groups represented in the class, school, community, and world.	
___ We draw on the home language(s) of our students to support their academic achievement and English language and literacy development as appropriate.	

___ Students participate in a wide range of teacher-directed and student-directed activity structures, including
   ___ whole group
   ___ small group
   ___ independent	

Observation	Evidence
___ Students use social and academic language orally and in writing for a wide range of purposes (e.g., to ask and answer questions, agree and disagree, seek information and inform, tell stories, give opinions, summarize, synthesize, classify, sequence, compare and contrast, justify and persuade, infer, solve problems, evaluate).	
___ ELLs are actively engaged in all classroom activities.	

We address the varied needs of our ELLs by differentiating and scaffolding instruction.	
Observation	**Evidence**
Teacher differentiates instruction to address ELLs' particular strengths and needs in terms of ___ English language proficiency (oral) ___ home language literacy development ___ English literacy development ___ content-area knowledge ___ cultural background ___ learning style	
Teacher scaffolds instruction to move from ___ oral language to written language ___ home language to second language ___ known concepts and skills to new concepts and skills ___ known genres to new genres	

We use classroom-based assessments of the performance and development of ELLs/bilingual learners.	
Observation	Evidence
___ Teachers use performance-based assessments that yield evidence of what ELLs know and can do relative to the big ideas and content objectives of the instructional unit regardless of their English language proficiency level.	
___ Teachers use evidence of ELLs' performance and development to guide their short term and long term content and language objectives.	
___ Teachers use evidence of ELLs' learning to inform their instructional choices.	

Strengths of our classroom instruction and assessment practices for ELLs/bilingual learners.

1. _____

2. _____

3. _____

Future Possibilities

1. _____

2. _____

3. _____

Action steps

1. _____

2. _____

3. _____

7

WHEN CHALLENGES ARISE

GUIDING PRINCIPLES

- We assess the particular needs of our English language learners (ELLs)/bilingual learners as challenges arise.
- We assess the particular needs of our school regarding ELLs/bilingual learners as challenges arise.
- We provide the most appropriate services available to address the student and school needs that we identify.
- We collect, analyze, and use valid and reliable data on the particular needs of ELLs/bilingual learners to drive our decision making when a challenging situation arises.

INTRODUCTION

English language learners (ELLs)/bilingual learners, like any other group of students, come from varied backgrounds and have extremely different skills and abilities. For example, ELLs/bilingual learners come from different language backgrounds, with different levels of proficiency in their native/home language, and with different literacy skills. ELLs come with different levels of English language proficiency, and they come with different types of schooling. Some arrive having experienced significant trauma in their lives. The ELLs/bilingual learners in our schools come from different socioeconomic backgrounds, and they bring with them varied cultural norms and values. They arrive at our schools at different times of the year, at different ages, and with different expectations and dreams.

Because of the social and political circumstances that lead ELLs/bilingual learners to enter the United States (and other English-speaking countries), the type of ELL population in our schools is likely to change over time. Thus, it is possible that after having students who come mostly from urban communities, schools begin to receive large numbers of ELLs who have lived in remote rural areas because of the economic conditions in a specific country. Or, because of political strife, large numbers of ELLs arrive from a language background that had not been represented before in the school or district. Or the ELL population may include ELLs who are not new to the United States but who have have migrated from another community in the United States because of changing political and socioeconomic circumstances. These fluctuations in the types of ELLs entering school create unforeseen challenges to school staff.

Despite the fact that diversity creates a richer environment for everyone, diversity can also bring challenges. Thus, ELLs/bilingual learners who seem to have higher levels of difficulty than would be expected in school, those who have specific learning disabilities, those who arrive at school past first or second grade not having had the expected level of education, and those who arrive in the middle of the year do pose challenges for their teachers and schools. ELLs who speak less commonly taught languages (Mixtec or Pashto, for example) may also pose challenges because schools may not have ready access to bilingual resources in these languages.

This chapter is organized around the questions that administrators are asking about how to address these kinds of challenges as they arise. The responses in this chapter are from experts who have experienced challenges like these in their schools, and they offer insight into ways that schools can meet the needs of all of their ELLs/bilingual learners while they enrich and strengthen the diverse environment at school for all of their students. The chapter concludes with a survey for reflection and action that administrators can use to determine how prepared they are to address the challenges that arise for their ELLs/bilingual learners and for their school overall.

■ **What do we do when English language learners seem to take a particularly long time to acquire English? How do we know what that is due to?**
NANCY CLOUD

In answering this question, it is important to remember that there is tremendous variation in the rate of language acquisition among children and youth. The statistics often cited indicate that it should take up to two years to develop everyday language for social interactions and five to seven years to develop academic English sufficient to compete with monolingual age-mates. However, these figures are averages compiled from a wide range of individual learning times. I have worked with students who took off like rockets and others who moved more slowly but continued to progress. Learning itself is often uneven, with periods of limited development followed by rapid growth spurts. Obviously, our programs, teaching expertise, teaching methods, and curriculum all interact to influence student progress.

With all of this in mind, I like to take a step-by-step approach to analyzing the situation when it seems that students are taking a long time to acquire English.

First: Look at the Student's Opportunity to Learn. To improve the learning situation, we have to understand (1) any significant disruptions in schooling, (2) the types of programs and services that have been provided, and the quality, comprehensiveness, and continuity of those services, (3) the expertise of the individuals working with the student, (4) the teaching approaches that have been used with the student and their effectiveness, (5) the responsiveness and known effectiveness of the curriculum for English language learners (ELLs), and (6) the level of involvement of the family and the supports that are available outside of school to extend school learning. Teachers should work on improving these elements first to improve students' growth in English.

Second: Look for Any Constricting Influences. Because the status of the primary language has a great effect on the development of the second language, we need to look closely at the first language. Is the student's first language well developed? Is the family clear on using their most proficient language with their child at home, rather than using an underdeveloped language that would constrict both the quantity and quality of language used in the home? If English is used at home, have we accounted for the characteristics of the child's speech community? Do we know what variety of English is spoken and any limitations (i.e., limited range of vocabulary) that may exist in the parents' proficiency that could explain patterns that we see in the child? When bilingualism is the goal, both languages must be well supported, rather than one favored at the expense of the other. We especially want to avoid the situation Jim Cummins calls the "square wheel deal" (picture a bicycle with two flat tires) in which neither language has been adequately developed to support learning.

What about motivation? Is the child motivated to learn English, and does the child feel accepted by and comfortable with English speakers? How is the affective climate in which the child is learning English? Is the child drawn in to communication with English speakers or rejected by them? Does the child feel encouraged and supported or negatively judged and overly corrected?

What about important learning differences? Have the child's experiential background knowledge and culturally determined learning characteristics really been taken into account in instruction or only given lip service? How is the room arranged? How are students grouped? What learning styles are favored? Are the participant structures (ways students are asked to participate) culturally compatible? Has the child been given sufficient learning opportunities and feedback for his or her unique needs? All of these things are known to influence language development, and to the extent that we strengthen these, we contribute to more successful English acquisition.

Third: Look for Learning Difficulties in the Child. Only after we have assurance that all of the requisite learning conditions are fully met—the programs, learning conditions, curriculum, and instruction—should we suspect learning difficulties on the part of the child. At that point we will seek to understand the possible disabilities that may be in our way (sensory, neurological, cognitive, social/emotional) so that we can account for them in the approaches and materials we choose to better support the learner.

ESTER J. DE JONG

English language learners (ELLs) face the challenge of simultaneously learning content and acquiring English, in addition to adapting to a new culture. Since their native English-speaking peers continue to progress cognitively and linguistically, ELLs are trying to catch up with a moving target. As a result, it may take a long time for ELLs to catch up with their peers and to be able to demonstrate their learning at age-appropriate levels on standardized achievement or reading tests. It is well known that a wide range of social and individual factors influence the rate of second language (L2) development. Furthermore, the quality of services offered to ELLs and the resources available to ELLs and their teachers play a crucial role. Together, these factors can either accelerate L2 development or significantly slow down the process of mastering English for academic purposes.

If a second language learner takes longer to acquire academic language proficiency, it does not therefore imply that the child has a learning or language disability. More information must be gathered to see if a student has a disability and should receive special education services. Determining whether the lack of progress is due to a disability or to normal second language development is challenging, particularly if the school or district does not have access to bilingual services. Standardized tests used for determining disabilities are generally inappropriate for ELLs because of issues of validity, norming groups, and language and cultural bias. As a result of inappropriate identification, many ELLs are overrepresented in special education services. More recently there has also been a trend toward failing to appropriately identify disabilities, leading to underrepresentation.

When setting expectations for L2 development, schools must carefully consider how the learning context may have affected a particular student's trajectory in English. Specifically, teachers and administrators need to take into account whether the following factors that define effective instructional practices have existed or are currently in existence:

1. High quality of services offered to ELLs.
    - A curriculum should be implemented that reflects ELLs' linguistic and cultural experiences and that has high expectations for ELLs.
    - The curriculum should value L1 as a resource and use the students' native language for instruction.
    - The curriculum should use appropriate sheltered English teaching techniques.
2. The use of ongoing assessments that document individual students' annual growth in language and content development.
    - Authentic assessments that assess the curriculum being taught should be used.
    - Scaffolding assessments for students' L2 proficiency as well as L1 skills should be undertaken.

We also need to take into account the influence of background variables on individual student's language and literacy development and content learning, including (but not limited to):

- L1 schooling experiences and L1 literacy background
- Sociopolitical context of the minority group in the United States and the immigration history

- Individual factors, such as age, personality, attitudes, and motivation

Given current trends in accountability, administrators play a key role in mediating the tension between standardized expectations of growth for ELLs and the actual growth that can be expected, given the learning context. They must ensure that all the elements of quality instruction are in place for ELLs and provide teachers with the necessary resources and professional development. They must also advocate for ELLs by understanding the limitations of standardized tests for ELLs and by being able to appropriately interpret achievement data within the context of their school. Finally, when it is determined special education services *are* needed, the special education teachers must be part of the team that develops an appropriate combination of bilingual/second language and special education supports.

■ How can we distinguish between a language difficulty and a learning disability?

CRISTINA SANCHEZ-LOPEZ

Administrators can create school environments that make it easier for school staff to find out what could be causing academic difficulties for English language learners (ELLs). Three factors can greatly affect the school-based problem-solving team's efficacy. First, an ELL's difficulty cannot be considered a disability when it is observed only in the student's second language (English). It is important that the problem-solving team have access to information in the student's primary or home language(s), no matter the age or grade level of the child. It is critical, then, that the school administrator create an environment in which students' languages and cultures are treated as resources at all times rather than as problems or barriers. Schools can successfully invite the students' languages and cultures into the school even in multilingual settings (see, e.g., Edwards, 2009; Schecter & Cummins, 2003; Walker, Edwards, & Blacksell, 1996).

The second factor that helps problem-solving teams sort out this issue is when school administrators schedule ongoing professional development programs that address second language acquisition, sheltered instruction, literacy, and language instruction across the curriculum, and other topics related to ELLs. All school staff, including general education and special education teachers, administrators, speech and language pathologists, school psychologists, social workers, counselors, and other staff, must have a working knowledge of these topics in order to accurately interpret the student's difficulty and be able to offer appropriate interventions.

The third factor that could influence the decision of whether to place an ELL in special education classes or not has to do with the extent to which appropriate literacy instruction has been provided for the ELL population. As ELLs become more proficient in English, they are able to "word call" but have limited reading comprehension. Teachers often misinterpret word calling as actual reading, which leads to difficulties across all content areas and sometimes to the incorrect diagnosis of reading disability. If administrators shared with their teachers the findings of the National Literacy Panel on Language Minority and Youth (August & Shanahan, 2006), then, (1) there would be a realization that instruction in the areas of phonics, phonemic awareness, fluency, comprehension, vocabulary and writing are necessary but not sufficient for ELLs to make progress in literacy, (2) there would be a greater emphasis on incorporating oral language into all aspects of literacy instruction, and (3) ELL students' home language would be used as a resource for developing English literacy.

There are many recommendations that influence how well a school does in diagnosing ELLs' learning disabilities and avoiding overrepresentation of ELLs in special education, but I have focused on three areas in which school administrators could have a great impact. Principals can create an environment at their schools that invites the students' languages and cultures into each classroom. The students' languages are viewed as resources, thereby ensuring that all school staff will have access to primary language data at any time and will be able to determine whether the difficulties that students evince when using English are also present when they use their other languages. If so, this observation might point to a more intrinsic cause of the problem. Principals can also seek out professional development opportunities for their entire staff related to second language learning. This would help team members better interpret the possible causes for an ELL student's difficulty. Finally, all staff should learn about how important primary language literacy is as a predictor of second language literacy development, as well as learn about how to support language and literacy across the content areas and throughout the grade levels as a means of avoiding unnecessary reading difficulties and hence providing ELLs access to academic content and concepts.

■ How can we best serve English language learners who do have special needs, such as a disability?
NANCY CLOUD

The best way we can serve English language learners (ELLs) who have special learning needs is to place them in classrooms with qualified teachers who can simultaneously address their cultural, linguistic, and disability characteristics. An "add-on" service approach, whereby ELLs are placed in unmodified special education settings (with special education teachers who have not been prepared to serve second language learners) and then receive some unmodified English as a second language (ESL) or bilingual support services (by ESL or bilingual teachers who have not been prepared to serve students with disabilities) does not make a quality program, despite everyone's best intentions.

What is needed are special educators (or inclusion teams of special and general educators) who can deliver well-integrated services because they have the specialized professional preparation required to fully meet *all* of the students' learning needs—as a second language learner, as a culturally diverse learner, and as a special needs learner. Such teachers would have knowledge and skills from the fields of special education, second language education, and bilingual/multicultural education.

These teachers would select teaching methods and materials that are known to be effective with students with disabilities and at the same time known to be effective with second language learners. Such methods might include (1) cooperative learning (a method used by special educators to promote social skills development while children work in small groups or teams to achieve learning goals), (2) visual learning approaches (use of graphic organizers, maps, webs, graphics), (3) multisensory and whole-body teaching approaches (arts-based learning approaches using music, drama, and the visual arts; total physical response), (4) experience-based learning approaches (such as the language experience approach; discovery learning), (5) process-based teaching approaches (i.e., writers workshop using traits-based writing approaches), and (6) technology-based learning approaches (assistive technology, interactive software; self-paced learning programs designed for struggling ELLs; smartboards and document cameras that promote multi-modal, interactive ways of learning). Curriculum materials would also be selected to match the child's learning needs, culturally and experientially determined background knowledge, and language characteristics. Multicultural materials would be plentiful.

Teachers would have clear goals for learners in terms of language development, literacy development, and academic learning, and they would know how to create culturally responsive learning environments (particularly when planning behavioral interventions) as well as how to scaffold instruction to bypass identified disabilities and to support learning through a second language.

To serve ELLs with special needs, we would carefully link in-school efforts with the student's other primary learning environment, the home. We would provide the best guidance to parents with respect to their language use with their child, namely, to consistently use their most proficient language with their child using communication that is developmentally appropriate for the child.

In cases where the language of instruction at school is different from the home language, we would link our efforts at the *learning objective level*, rather than ask parents to use a language in which they have limited proficiency, which would restrict both the quantity and quality of the language used. This would mean that if at school we are working in English on labeling objects or describing actions or practicing particular mathematics skills, these objectives would be worked on at home in the native language. In other words, we would link our efforts at the goal or objective level and let the language of instruction vary. In this way, the child would be assisted to build and transfer desired skills across the two primary learning environments.

Finally, all service providers working with the student (speech and language clinician, counselor, occupational therapist) need to be on the same page regarding the culturally responsive learning conditions and teaching approaches to be used. They must be given the time needed to carefully coordinate their efforts so that together they fully address the child's cultural, linguistic, and learning needs. These are the major guidelines to follow in providing quality services to ELLs with special learning needs (Cloud, 2002, 2005; Fisher, Frey & Rothenberg, 2011; Hamayan, Marler, Sanchez-Lopez, & Damico, in press; Hearne, 2000).

■ How can we ensure that response to intervention (RTI) is appropriate for English language learners?
JACK S. DAMICO and RYAN L. NELSON

One of the most promising changes from the last to the current reauthorization of *Individuals With Disabilities Education Improvement Act* has been the movement away from the use of norm-referenced standardized testing and discrepancy formulae toward the use of response to intervention (RTI) to identify challenged learners (especially students to be referred for special education). For years English language learners (ELL) have been inappropriately placed and over-represented in special education programs due to biased and ineffective standardized tests of academic and language ability. RTI enables an alternate and potentially much more effective approach for determining why an ELL is experiencing difficulties in the classroom, what interventions are needed to assist an ELL with academic language, literacy development, or general learning difficulties in the classroom, and whether special education placement is a viable option. Appropriately employed, RTI provides the context for the sort of creative problem-solving that addresses ELLs' needs in our schools.

While the application of RTI is promising, however, care must be taken to ensure that this innovative approach for addressing learner problems is actually innovative (Hamayan, Marler, Sanchez-Lopez, & Damico, in press). In our experience, the promise of RTI may often be crushed by poor implementation that merely retreads old concepts and practices under the banner of RTI. The great advantage of RTI approaches pivot on the application of appropriate and innovative teaching strategies and authentic monitoring and assessment.

To ensure appropriate implementation, the following practices should be employed within any RTI framework assisting ELLs:

- It should be the operating assumption that any ELL placed within the multi-tiered RTI framework possesses intrinsic competence. That is, each individual should be considered initially as a normal learner who merely falls prey to external variables that interfere with learning.
- The interventionists used within RTI should be well trained for dealing with ELLs' needs. Interventionists not only need to know various evidence-based instructional approaches that are effective for teaching ELLs (including first and second language acquisition strategies), but they also must be able to make appropriate accommodations in the learning context(s) so these contexts are culturally and linguistically meaningful for individual ELLs.
- Any efforts within the RTI should be collaborative in nature; the involved school personnel should combine their expertise, step outside of their traditional roles, and share their perspectives, knowledge, and experiences for the benefit of the ELL.
- Rather than employing a "standard treatment protocol" wherein every student with similar problems receives the same empirically validated treatment, RTI with ELLs should employ the "problem solving approach." This means the RTI personnel identify strategies for adapting instruction and/or the classroom environment to increase the success of each student who has academic or behavioral difficulties.
- Within the "problem-solving" format, (1) problems are defined behaviorally, (2) intervention is planned specifically for the targeted student and planned over a reasonable period of time, (3) performance is measured in the natural setting using authentic measures, like oral miscue analysis or running records, rather than standardized measures, like *Dynamic Indicators of Basic Early Literacy Skills (DIBELS)*, and (4) student progress is compared to that of peers (Xu & Drame, 2008).
- Close attention should be paid to the quality of the ELL's social interactions with their peers, the instructional environment, and the teacher variables that directly impact their academic and social achievements.
- Accommodations should include incorporation of the home culture of the individual. ELLs often excel academically when their culture, language, heritage, and experiences are part of high-quality education facilitating their learning and development (Brown & Doolittle, 2008).

BARBARA MARLER and CRISTINA SANCHEZ-LOPEZ

Before contemplating the appropriateness of interventions for English language learners (ELLs) used in Response to Intervention (RTI), we must look at the learning environment created for these students. RTI functions on the premise that all children, including ELLs, have access to an optimal learning environment. The current learning environment should be effective for the majority of ELLs it serves using instructional practices reflective of the research in the field of ESL/bilingual education. Our first step is to fortify and improve the learning environment we provide to all ELLs.

Once certain that the learning environment is effective for most ELLs and reflective of "best practice" for ELLs, teams of educators (including professionals with training in ESL/bilingual education) can craft interventions for those ELLs that are experiencing difficulty in school. Interventions should be directly linked to the area(s) in which the ELL is experiencing difficulty.

The team should consider the student's social and academic language proficiency in listening, speaking, reading, and writing domains in all content areas (both the first and second languages and, when appropriate, the third language), background experiences, preferred ways of interacting and communicating, areas of linguistic and academic strength, previous schooling, home literacy practices, personality, family dynamics, and the home culture. The team should also consider who could best implement the intervention and when and how the intervention should be implemented for cohesive, optimized results.

We offer seven key factors that can be used to craft or to evaluate commercially published interventions at any tier as to their appropriateness for ELLs. It is important to realize that as we move up the RTI pyramid, interventions at Tier II or III are not substantially different from those utilized at Tier I; rather, they require more substantive support sustained over time (increased intensity, more frequent progress monitoring, smaller student-teacher ratio, etc.). An intervention that does not address all seven factors, in addition to the considerations mention previously, has little likelihood of being appropriate for ELLs.

1. *Comprehensibility*: Comprehensibility is fundamental to instruction and assessment for ELLs. Is the intervention presented in a context that is comprehensible at the ELL's level of language proficiency?
2. *Active and Authentic Engagement*: Instructional and assessment activities that are reflective of authentic, real-world activities promote active interaction among students and between students and materials, which is essential to language acquisition and concept learning. Does the intervention present tasks in ways that are familiar to ELLs, that are reflective of their life and culture, and that are meaningful, interesting, and functional?
3. *Transfer of Skills: Skills and concepts learned in one language have the potential to transfer to the second language.* Does the intervention facilitate the transfer of what was learned in one language over to the other language? Does the intervention take into account similarities and differences between the home and second language?

4. *An Additive Context*: In a constructivist approach to learning, the acquisition of a second language builds on home language development without detriment or diminishment of the first language. Does the intervention seek to build upon the ELL's linguistic and academic strengths? If instruction has been offered in the home language, has the intervention been implemented in that language to support the student and validate the difficulty?

5. *Social and Academic Language Proficiency*: A focus on developing academic language is necessary to make it easier for ELLs to understand new concepts. Does the intervention address social and academic language proficiency as well as skills and concepts associated with the content area?

6. *The Typical Length of Time to Acquire Language Proficiency*: Some ELLs may take more than five years to develop a high enough level of academic English proficiency to survive, let alone flourish, in a general education classroom. Does the intervention and its accompanying progress monitoring take this into account?

We should provide our teams with this information and hold them accountable for its use in the context of problem solving and crafting interventions to ensure that the interventions suggested for ELLs experiencing difficulty in school are appropriate as well as linguistically and culturally responsive.

■ How do we address the challenges of adolescent English language learners?

JUDAH LAKIN and NANCY CLOUD

Adolescent English language learners (ELLs) face many challenges when entering an English-medium schooling environment at the upper grades. They face the challenge of meeting graduation requirements, learning academic English, being a new arrival in a complex social environment, and often balancing the demands of school, home, and work. There is a lot administrators can do to make middle and high school experiences go more smoothly for these learners.

There is probably no more diverse population of students in your school collected under one heading—that of English language learner. Among this category are immigrants, some of whom have been well educated in their country of origin and made a planned move to the United States, refugees and migrants who were driven here by social forces and often have gaps in their education (e.g., students with interrupted formal education), as well as ELLs or former ELLs who are not new arrivals but who still struggle with academic English (long-term ELLs). It is because of this diversity and the different services that each type of student may require that we need to plan for these learners first when programming students each year.

Adolescent ELLs defy typical grade-level programming patterns. Secondary guidance counselors need to schedule ELLs first so that these students can earn the credits they need to graduate. Unlike other adolescents, they often need classes that span all four grade levels, which makes scheduling them difficult if this is done after most classes are full. In scheduling them first, you can guarantee they are not locked out of any courses they absolutely need to graduate. Keeping some space in each class also insures that new arrivals who come during the school year can get the classes they need.

Learning English takes time, and different teaching methods and materials are needed to educate ELLs. Adolescent ELLs need bilingual or sheltered content classes (taught by certified and trained teachers) in order to access rigorous academic content while in the process of learning academic English and building the background knowledge that native speakers built over many years (e.g., about U.S. history, geography, literature, etc.). Additionally, adolescent ELLs may need help with adjusting to life in the U.S., help understanding why a high school diploma matters, and strong support from guidance counselors to meet their expected social adjustment needs. Your best and most responsive staff should be working with adolescent ELLs. After all, their success is your success, as it is often the ELL population's yearly progress that prevents the school or district from meeting growth targets.

High school is demanding for all students, but even more so for ELLs. Being a new arrival and/or having families that are under tremendous pressures lead to many demands on our students, not just school. Often they work and are a main resource to their families in navigating a new language and culture. Because of this, it is very important that schools create flexible options for ELLs. This might mean modified schedules, before or after school support, mentors, translation services, etc. When we really see the entirety of what they face, then we can help them navigate their many demands and give them good support. We can create welcoming environments that include native language signage, and demonstrate respect for the communities, cultures, languages, and countries from which our students come so that we increase the likelihood that parents can really engage with the school.

Because adolescent ELLs are faced with many pressures to make it to graduation, your intervention and support can make all the difference—especially programming for the ELLs first and providing them with the programs and services they need to really succeed and feel a part of the school community (see Cloud, Lakin, Leininger, & Maxwell, 2010, for a detailed discussion of teaching and guidance strategies for adolescent ELLs).

How should we deal with overage English language learners who come to school with a low level of literacy in their first language?
YVONNE S. FREEMAN and DAVID FREEMAN

Older English language learners (ELLs) present a challenge for teachers. Some arrive with adequate formal schooling, but many others have limited formal or interrupted schooling. Felipe is a typical overage ELL. He attended a rural school in Mexico for two years. When he came to the United States, he was placed in second grade. His education has been frequently interrupted by return trips to Mexico and by absences when the family moved to other parts of the country with the crops. Felipe will enter middle school next year. He cannot read or write in Spanish. His English literacy is below grade level, and he is behind his classmates in math, science, and social studies. There are many overage ELLs like Felipe in U.S. schools (Freeman & Freeman, 2002).

Teachers frequently ask, "How can I help my older ELLs read and write in English when they cannot read or write well in their first language? What strategies and texts should I be using with overage ELLs?" We have found that successful teachers follow certain practices. In addition to teaching language through content and organizing curriculum around units of inquiry, these teachers do the following: they draw on and validate their students' strengths; they engage students in hands-on activities, working in cooperative groups; they use materials that are culturally relevant; and they use the preview, view, and review strategy.

1. Teachers can draw on and validate students' strengths by recognizing their life experiences and using their first language. When teachers draw on their students' life experiences and recognize common cultural values, struggling students respond positively. Teachers can also use strategies with students to help them recognize cognates, which often include important academic vocabulary.
2. Many studies have shown the benefits of cooperative learning for language minority students. Many teachers organize students into same-language groups or pairs so that students can use their first languages to help one another. When academic assignments include projects during which students work together, overage ELLs become more involved and experience more success. Teachers can differentiate their instruction by having limited-formal-schooling students participate by illustrating concepts, labeling, and writing short contributions.
3. Teachers can read aloud or have available in the classroom books that include events, settings, and characters that are familiar to the students. Students want to read and are willing to work hard to read culturally relevant texts, including culturally relevant bilingual

books, because they reflect the here and now of their lives (Freeman, Freeman, & Ebe, 2011).
4. Preview, view, and review is an excellent strategy for working with limited-formal-schooling students. If the teacher, a bilingual peer or cross-age tutor, a bilingual aide, or a parent can simply tell the English learners in their native language what the upcoming lesson is about, the students are provided with a preview. During the view the teacher conducts the lesson using strategies to make the input comprehensible. With the help of the preview, the students can follow the English better and acquire both English and academic content. Finally, it is good to have a short time of review during which students can work in same-language pairs or groups to clarify and summarize the lessons and then report back in English.

Teachers who are successful with working with overage students use the preceding strategies to help their students move towards academic success (Freeman & Freeman, 2009).

■ How can we best serve students who come with interrupted formal education (SIFE) or limited prior schooling?
BARBARA MARLER

Students with interrupted formal education (SIFE students) can be well served through a newcomers' program that takes into account the unique needs that such English language learners (ELLs) bring to our schools. Many of these students are at risk of failing in their academic subjects if adequate support services are not provided to address gaps in their academic development. Additionally, older ELLs with interrupted or limited prior schooling, are at greater risk of dropping out of school. Still others have had limited opportunities to fully develop literacy in their native language. Additionally, the need to become fully cognizant, competent, and savvy in the new, non-native culture can be a daunting task, especially when fluency in the target language is limited and when little support is available in the students' native language. A portion of the existing bilingual/English as a second language (ESL) program should be devoted to the needs of these unique ELLs

This programming can take the form of a Newcomers' Center (usually in the same vein as a "school within a school") or a series of courses that new arrivals are expected to participate in during the first few months of enrollment (Short & Boyson, 2004). Newcomer Centers are usually set aside from the rest of the school, but successful models have also been established where the newcomers are integrated with their English-speaking peers or other ELLs who have been in U.S. schools for a few years. Regardless of the degree of separateness of the Newcomer Center, such programming options are to be considered short-term, intensive interventions, designed to give such students an added advantage as quickly as possible. Once students reach a certain level of English proficiency and become skilled in the culture of school, they can be gradually transitioned into the existing bilingual/ESL classes or the mainstream.

Newcomer programming includes the following components:

- Instruction in the native language (whenever possible) in academic areas and literacy. At this entry point in the newcomers' life, the native language is going to be the most efficient route to literacy and to content-area knowledge attainment.
- Survival English and initial English literacy instruction. This must be given by a highly skilled ESL teacher who knows how to integrate language with content instruction and how to connect oral language development with beginning literacy. Intensive survival English (for six to twelve weeks) prepares students for the demands of U.S. schools and allows instruction to move more rapidly from social language to academic language.
- Understanding American culture and U.S. schools. Newcomers must be introduced to the way things work in their new community and the larger society, such as public services and public transportation, as well as in their school, such as lockers and cafeteria rules. When students are prepared to deal with the cultural chasms they are likely to encounter they are better able to focus comfortably on academic and linguistic pursuits.

For older students, career/vocational/post-secondary schooling awareness and planning is important. This helps to contextualize learning for new arrivals and guide them as they begin to make choices that influence their future.

Newcomers' programming cannot remedy lost years of formal schooling, but it can help students reach a level where content area instruction in regular bilingual/ESL classrooms becomes more meaningful and can be provided closer to the age-appropriate grade level.

PAULA MARKUS

UNDERSTAND THE BACKGROUNDS AND NEEDS OF ENGLISH LANGUAGE LEARNERS WITH LIMITED PRIOR SCHOOLING

English language learners (ELLs) with limited prior schooling come to us from countries all over the world. They will have varying degrees of literacy in their first language. They may have gaps of several years in formal schooling, or they may have never had the opportunity to attend school at all. These gaps in prior schooling can result from a number of difficult contributing factors: situations of war and conflict; political oppression and instability and its accompanying emotional trauma; life in refugee camps sometimes stretching back as far as the child can remember; natural disasters and famine; several economic hardships; and continuous migrant living.

The needs of learners with limited prior schooling may extend beyond the academic: they and their families may be waiting for the resolution of refugee claims; they may be experiencing reunification with family members after a long period of separation; they may have lost family members as a result of war and conflict, or still be uncertain as to the whereabouts of loved ones; they may be living under severe financial restrictions in their new country; and they may be going through a period of mourning for their former lives as they adjust to a new country and life which they did not foresee in their future.

Regardless of the individual backgrounds of ELLs with limited prior schooling, the overarching vision for working with such students must be that they are all capable of learning and achieving success given the appropriate supports and opportunities in school. Learners with gaps in formal schooling will most certainly have acquired other knowledge and skill sets that go beyond formal learning, and will have strengths in areas as diverse as problem solving and decision making, oral proficiency in perhaps several languages, and finely-honed survival skills, all of which should be surveyed and built upon. These students need to have their backgrounds and skills acknowledged and used as a starting point for their journey in becoming academic learners with a secure place in the school community.

DISTRICT OR SCHOOL SUPPORT FOR ENGLISH LANGUAGE LEARNERS WITH LIMITED PRIOR SCHOOLING

Accelerated learning programs can be designed to help ELLs with limited prior schooling make significant gains in second language learning, literacy and numeracy skills, and academic knowledge and skills, so that they can move towards successful integration into the mainstream program. When there is a critical mass of such learners in one school, the program can be located on site, or when there are smaller groups of students in several schools, a congregated program can be established in a designated school serving a specific geographical area, or in a district Newcomer Center. Such an accelerated learning program should have clearly articulated goals for students to make specific annual gains in literacy and numeracy development. It should also include sheltered academic upgrading in core subjects such as social studies and science to enable learners to gain access to the full academic curriculum. Social and emotional support for students as they adjust to the school environment, and counseling with a view to future goals, should also be part of a program focused on the needs of ELLs with limited prior schooling. It is very important to realize that ELLs with limited or interrupted prior schooling will require more time to achieve academic proficiency in English than their peers who have had uninterrupted school careers. It may take a number of years for ELLs with limited prior schooling to begin to approach their peers in literacy and academic skills. But through a supportive program, ELLs with limited prior schooling can develop a strong sense of themselves as lifelong learners who will be able to build and further develop their skills and knowledge all during their lives.

SUPPORT FROM THE SCHOOL ADMINISTRATOR TO FACILITATE STUDENT SUCCESS

To provide support for the success of ELLs with limited prior schooling, the school administrator can do the following:

- Inform parents and students that placement is being considered in an accelerated learning program for students with limited prior schooling and seek their written consent (using an interpreter when required).
- Ensure that students and parents sign a program contract which clearly sets out the expectations from students, parents, and staff with regards to attendance, homework, and putting forth best efforts.
- Structure the timetable so that ELLs with limited prior schooling are able to participate in the mainstream grade-level program for one-third to one-half of the school day, to ensure integration and learning with grade-level English-speaking peers.
- Facilitate professional development so that the whole staff has a shared understanding about meeting the needs of ELLs with limited prior schooling.
- Encourage teachers to use exemplary classroom techniques for facilitating successful learning by students with limited prior schooling. The following encourage teachers to:
  - establish clear and firm classroom routines and safety rules to help students with limited experience in school understand and learn what is expected of them;
  - use the language experience approach to assist students in learning to read through composing their own meaningful texts;
  - build regular co-operative learning groups and tasks into the classroom;
  - compile a collection of audio books with matching texts so students can read and listen concurrently to build literacy skills;
  - take students on meaningful field trips in the community to help fill in gaps in their experience;
  - facilitate the writing of personal stories to share students' experiences with the classroom and school community; and
  - provide opportunities to use digital technologies for literacy and numeracy skills development.

◼ How can we best serve migrant English language learner populations?
NADEEN RUIZ

In 2002, the U.S. Department of Education commissioned a report on the educational context of migrant students, *The Same High Standards for Migrant Students: Holding Title I Schools Accountable.* The three-volume report highlighted a number of contextual features of schools with high numbers of migrant students. Such schools are poorer. There are differences in curriculum between districts "sharing" migrant students that add to the serious problem of academic discontinuity. There is also an inability to estimate the percentage of migrant students who actually participate in statewide and district accountability systems and an inability to disaggregate their scores. These school-site features, along with migrant families' mobility, low income levels, and lack of English proficiency, led the National Commission on Migrant Education to note, "Some educators view both currently and formerly migratory children as having greater needs than other disadvantaged populations" (p. 31). In turn, the U.S. National Migrant Office has documented the academic outcomes of these ineffective educational contexts over the past decade and a half, showing a persistent and dramatic achievement gap between migrant and nonmigrant students.

Despite this sobering picture of migrant students' educational needs at the national level, we have found through our own work in the *Migrant Optimal Learning Environment (OLE) Project* (Migrant/OLE Project, 2004) that these patterns of underachievement can be reversed. Our research shows that when educators offer *optimal learning environments* to migrant students, that is, evidence-based literacy instruction and practices, migrant students traverse the achievement gap and actually outperform nonmigrant students matched for language background in areas such as emergent literacy skills, standardized writing scores, and overall academic achievement. The optimal conditions for instruction of migrant students used by the Migrant/OLE Project are shown in Figure 7.1 (Ruiz, García, & Figueroa, 1996).

How can administrators put in place what is needed to replicate the success of schools and programs like those in the Migrant/OLE Project?

1. Working with your local migrant director or coordinator, disaggregate the achievement data for migrant students in each school, at each grade level, and closely examine the instructional programs offered to migrant students.

Brad Doyle, Migrant Education Director for a Northern California region, conducts what he calls "reading audits." Brad literally sits down with

1. Student Choice
Students exercise choice in their learning when possible: writing topics, books, research projects, and thematic cycles.

2. Student-Centered
Lessons begin with students' personal experiences, background knowledge, and interests.

3. Whole Texts for Explicit Teaching of Skills and Strategies
Lessons begin with whole, communicatively functional texts (e.g., books, poems, newspaper articles) to maximize the construction of understanding; then move to the analysis of components of reading and writing processes, such as strategies, text organizations, or smaller units of language forms (e.g., phonics, spelling, punctuation).

4. Active Participation
Students actively engage in lessons with frequent and long turns at producing both oral and written language.

5. Meaning First, Followed by Form
Students construct meaning from (reading) or through (writing) text first, then move to a focus on correct forms of language such as spelling and grammar.

6. Authentic Purpose
The end-products of lessons have a real-life function that often extends beyond the classroom; real audiences, real purposes.

7. Approximations
Students are encouraged to take risks and successively approximate language and literacy skills (following a developmental course).

8. Immersion in Language and Print
The classroom is saturated with different print forms and functions, and with opportunities to understand and use language for a wide range of purposes. All teachers act on their charge to teach language across the curriculum.

9. Demonstrations
Teachers demonstrate their own reading and writing, and share their ongoing efforts with students. "More expert" students also serve as models for their peers.

10. Response
Students receive timely responses to their oral and written texts that go beyond letter grades to personalized and thoughtful acknowledgments of their ideas, experiences, and efforts.

11. Community of Learners
Students, parents, and teachers form a community of readers, writers, and learners who explore a range of questions relevant to them. Students have the opportunity to discover and develop their academic identities.

12. High Expectations
Teachers, parents, and the students themselves expect that students will become proficient and independent speakers, readers, and writers. Teachers make sure that scaffolds are in place to help students meet these expectations.

FIGURE 7.1 Optimal conditions for language and literacy learning
(*The Migrant/OLE Project*)

administrators in each of the schools in his region and closely examines the literacy program offered to migrant students. The audit focuses on identifying the primary literacy program and supplemental programs, the profiles of students receiving native language reading support, assessments that are curriculum-based evidence of reading performance, and expected and actual reading levels for each migrant student in grades K–3. In a study conducted by the Migrant/OLE Project we discovered what we believe is an outcome of this region's reading audits and emphasis on evidence-based literacy instruction: the migrant students in this particular region outperformed the students in any other region in California in numbers reaching the 50th percentile in reading achievement scores (Figueroa, 2004).

2. Offer an evidence-based literacy instruction to migrant students.

Unfortunately, in a recent meta-analysis of 38 studies from the National Reading Panel, only one included English language learners (ELLs) (Ehri, Nunes, Stahl, & Willows, 2001), and consequently it cannot be considered scientific or evidence based because of the lack of fit between the children in the studies and ELLs such as migrant students (International Reading Association, 2001; Ruiz & Figueroa, 2004). There is, however, a robust body of literature on best literacy practices with ELLs as cited throughout this volume and reflected in Figure 7.1. That information should be used by schools to create optimal learning environments for migrant students wherein, despite the often harsh realities of migrant life circumstances, migrant students can academically thrive.

■ **How can we best serve older English language learners who are returning to school after having dropped out, or who have arrived in the United States after age 18?**
JOE REEVES LOCKE

Older English language learners (ELLs) in pursuit of a high school diploma find themselves dealing with not only the intricacies of an academic learning experience in a non-native language but also with the day-to-day grind of life in an alien environment. They may be faced with seemingly overwhelming issues at home or at work, and now they have taken on the pursuit of a high school diploma! An adult high school format provides the needed venue for the older ELL in pursuit of an academic learning experience. Like all ELLs, but even more so for adults, they need encouragement, support, and flexibility.

Encouragement should begin with the initial contact of the learner with the program. Assure the learner of his or her ability to be successful in an academic endeavor. Make it simple to get started in the learning experience. Keep registration and assessment to a minimum, and if possible have them occur at the same location as the learning experience. Apprise the learner of the number of credits, required classes, and electives needed to graduate. Detail for the learner not only the daily class schedule but also the possible amount of time it will take to reach the ultimate goal of a high school diploma.

Support for the older ELL, as for all older learners, is intrinsic in the adult high school venue. When the adult high school is able to offer ELL classes, then that support is enhanced for the older ELL. Adult learners often are more focused, more motivated, and more likely to be supportive of each other in the classroom. Adult learners are in the adult high school because of a self-perceived need to obtain their high school diploma. The climate of an adult high school enables teachers, ELL as well as mainstream, to provide individualized attention at particular points of need.

Flexibility in attendance, scheduling, and statute of limitations greatly aids older ELLs in their academic learning experience. Older ELLs have so many calls on their time that an illness in the family, a change in transportation arrangements, or a change in a work schedule may mean missing days of class, or may even necessitate a hiatus in attendance. Make it possible, if needed, for students to easily arrange for make-up sessions with teachers for time missed. Simplify the process of schedule changes, so that students will not dread the procedure and will not hesitate to do it. Reduce the amount of paper work connected with re-entry into the program. Give credits the longest possible life, so that re-entry will be a continuation and not another new beginning. The encouragement, support, and flexibility in the academic learning experience for the older ELL does not mean a reduction in the quality of the instruction. The older ELL, just as the under-18 ELL, should be held to district, state, and national standards. Older ELLs are in the class because they are taking the time and making the effort to be there, and they want quality learning that will make a meaningful difference in their lives.

■ What can we do when there are only a few English language learners in a school district?
SUZANNE WAGNER and TAMARA KING

Immigrant families from different cultural and language backgrounds sometimes arrive in school districts that have so few English language learners (ELLs) that there is no specific program for them. This is both an advantage and a challenge. It is an advantage in that the few ELLs can receive more individual attention. It is a disadvantage since the school typically does not have the resources necessary for educating these students and the staff has not been trained how to best educate ELLs. Administrators and teachers who have the task of developing a program for these new learners need to begin by finding out what the ELLs already know and can do in order to plan instruction which addresses three academic needs: (1) how they will learn grade level concepts, (2) how they will learn (or continue to learn) to read and write, and (3) how the students will develop academic English language proficiency.

ASSESSING LITERACY, SCHOOL KNOWLEDGE, AND LANGUAGE SKILLS

When new ELLs arrive at school, the principal and the receiving teacher can have a "getting to know you" conversation with the parents and the new ELLs. Using an interpreter, find out where they are from, and ask about their families. (Meetings with parents of ELLs should always begin by building relationships.) Then, find out more about the schools the children have attended and the children's learning experiences. Speak directly (through the interpreter) with older ELLs.

Whenever possible, conduct an informal literacy screening process. Using a children's book in the student's language, ask the new ELL to read a paragraph and retell the information. Then, ask him/her to write a paragraph about the family. Even without understanding the home language, the principal and teacher will be able to observe the student's fluency and ability to retell what he/she read. The student's handwriting (fine motor ability, sentences, punctuation, and/or diacritical marks) will indicate if the student has been in school regularly. (ELLs arrive with varying amounts of school knowledge and literacy experiences—even if they do not appear to have age-appropriate skills, they need to be placed at the grade levels of their age-group peers.) Later, after the ELL is comfortable in school, the teacher can conduct the state-adopted English language proficiency test. However, the authentic measures described previously may be more useful in developing an instructional plan.

LEARNING GRADE LEVEL ACADEMIC CONCEPTS

If the new ELLs have a history of irregular school attendance, low literacy skills in first language, and have missed major concepts in school, providing instruction through the native language is the most effective way to help them catch up to the academic knowledge of their English-speaking peers. For ELLs who come to the school with age-appropriate knowledge and literacy skills, initial support through the native language will help them continue to learn academic concepts. Their literacy and academic knowledge will serve as a strong foundation that will help them learn further.

Administrators and teachers can find creative ways to provide native language support even when resources are limited. Perhaps there are bilingual community members from the language group who would work for a few hours a week as tutors. Older bilingual children who are more proficient in English can be trained as cross-age tutors. Parents can be native language tutors when they support their children's learning at home. Encourage teachers to write an "Apple Letter" to the ELLs' parents once a week. Through an interpreter, explain to the parents that their children will be bringing home special letters that tell the parents what their children are learning—the letters suggest ways to help their children. Explain that this letter will have a graphic apple drawn around the message. Since the teacher does not know the family's language, the letter will be in English so the family interpreter will need to read the letters to the parents.

Federal law mandates that all English language learners in grades K-12 receive instruction to help them become proficient in English (NCLB, 2001). Therefore, it is important that at least one teacher receive training to become certified as an English as a second language (ESL) teacher. This teacher, who may be a reading teacher, an instructional coach, or have previous experience teaching languages, can be assigned to provide daily ESL instruction in addition to his/her regular teaching assignment. Administrators can also make sure that professional development in ESL strategies such as sheltering and differentiating instruction is provided for elementary general education and secondary content teachers who have ELLs in their classrooms. This training will help all teachers make their instruction comprehensible by modeling and using comprehensible language just above ELLs' current proficiency level; using pictures, charts, and other visuals; differentiating classroom tasks and assessment; and selecting materials and readings according to the students' English language proficiency levels. With few ELLs to serve, the ESL teacher can work closely with the general education teacher to develop language lessons that are focused on the big ideas and vocabulary of the content topics that the children are learning in the general education classroom.

LITERACY DEVELOPMENT

Research suggests that initial literacy instruction be provided in the child's native language whenever possible. In districts which do not have the resources to provide formal literacy instruction in the native language, it is important that the ELLs have meaning-based literacy instruction. Learning to read in a second language is meaning based when the texts, writing activities, skills, and tasks are meaningful and functional for the emergent reader. First, the literacy teacher and the ESL teacher must work together closely to help the ELLs develop oral English fluency. The teachers can write down and display the words, phrases, and sentences that the ELLs understand and are producing orally. With this information, the teachers can (1) conduct assessment procedures to find out what the children already know about reading and writing, (2) plan activities that help the ELLs build and integrate oral language with literacy tasks, (3) use the ELLs' writing as a pathway to reading, (4) plan multiple vocabulary building activities, and (5) provide multiple prior knowledge activities using visual and interactive instructional supports.

LEARNING ACADEMIC ENGLISH

Regardless of how few ELLs a district has, the students will need daily ESL instruction that is related to what their peers are learning in the general education classrooms. Principals can make sure that the new ELLs are not placed at the computer to learn English through second language websites or software. They can also make sure that the ESL teacher uses a content-based ESL instructional approach rather than a traditional ESL approach that teaches social language that the children are likely to learn on their own. ELLs need structured activities to develop oral language around classroom tasks and topics. Placing them in small groups with more proficient English speakers can provide low-risk opportunities for classroom talk.

■ How can we schedule English language learners when we do not have enough students to make up a class or a program?
BARBARA MARLER

One important issue that administrators need to be concerned about is different patterns of grouping English language learners (ELLs) for instruction. Administrators should be cognizant of the many ways of grouping students, aware of each grouping pattern's advantages and disadvantages, able to communicate this information to teachers, and willing to provide teachers with the support they need to carry out a variety of student grouping patterns. Teachers may group students according to grade level, language proficiency level, interests, or tasks. Teacher should make student-grouping decisions based on instructional goals and reflective of the strengths and needs of the students they are teaching.

Administrators can provide teachers with support simply by changing the way in which they approach scheduling of classes in their building. Most building administrators typically begin to plan their building's schedule by first plotting the days and times of the "specials classes" (typically physical education, music, art, library time, and computer instruction). The practice is understandable: many of the "specials" teachers are itinerant, so the way buildings share their services should be well planned. Additionally, most of the "specials" teachers provide instruction to every student in the building, and therefore their schedules do influence the daily schedule of every other teacher. After the "specials" classes are scheduled, administrators typically go to the general education teachers to incorporate reading, math, science, and social studies into the building schedule plan. Generally, teachers of ELLs are invited to create their teaching schedules (which include student-grouping patterns) after the entire building schedule is set. When there are many language groups represented in each class or throughout the school, this becomes a daunting task. The resulting schedule is not geared to the needs of the ELLs but rather is a reflection of instruction offered when the students or teachers are available. If administrators consider the academic and linguistic instructional needs of the ELLs served in the building before establishing the building schedule for the "specials" classes and the general education classes, many more student-grouping patterns can be supported. Administrators should meet with the teachers of ELLs prior to establishing the building schedule to become fully aware of the grouping patterns the teachers intend to pursue during the following school year to meet the academic and linguistic instructional needs of their students.

In a pull-out program, administrators can also provide support to different student grouping patterns by clustering ELLs into targeted general education homerooms. Many administrators believe that assigning students randomly to homerooms is a good idea: student diversity and student needs are distributed equitably throughout the school. Actually, assigning ELL students randomly into general education homerooms compromises their instructional program. In an elementary school with five or six grade levels, the teacher of ELLs is expected to communicate and collaborate with upward of ten to fifteen teachers. In a middle school with teams, the teacher of ELLs is expected to communicate and collaborate with more than two teams. Both situations are impossible to manage, and the resulting lack of communication and collaboration seriously compromises the effectiveness and efficiency of the educational program for ELLs. Instead, the administrator should implement a practice of clustering ELLs students at a given grade level into a targeted homeroom or into a targeted team. With clustering, resources (both instructional and professional development) can be easily shared with the students and staff involved, and the teachers can more easily find time to communicate and collaborate. Additionally, ELLs may be grouped, either in and out of the clustered general education homeroom or in and out of the team, according to the instructional goals and the student's strengths and needs.

Even though there may be many different languages or language groups in each class or throughout the school, such a situation does not preclude the need for native language instruction and support. Administrators should attempt to recruit and hire bilingual and ESL teachers that have fluency in the largest language groups. For example, in a facility with twelve Gujarati speakers, six Polish speakers, four Japanese speakers, and three Russian speakers, a bilingual or ESL teacher with fluency in both English and Gujarati can provide ESL instruction to all twenty-five ELLs and native language instruction and support to the twelve Gujarati speakers.

For the students who do not have native language representation among the building staff, the school should take full advantage of the fact that there are many cultures and languages represented in the student body. All students in the building, be they ELLs or not, will benefit from a linguistically and culturally rich environment. School staff must communicate to parents the value of the native language and culture and actively encourage parents to continue to use the native language at home with their children. All school staff should endeavor to make sure that parents have access to instructional or content materials in their native language, whether on the Internet or in materials that the school provides in their learning center or library. In addition, schools should work in partnership with other community agencies, such as the community library and other local schools. Administrators who work with their community library will be certain that the library is cognizant of the native language concerns and needs of the community. An active relationship with the local high school may lead the administrator to discover that many sophomores have service learning requirements. Such graduation requirements can be linked to foreign language study for many students who wish to practice their foreign language skills but cannot afford an AFS experience or a summer living in a foreign country. These students can be engaged to provide cross-age tutoring or hired to assist teachers during summer school programs. Schools should foster relationships with all residents of the community, not just the parents of the students they are currently serving. Fostering such relationships expands the pool of volunteers as well as the pool of individuals willing to translate, interpret, and provide native language support to students.

SURVEY FOR REFLECTION AND ACTION

This survey is based on the guiding principles that were articulated in the Introduction to the chapter. Read the following statements about how your school addresses challenges regarding the education of ELLs. Indicate the extent to which each of the following applies to your school: DK—don't know; 1—strongly disagree; 2—disagree; 3—agree; 4—strongly agree. Use the results of your survey to identify strengths and future possibilities relative to the challenges you face. Then identify one to three actions you can take to improve these efforts.

We appropriately assess student, school, and district needs to determine the nature of the challenge.

- Personnel who are responsible for assessing the challenge have   DK 1 2 3 4
  an understanding of second language acquisition and the area
  for which they are assessing (e.g., for a learning disability or
  having many languages represented in each classroom).

- In the case of an individual challenge, outside contextual   DK 1 2 3 4
  influences have been explored (e.g., home factors, prior
  schooling, first language) before a special education referral is
  initiated.

- In the case of an individual challenge, students' opportunities   DK 1 2 3 4
  to learn have been explored.

- In the case of a school/district level challenge (e.g., limited   DK 1 2 3 4
  resources in a given language), resources within the entire
  community have been explored.

We provide appropriate services to address the needs we identify.

- Services provided to address the challenge (e.g., lack of records   DK 1 2 3 4
  from past schools, the academic needs of overage ELLs) are
  based on appropriate assessment of the challenge.

- Services to address the challenge are provided by highly   DK 1 2 3 4
  qualified personnel.

- Services to address the challenge are implemented with the   DK 1 2 3 4
  necessary resources (e.g., materials, time).

We use valid and reliable data to drive decision making.

- Educators collect valid and reliable data on students'   DK 1 2 3 4
  performance and development over time.

- Educators use that data to drive decision making (e.g., to inform   DK 1 2 3 4
  instruction, program and professional development, and policy).

Strengths of the way we meet challenges

1. _____

2. _____

3. _____

Future Possibilities

1. _____

2. _____

3. _____

Action steps

1. _____

2. _____

3. _____

8

ADVOCACY

GUIDING PRINCIPLES
- We keep ourselves well-informed about all issues concerning English language learners (ELLs), including their rights, the policies and legal mandates that affect them, and the programs and practices that most effectively serve them.
- We maintain an ongoing relationship with individuals and groups that make decisions regarding ELLs/bilingual learners.
- We determine the appropriateness of policies and decisions regarding ELLs/bilingual learners on the basis of what research and our experience suggest are most effective.
- We have a strategy for advocating on behalf of ELLs/bilingual learners and for building their power to advocate for themselves.

INTRODUCTION

Public education, schooling provided by the government and paid for by taxes as well as other sources, is a right that we have come to take for granted in the United States. However, English language learners (ELLs) do not represent and are generally not well represented by the brokers of power in public education. As long as ELLs do not constitute the powerful majority in this society, they remain, in most states, an afterthought in educational policy and planning. To make things worse, many people see ELLs as a burden to society, and they perceive diversity as a challenge to schools rather than a source of richness. Thus, as long as ELLs remain an afterthought, and as long as there are people who see these students in a negative light, we need to advocate on their behalf as well as on behalf of their families, their teachers, and their program administrators. This advocacy must be all-inclusive because just as ELLs are an afterthought in many cases, so are the individuals and the programs associated with them.

Advocacy on behalf of the program for ELLs must be comprehensive. Instruction, assessment, and accountability are the primary foci for most districts, but other aspects, such as extracurricular activities and physical building issues, are also candidates. Advocacy must also happen in every phase of the development of the program. When a school is starting a new program for ELLs, it must begin by advocating for the program. As the program is developing, administrators need to advocate for changes in that program that are necessary for its success. Even for well-established programs, there is a constant need to make sure that the effectiveness of that program is advertised and understood by everyone involved in the school community. Advocacy must reach the widest range of individuals involved in the school community. The range can include parents, local business owners and community members, and state and Federal legislators.

New legislation is something that all schools have to accommodate almost annually, and sometimes the appropriateness of new legislation and policies for ELLs is questionable. It is essential that we assess new legislation and policies in light of what we know is best for ELLs/bilingual learners. Just as schools need to be held accountable for what they do with ELLs using a system such as the *Castañeda v. Pickard* test (see Crawford in Chapter 3), legislation and policies should similarly be based on sound theory and practice.

With respect to advocating on behalf of ELLs, two issues emerge. First, it is essential that we advocate for all ELLs/bilingual learners equitably, remembering that the same treatment for everyone does not constitute equal treatment. Second, and perhaps most important in all discussions of advocacy, we must keep in mind that advocacy on behalf of people must have as a primary goal the empowerment of those people to become activists and advocates themselves. We advocate on behalf of ELLs/bilingual learners, their parents, and their teachers so that they may in the future advocate on behalf of themselves.

This chapter is organized to answer questions that administrators and other educational leaders ask about advocacy for ELLs/bilingual learners. The answers that experts provide offer insight into strategies that administrators and leadership team members can use to advocate and stimulate action in their schools and communities. Effective advocacy is critical in light of the confusion, conflict, and controversy surrounding the education of ELLs that we hear in the popular media today. The chapter concludes with a Survey for Reflection and Action that administrators can use to consider their approaches to advocacy, and to identify action steps they can take to improve this important aspect of educating ELLs/bilingual learners.

■ Regarding English language learners, whom do we advocate with, and about what?

MARÍA JOSEFINA (JOSIE) YANGUAS

With all the different stakeholder groups, one of the most important elements of advocacy begins with putting forth positive and accurate information about programs for English language learners (ELLs) in your school and district. All too often there are negative perceptions regarding programs for ELLs that can be countered with a school visit or a school report. Therefore, whenever there is an opportunity to showcase ELL students in a school, not only should notices be sent to the parents, school officials, and school board members, they should also go to other groups in the community, including the media, local elected officials, and local business and community groups. Any follow-up reports about such events or additional documents that describe the academic progress and other accomplishments of ELL students (including those accomplishments not easily measured by standardized tests but that may be socio-affective in nature, e.g., outstanding parental involvement at different events, former ELLs becoming teachers in the school district,) should also be sent to these different stakeholder groups. Such reports need not be long and elaborate but rather brief and to the point.

Table 8.1 lists the various stakeholders and the most crucial information administrators need to obtain about them, as well as the information stakeholders might be most interested in.

■ What are some key elements in advocating for educational programs for English language learners?
STEPHEN KRASHEN

Language educators have serious public relations problems. This is because the views of professionals are often very different from personal theories held by the public, and the "commonsense" views of the public have won all the recent battles. Despite consistent evidence supporting bilingual education, voters in three states voted to dismantle it. Despite substantial evidence showing the limits of phonics and the power of real reading, intensive systematic phonics is strongly supported by state departments of education and the Federal government.

In addition, there is the familiar problem of dealing with the media. In general, reporters, often overworked and facing deadlines, cannot study educational issues in depth, and get their information from other newspapers, press releases, and conservative think tanks (Stafancic & Delgado, 1996). Although it is possible to inform the public and even change public opinion, this will never happen if we don't try. Here are some steps we might take.

STEP ONE: BE INFORMED
Many educators feel that they are too busy to read professional literature, or don't know where to find it. But we can inform ourselves quickly and easily, thanks to some high-quality websites and reader-friendly books.

STEP TWO: SHARE WITH ALLIES
If our colleagues are not aware of what we and others are doing, there is no hope. All too often professionals find out about significant events only after they have appeared in the press, and have been misrepresented.

In sharing information, we discover groups that either already hold similar views or are open to hearing our point of view. This results in a rapid diffusion of ideas. Similar battles are being fought in different areas of education, and the arguments and data that help in one area can help in another.

Sharing ideas these days is easy, requiring only forwarding items to others electronically. An easy way to pass information along is to get on twitter. Retweeting is a fast and easy way to share. I have been following,

(text continues on page 232)

TABLE 8.1 Regarding English language learners, with whom do we advocate and about what?

What Level?	Who?	What Would Be Useful to Find Out?	What Do We Advocate About?
State elected officials	Governor	Who are gubernatorial staff members that help shape state education policy and budgets?	• Adequate funding for ELL/bilingual education. • Lobby in favor of/against specific legislative and budgetary proposals that affect ELLs. This would also include possible anti-immigrant legislation that has been approved in some states.
	State representatives and state senators	Who are the key leaders at the House and Senate level knowledgeable about education? Who are educators and parents who reside in the districts of these officials who can speak/serve as advocate for ELL/bilingual education? Do these elected officials have constituency-based education committees that help shape local educational policy? Who are elected officials who are well-meaning but have little knowledge/information about ELLs?	• Have elected officials sponsor specific legislation that would be favorable for ELLs; e.g., if there is no provision in state law for ELL/bilingual education, find an elected official willing to sponsor such legislation. • Lobby in favor of/against specific legislative and budgetary proposals that affect ELLs. This could also include possible anti-immigrant legislation that has been approved in some states, such SB1070 in Arizona. • Consider volunteering for (or even forming) such committees to assist with the formulation of possible ELL/bilingual education legislation.
Federal elected officials	U.S. Senators and U.S. Representatives	Make the distinction as to whether a policy is a Federal or state mandate; e.g., Title III monies are Federal monies that support ELLs, yet at the same time the majority of funds that support ELL education come from state/local monies.	• Keep Federal officials apprised of how the state is supporting the needs of ELLs. • Lobby in favor of/against specific Federal budgetary proposals that affect ELLs.
State Board of Education or State Department of Education		• Is the state superintendent an elected position? An appointed position? • Is there a designated individual/department at the state level that supports ELL education?	• Statewide policy decisions related to ELLs, particularly critical within the context of NCLB and its high-stakes accountability and assessments expected for ELLs. • Supplemental funding for ELL education. • Expansion of bilingual/ESL services to specific populations such as pre-school students[1]
Local school board		How many members understand and/or are supportive of ELL policies?	• Encourage parents knowledgeable in ELL programs to get elected to the school board.

Stakeholder	Description / Examples	Questions	Actions
Parent groups and parents	PTAs, school-based committees with parent members (e.g., NCLB and/or bilingual parental advisory committees, local school councils), other formal or informal parent groups at a school.	How many parents/parent leaders in these various committees understand and/or are supportive of ELL policies? How many parents/parent leaders articulate some opinion (favorable or unfavorable) regarding instructional programs for ELLs at the local school level?	• Encourage parents to participate in some kind of formal/informal group at school that will help parents better understand (and ultimately advocate for) ELL. • Encourage parents knowledgeable about ELL programs to testify at school board meetings for any new policy initiatives for ELL students.
Media	Print, TV, social media	Are there local community newspapers, cable stations, bloggers who have articulated either a favorable or unfavorable report regarding ELLs?	• Invite the media, especially local community newspaper or cable stations, to visit the school, and send reports to different media sources that highlight ELL students and their accomplishments.
Local community/ business groups/ local chambers of commerce/ community-based organizations	Some community or business groups may have significant ties to local schools, such as helping to coordinate after school programs or community schools initiatives. They may also be affiliated with the creation of a local charter school.	Has the local community or business group articulated some position (favorable or unfavorable) regarding ELLs? If such groups are closely tied to concrete activities at schools, are such initiatives favorable or unfavorable for ELLs (e.g., equitable access to activities; language(s) used).	• Could be a source of income to help support small projects related to ELLs. • Can talk and testify to other stakeholders (such as school board members and elected officials) on behalf of ELL students and any possible program needs.
Education associations and national advocacy groups	Some examples include MALDEF, Aspira, NABE, TESOL, NAEYC, and state associations of these national groups.	What are the position papers, if any, written by such groups that articulate a specific stance toward ELLs?	• Can advocate for different ELL/bilingual education policies through position papers, member newsletters and events. • Can talk and testify to other stakeholders (such as school board members and elected officials) on behalf of ELL students and any possible program needs.
School district level	District superintendent and other central office administrators, teacher unions, teacher leaders within a school, departmental chairs, teacher assistants, other school support staff.	How many school-level administrators, teachers and other education personnel understand and/or are supportive of ELL policies? How many school-level administrators, teachers, and other education personnel articulate some opinion (favorable or unfavorable) regarding instructional programs for ELLs at the local school level?	• Can advocate for different ELL/bilingual education policies through membership newsletters and events. • Can talk and testify to other stakeholders (such as school board members and elected officials) on behalf of ELL students and any possible program needs.

1 For example, the Illinois legislature in 2009 clarified the definition of ELLs to include pre-school students, beginning at age 3, who are served by pre-K programs, thus making this student population eligible for bilingual/ESL services.

and retweeting, Susan Ohanian, Alfie Kohn, Diane Ravitch, and a number of others. We may not have as many followers as Charley Sheen does (over 4 million) or Lady Gaga (now over 11 million), but twitter will allow us to reach thousands of people right away.

STEP THREE: EXPRESS YOUR OWN POINT OF VIEW, FROM YOUR OWN EXPERIENCE AND EXPERTISE

To paraphrase Susan Ohanian, the public needs to hear from those who have been in the classroom, not from those who have never in their lives been shut up in a room with a large group of seventh graders for a full day. I suggest you write (or talk) about any issue in which you, as a professional, have knowledge that the public does not have and needs to have.

Publish your opinions anywhere you can. At least tell us, your colleagues, by posting on listservs. Others will learn from your ideas and might be able to use them. There are of course other possibilities: letters to the editor, op-eds, blogs, articles in professional journals, general-interest magazines, newsletters, and so forth.

Each person has to discover what is comfortable for him- or herself. I like to write journal papers and letters to the editor, and I stick to these formats. For some reason, I find it hard to write op-eds or general-interest articles. (Thomas Feyer, letters editor for the *New York Times*, has provided some good advice on writing letters to the editor; Feyer, 2004.)

Right now, the public is hearing only from amateurs with little or no experience in educational practice or research. The public needs to hear from the real experts.

The acceptance of new ideas depends on a variety of factors: One factor is obvious—how much people know about the new idea. Rogers (1983) notes that we see no acceptance of new ideas until potential "adapters" have a minimum amount of information. But once a certain threshold is reached, increases in information result in substantial increases in acceptance of the new idea (p. 235). We are, in my view, far below the minimum. Getting information to the public and, eventually to opinion leaders is a task we must all take part in.

■ **What are some concrete strategies that administrators and teachers can use to guide advocacy for English language learners on the local level?**

ESTER J. DE JONG

Teachers are important language decision makers in their classroom and their schools. Through their daily decisions about language and language use, teachers help shape students' linguistic and cultural identities as well as their academic and language and literacy development. They do not make such language decisions in a vacuum. Federal, national, state, and local policies direct language choices and possibilities at the school and classroom levels. While teachers have considerable agency, broader structures, such as state and Federal law as well as local district policy, can expand and constrain the language options teachers can explore.

Understanding and valuing the diversity of students' and families' linguistic and cultural practices and experiences and using this diversity for organizing schools and classrooms is key to providing multilingual learners with equal access to high-quality schooling. How can educators contribute to moving away from deficit-oriented, assimilationist policies and practices to enrichment-oriented/pluralist practices that respect and build on bilingual students' and their families' linguistic and cultural resources? I argue that this kind of shift may need two pathways for advocacy.

PATHWAY 1: ENGAGING WITH DOMINANT DISCOURSES

The first pathway focuses on uncovering discontinuities and ambiguities within the assimilationist view of diversity itself. The goal is to engage in a conversation based on the explicit and implicit assumptions about education, language, and language learning within this view. For example, instead of framing the effectiveness debate as one that must prove that bilingual education is better than English-only programs, the issue can be rephrased in terms of how different English-only programs reach long-term social, language, and academic goals for linguistically and culturally diverse students. When the comparison with bilingual education is excluded from the policy discourse, this question calls for careful analysis of the strengths and weaknesses of English-only policies and their positive and negative impact on student learning. Engaging in the analysis of data that would highlight key features of effective practices in English-medium schools could provide different insights about what schools can do to support English language learners (ELLs) and educational attainment. Linking these discussions to short-term and long-term educational outcomes (language, literacy, content, and sociocultural development) would also more meaningfully inform policy and practice.

PATHWAY 2: FRAMING PLURALIST DISCOURSES

Simply engaging thoughtfully with assimilationist frames will be insufficient, however, to accomplish a shift to more pluralist discourses. The second pathway for advocacy aims to articulate a multilingual discourse "in its own right," with its own agenda. This discourse would promote policies and practices that reflect, first, a view that bi/multilingual systems are interconnected, integrated, and creative rather than the simple addition of two or more discrete, monolingual systems. Second, this discourse recognizes that multilingual practices are always embedded within localized and broader sociopolitical contexts.

For multilingual discourses to find their way into policy and practice, educators need to formulate policies and identify practices and conditions for multilingual students' success that are informed by scholarship that takes a multilingual and bilingual perspective (Castek et al., 2008). The four principles defined in de Jong (2011)—the Principles of Educational Equity, Affirming Identities, Promoting Additive Bi/Multilingualism, and Structuring for Integration—also take a pluralist approach. These principles can be applied separately as analytical lenses for reflection on scholarship, policies, and practices, but they also must be considered together to create equitable, optimal learning environments for all students.

WAYNE E. WRIGHT

English language learners (ELLs) and their families, many of whom are from lower socioeconomic homes and communities, typically are among the least empowered individuals in our society. When policies at the school have a negative impact on ELL students or their families, parents, for several reasons, may be discouraged from speaking out: (a) they may be unfamiliar with the educational system and may not fully understand how policies affect their children; (b) if they do not speak English and no one at the school can speak their language, they may be unable to speak out; (c) they may be hesitant to raise their concerns because their culture emphasizes respect for teachers and the school; and (d) many work full-time or even work two or more jobs to support their families, making it difficult for them to find time to go to the school to express their concerns.

For these and other reasons, it is important for teachers of ELLs to become advocates for their students. The following are a few ideas for doing so.

- **Take advantage of the positive aspects of Federal and state policies for ELLs.**

There are many problems associated with Federal and state policies for ELLs, particularly as they relate to mandates for high-stakes testing and accountability. These policies, however, have at least raised awareness that schools are responsible for meeting the needs of ELL students. Education for ELLs has had an unfortunate history of underfunding, and teachers have found it difficult to get the resources they need for their ELL students.

You can take advantage of No Child Left Behind (NCLB) and other Federal education programs by going to your district leaders. Ask how Federal Title III funds, stimulus funding, Race to the Top grants, and state funds for ELLs are being used in your district. Provide a list of needed resources. Does your school lack English as a second language curricular programs? Search for one you like, give the details to your district leaders, and recommend it for purchase. Are there supplemental materials, software programs, or other technologies you think would help your students? Put a list together, write out the rationale, and explain to your district leaders how such materials would help your ELL students make progress in meeting language proficiency and content area standards. Got an idea for an afterschool program that would benefit the students and their families? Approach your district leaders and ask them for funding, or apply for an external grant to fund the program.

- **Keep data to show the progress of ELLs in learning English and academic content.**

Collect data from multiple authentic alternative assessments for your ELL students and synthesize the information in ways that can be shared with parents, school and district administrators, and the public. This process is particularly important when the results of invalid high-stakes tests create a false depiction of the quality of teaching and learning in your classroom or school. Teachers whose ELL students obtain low scores on statewide high-stakes tests can turn around and provide strong evidence of the students' growth.

- **Work to change policies that are potentially harmful to your students.**

Educators often feel helpless to change bad education and language policies that have adverse effects on their students, on their classrooms and schools, and even on themselves. Educators who feel it is wrong to force ELLs to take high-stakes tests in English before they reach a level of proficiency in their new language sufficient to comprehend it—and hold teachers and administrators accountable for the results even if they are likely invalid—nonetheless feel they have no choice but to go along with the system. I agree that teachers and administrators must comply with what is required in their state and in their school. They also have a responsibility to try to minimize the harm as much as they legally can within the confines of their own classrooms and school. However, outside of school hours, teachers and administrators are private citizens who have the full right to advocate for change. If policies are harming your students, speak up! Gather evidence from your school that documents harm being done. Take this evidence to district administrators. Start a blog. Talk to parents. Organize colleagues and parents to testify at district and state school board meetings. Write letters to the editor of the local newspaper. Write letters to local and state policy makers. Invite them to your school. Join local and national networks of educators working for change.

- **Serve on key school, district, and state committees.**

Most schools and districts have several committees that make important decisions—or at least important recommendations to decision makers—

that can impact ELL students. These committees address policies, programs, standards, assessments, curriculum adoption, reclassification of students, and other issues. It is imperative that educators who advocate for their ELL students serve on these committees as well as on those at the state level that also consider issues that can impact ELLs.

■ How can we use information about the program for English language learners to advocate for further development?
ELSE HAMAYAN

Having information about your English language learner (ELL) program is essential for advocacy purposes. Gathering that information should be part of the routine functioning of every school that has an ELL population. This way, you have access to the information you need when you need it. You cannot go back in the spring when budgetary decisions are being taken by the school board and assess the level of proficiency that students started the academic year with. That information has to be there from the very beginning of the year.

The following is a partial list of the information that could be useful to have to advocate on behalf of the program for ELLs.

- Scores on tests: Make sure that you can show development and growth over time. Interpret the scores or performance levels relative to state content and language proficiency standards and accountability requirements.
- Scores obtained from qualitative data such as checklists, rating scales, and rubrics: Again, explain what different levels of scores mean in terms of performance on a given subject matter.
- For programs where ELLs exit the services provided once they reach a certain level of proficiency: Provide a description, either numeric or qualitative, of how well students who are functioning in the mainstream with little or no specialized support are doing.
- Student work samples: Select students' best work that clearly represents parts of the curriculum. Use common rubrics to assess student work.
- Gather success stories from individual students, either those who are still in the program or those who have graduated.
- Save testimonials from parents of ELL students.
- Save testimonials from employers of ELL students.

When it comes time to present this information, an administrator must be sure it is done in a way that appeals to the particular audience to whom it is being presented. Finally, it is easiest for people to relate to someone who is like them. If you are appealing to your superintendent, get another superintendent to talk to him or her. If you are talking to parents, get another parent to do the presentation, or talk to them yourself as a parent rather than as a researcher or administrator.

■ What are some resources to help us advocate on behalf of English language learners?

NANCY CLOUD

Language-minority students and parents may not advocate for themselves, for many reasons. First, they may lack the proficiency in English to engage in this sophisticated verbal interplay, or for cultural reasons they may shy away from speaking up. Second, they may not fully understand the expectations of democratic institutions and may instead believe that the institution will respond to their needs without prompting. Third, they may have other reasons for nonparticipation, such as fear of reprisal based on their residency status or ethnicity, or negative past experiences. For all these reasons, administrators and teachers need to advocate on behalf of this student group to ensure that they get the best education possible.

What does it take to advocate for this group? First, we must be familiar with the relevant laws and legislation to make certain children and parents get all of the services and protections to which they are entitled. To get this information, we can start at the U.S. Department of Education, Office for Civil Rights, which has issued guidelines for program development and evaluation (*Programs for English Language Learners: Resource Materials for Planning and Self- Assessments*, updated through March 28, 2000, available at http://www.ed.gov/about/offices/list/ocr/ell/index. html). Another helpful contact is the National Clearinghouse for English Language Acquisition and Language Instruction Educational Programs, which has published a fact sheet entitled "What Legal Obligations Do Schools Have to English Language Learners?" (available at http://www.ncela.gwu .edu/expert/faq/23legal.htm). Finally, we can contact the Council of Chief State School Officers, which has published "Summary of recommendations and policy implications for improving the assessment and monitoring of students with limited English proficiency" as well as other policy-oriented documents directed toward the appropriate education of English language learners (ELLs) (available at http://www.ccsso.org).

Second, we need to understand best practices for ELLs. For this, we can turn to our professional associations to learn of the position statements they have issued with respect to the assessment and education of language-minority students. We can also join with them in their advocacy efforts on behalf of ELLs. There is a great degree of consistency among the recommendations they make, which should give us the ammunition we need to defend the policies and practices we wish to implement on behalf of ELLs. Associations that have issued policy statements of interest include Teachers of English to Speakers of Other Languages (TESOL), the National Association for Bilingual Education (NABE), the International Reading Association (IRA), the National Council of Teachers of English (NCTE), the National Association for the Education of Young Children (NAEYC), the National Education Association (NEA), the American Educational Research Association (AERA) , the National Council on Measurement in Education (NCME), and the American Psychological Association (APA). Collectively, they support the use of the native language in instruction and assessment, the active development of bilingualism/multilingualism in our multicultural society, respect for and responsiveness to children's primary languages and cultures at school, and the active involvement of language-minority parents.

Finally, to advocate effectively, we need to understand the goals and requirements of the major program models designed to serve ELLs so that we can select appropriate models and implement them well. A great source for this purpose is Fred Genesee's *Program Alternatives for Linguistically Diverse Students* (Center for Research on Education, Diversity & Excellence, University of California, Santa Cruz, 1999, available at http://www.cal.org/crede/pubs, along with many other helpful publications).

Being well-informed should form the foundation of our advocacy efforts at all levels of the educational system—state, district, and school. All issue policies and establish practices that need to work for ELLs. Obviously, it works best if our advocacy happens early on, as policies are being formulated and practices are being determined. Whether it is high-stakes testing or curriculum decisions, advocacy is needed to make sure that the needs of ELLs are fully considered. Administrators are in an ideal position to advocate on behalf of ELLs, and it is in their best interest to do so, as their success hinges on doing the right thing for the populations they serve.

■ **How can we move from advocacy for English language learners to activism by English language learners and their families?**
NANCY SANTIAGO-NEGRÓN

Advocate: one that pleads the cause of another; specifically: one that pleads the cause of another before a tribunal or judicial court
Activism: a doctrine or practice that emphasizes direct vigorous action especially in support of or opposition to one side of a controversial issue
—Merriam-Webster Dictionary

So many of us who work in education like to think of ourselves as advocates for the children we teach, for the families in our schools, or for the community our schools serve. But how many of us think of ourselves as activists? I believe that to truly change the world of the children we serve, we cannot continue to simply advocate or speak for the community. Instead, we need to help the community speak for itself.

As an advocate, your pleas may still go unanswered, your requests for support unmet, and your sole voice ignored. But if you wish to create change for your students, you must move a community to speak together. To be a true agent of change you must create situations that allow the community to speak together loudly and allow the community to be understood regardless of the language spoken.

The summer that the state took over control of the School District of Philadelphia taught me many things, but the most important lesson was how to create real change. Philadelphia was in the beginning phase of the most unprecedented experiment in public education in many generations. The very face of public education was about to change forever in Philadelphia, yet when I looked around my community during this very tense period I noticed something very worrisome—silence. The public education system was about to undertake the most drastic change in its history, yet the community had very little to say on the matter. I, along with some fellow advocates, started to voice our concerns over the impending changes. We called meetings, wrote letters, and made telephone call after telephone call to school district and state officials requesting help, to no avail. After several months of advocating, I realized that we had to regroup and try another strategy quickly.

I then tried to "preach from the pulpit," spewing out information on what was happening to all who would listen. I tried to get the community and parents to write letters and make telephone calls, hoping that this would draw more attention to the issue. What I did not realize then was that listening and engaging are two very different things. Parents and community residents politely listened to me and my colleagues, but nothing of what we said made a difference in their behaviors because they were not invested in us. Actually, when I review these events more objectively today, I realize that I was not invested in them either—at least not at that time. I was invested in the "cause," in the issue of equal access to quality education. I was invested in the issue that I thought automatically translated to being invested in children, but I was wrong. I needed to become invested in the day-to-day lives of my students and the community, both inside and outside of the school walls. Once parents felt me reach out to them in a sincere way, in a way that said "we are partners," not "I am that expert here to help you," they felt comfortable. Once I invested my time and energy to build a relationship that felt safe for both of us, parents started to invest their time and energy in me and our school district.

The building of these relationships started with a simple question. Instead of running in and out of schools "raising awareness" about the impending takeover, I decided to ask questions. Our road toward real change started with one question: Do you know what is happening to our schools? It seems like such a simple question at first, but it opened floodgates of ideas, opinions, and insights into what makes a community work. The question almost never received the answer that I thought that I would hear—the way that I thought it should be. I received one answer when I visited a church, another answer when the question was asked in a community-based organization, and yet another answer altogether when I met with parents at the park for a community event. What I realized is that the answer was more complex than I had originally thought, but the solution seemed closer with each person I talked to that summer.

The question began a dialogue, a true exchange with parents, students, community leaders, and residents. This dialogue took me out of the safety of a central office building and into community-based organizations, community and civic meetings, churches, grocery stores, and parents' homes. This new conversation helped me understand the importance of opening my schools' doors to the community. I learned to open the doors of our schools to basketball games, first-time homebuyer workshops, and community aerobics classes. I let the community into my home, and they welcomed me into theirs. This exchange eventually took us to marching in the streets and speaking up at board meetings. The shared communication led to "actions" that guaranteed that our parents, not outside advocates, would be listened to. Parents and community residents were the activists that caused actions (and reactions) that later made all of the difference in their children's schools and educational process.

If I try to organize the steps we took on our road to change together, it would probably look like this short list:

Leave Your Building: Take a walk or drive in your school's community and conduct a survey. See what resources exist. Make a list of those resources, including names and contact numbers. Drop in at the community grocery store. Visit community landmarks.

Reach Out to Your Neighbors: Find out what services the community-based organizations in the area provide. See if they have something they can offer to your students and families. If they conduct workshops, offer them your space to provide one of those workshops. Many of these organizations are trying to reach the same families that you serve. Keep a contact list handy and available to your staff at all times.

Support Your School's Community: Buy your breakfast, lunch, snacks, and lottery tickets in that neighborhood grocery store. Listen to the conversations while you are there. Pick up the local newspapers while you are there. Get into the habit of talking regularly to the store owners and ask them questions about the community. Leave information about your school and school events at the stores. Make sure that community residents always have a way to contact you should they need you.

Bring People, Other Than Students, Into Your Schools: Offer the community different workshops in your schools via your community partners and municipal agencies (how to purchase a home, tax prep, CPR/ first aid, and so forth). Sit in on those workshops as a participant and not just the coordinator. Have these workshops take place during hours that allow working parents to attend. Open student performances and special events to community leaders, business owners, and volunteers. Build relationships with adults outside of your school staff and parents.

Create a Climate of Trust and Reciprocity: Ask questions and allow folks to be as honest as possible. Gather information from all sources— parents, students, and school volunteers. Have a feedback loop that allows people to give you information in an anonymous way (such as a suggestion box or email address), and then act on those suggestions if appropriate. Organize community forums on education with a partner (and make sure that you always have someone there who can translate if necessary). The creation of the forum agenda should not be up to the school staff. Have a community-based partner take on this responsibility; you just help them get the word out.

Share: Share information, share space, share time, share history, and share celebrations. Share information in the languages that all parents can understand. Share your concerns and causes with them. Chances are they will share the same concerns with you.

Our time frame was relatively short, and things did not take place in the most organized or sequential of timelines, but they happened. One at a time, great new partnerships started to form and take hold of parent groups, of community meetings, and eventually of the issue of the state takeover. When it was time to fight for change, parents, community residents, business owners, leaders, and elected officials were ready. They were armed with information and whole community support. The state and district entities now realized that they could not move on this very prickly issue until they listened and reacted to the concerns being raised by the local community.

■ How have recent policies affected the way we perceive English language learners' performance in school?

ELSE HAMAYAN

Many policies in education, beginning with the infamous No Child Left Behind, have adversely affected the way we perceive English language learners' (ELLs') performance in school. Interpreting how well ELLs do in school is usually influenced by the question: How long does it take for an ELL to become proficient in English? This question is itself embedded in a much larger and thornier issue: How long does it take any student to learn anything? When can we expect a student to attain academic concepts for a given grade level? This issue has become critical, and three trends in education have led to pedagogical decisions and practices that are counterproductive to learning. None of these trends make developmental or humane sense for any student, but the implications are dire especially for ELLs.

1. *High-stakes tests are becoming the primary if not the sole method of determining success in meeting expectations.* Worse, students who fail to meet standards measured by high-stakes tests are penalized, or they cause their schools to be penalized. ELLs, who are likely to perform poorly on standardized paper and pencil tests for a variety of reasons that do not reflect these students' ability to learn, fall into this category. This dependence on norm-referenced tests has become an accepted part of the educational system in the U.S., but it is not the norm in many other countries. In my experience as the parent of a young student in the public school system in Argentina, I see that teachers' own assessments and evaluations of their students are given as much importance as formal testing results.

2. *More and more is being expected of younger and younger children.* Children are now expected to enter kindergarten with skills that were not expected of them in the recent past. The notion that five-year-olds need not do more than play and learn the rules of socialization has long disappeared in U.S. kindergartens and has been replaced by the absurd notion that the earlier children begin to master the basic elements of reading, such as phonics and letter recognition, the more likely they are to succeed in school (Ohanian, 2002). In educational systems of many other countries (see for example the article on Finland, Alvarez, 2004), formal instruction on literacy and abstract concepts does not begin until children have reached the age of seven or eight. In Argentina, play and recreation have a major role in the early grades, and teachers give themselves six years to develop literacy as a tool for learning. This push for younger children to do more is particularly problematical for ELLs because many of them enter kindergarten or first grade lacking some academic skills but bringing with them other skills such as socializing with others, negotiating, and turn-taking. When these nonacademic skills lose their value in the eyes of legislators and administrators, ELLs are at a disadvantage. In an atmosphere where kindergarten education has become heavily focused on teaching literacy and other academic skills, ELLs are likely to be seen as "at-risk." Unfortunately, this downward move of expecting younger children to do more has begun to influence even preschool education in the U.S., which is rapidly following the trend of more academics and less independent and imaginative play (Miller & Almon, 2009).

3. *Same-age children are expected to meet the same expectations at the same time.* This trend has resulted in unjust consequences for all children who happen to be a step or two behind their peers. Children who are sim-

ply late readers will appear as failures. Waiting a year or perhaps even two years for these late readers to meet the requirements would give them the benefit of being seen as successes rather than failures. Many ELLs, simply by virtue of coming to school with a language other than the language of instruction and from a cultural context that may be quite different from the culture of school, are nonstandard students. They will not fit into the rigid mold that has been created for "the average child" and will need the extra time that unfortunately the system rarely gives them.

It may take some students as little as two or three years; it may take others as long as ten to learn enough English and to the level that their potential allows. To expect all students to attain the proficiency they need in either of the two extremes of the range (two or ten years) is foolish. To calculate an average, use it as a standard, and expect all students to have attained proficiency in five or six years is to act on the basis of a statistical illusion.

So, what needs to happen?

- Become activists and advocate for a more sensible expectation of ELLs from kindergarten to high school at the school, district, state, and Federal levels.
- Base your pedagogical decisions on sound research and experience and demand the same of your legislators and policy makers.
- Collect classroom-based data to use as additional sources of information on students.
- Document your students' stories and use them to advocate for an educational system that takes into account the individuality of ELLs.

■ What is bilingualism worth, and how much should we be willing to invest in it?
REBECCA FREEMAN FIELD and ELSE HAMAYAN

The fact that we are asked what bilingualism is worth and how much we should invest in it is an indication that we are far from being a society that values expertise in two (or more) languages. Yet in this day and age we should be very concerned that despite the fact that many students in U.S. schools speak a language other than English at home, few of these students graduate from high school with proficiency in that language. Since the early 1900s, immigrants have experienced strong pressure to assimilate to monolingualism in English. Even among the Spanish-speaking population today, we see clear evidence of an ongoing language shift toward English, despite the large numbers of immigrants that revitalize this language throughout the country. For the majority of immigrants, today as in the past, the native language is generally lost after three generations (Peyton, Ranard, & McGinnis, 2001).

The cost to the individual of losing their home language is serious and significant. When children refuse to speak the language of their home, family, and community because English has more prestige, they can become alienated from these critical connections that help them understand who they are relative to others in the world. When children believe they must reject their home language and culture in order to participate and achieve in a monolingual, English-speaking world, they deny an important part of their sociocultural identity. They also limit opportunities that could be readily available to them if they were to maintain and develop their home language.

Contrary to popular belief, maintaining and developing a home language by no means hinders an English language learner's ability to acquire English. Add to that the evidence that shows tremendous benefits to bilingualism, both individual and societal. A wide range of research shows educational, cognitive, sociocultural, and economic benefits of bilingualism for the individual. Bilinguals tend to perform better than monolinguals on cognitive tasks that call for divergent thinking, pattern recognition, and problem solving, and they tend to demonstrate sophisticated levels of metalinguistic awareness. People who can use more than one language can generally communicate across language and cultural boundaries more effectively, and they generally have a wider range of professional opportunities available to them in the global economy (Cloud, Genesee, & Hamayan, 2000; de Jong, 2011).

The evidence about ELLs in particular and Latinos in general demonstrates that these student populations score disproportionately low on standardized tests and drop out of school at disproportionately high rates (Genesee, Lindholm-Leary, Saunders, & Christian, 2006). At the same time, the evidence on well-implemented dual language programs (such as two-way immersion and one-way developmental bilingual programs) shows that these programs enable ELLs to close the achievement gap with their English-speaking peers in five to seven years (Lindholm-Leary, 2001; Thomas and Collier, 2002; Collier & Thomas, 2009). These data suggest that when schools have the linguistic resources available to implement dual language programs that lead to additive bilingualism and biliteracy, they are well worth the investment.

Promoting bilingualism is not only good for the individual, their families, and the local community, it is good for the nation overall. According to the National Foreign Language Center,

> . . . the United States has critical needs for genuine communicative competency in a range of languages, a level of competency that can rarely be attained by native English speakers in a classroom setting. The ethnic communities constitute a valuable and unique resource in producing true multilingual ability in English and languages that are essential to the national interest (National Foreign Language Center, 1995, p. 1).

Peyton, Renaid, & McGinnis (2001) argue that a national policy that viewed these languages as resources to be preserved and developed rather than as obstacles to be overcome could contribute significantly and in a relatively short time to America's expertise in foreign languages.

Bilingualism is the expectation and the norm in most other countries in the world today. Many countries have language policies that promote the teaching of additional languages beginning in elementary school. Although there is no such language policy or expectation overall in the United States today, schools can challenge the assimilation process on the local level by investing in bilingualism. In our opinion, the benefits clearly outweigh the costs.

SURVEY FOR REFLECTION AND ACTION

This survey is based on the guiding principles about advocacy that were articulated in the Introduction to the chapter. Read the following statements about your school's advocacy efforts on behalf of your ELLs. Indicate the extent to which each of the following applies to your school: DK—don't know; 1—strongly disagree; 2—disagree; 3—agree; 4—strongly agree. Use the results of your survey to identify your advocacy strengths and needs to determine what, if any, actions you should take to improve these efforts.

Everyone at our school is well informed about legal mandates and the rights of English language learners.

- Everyone at our school understands the program for ELLs to be able to advocate on its behalf.   DK 1 2 3 4

- There is a system in place through which new information is gathered and disseminated efficiently.   DK 1 2 3 4

We assess the appropriateness of policies and decisions regarding ELLs in light of what we know is best for them.

- We ensure that our polices and decisions regarding ELLs are aligned with credible research about ELL education.   DK 1 2 3 4

- We assess whether policies and decisions regarding ELLs seem appropriate in light of our experiences teaching these students.   DK 1 2 3 4

Members of our staff/school leadership team have an ongoing relationship with the following constituents.

- Parents and community members   DK 1 2 3 4

- District level administrators   DK 1 2 3 4

- State legislators   DK 1 2 3 4

- Federal legislators   DK 1 2 3 4

- Mass media (newspaper, radio, etc.)   DK 1 2 3 4

- Other advocacy groups (organizations, resource centers)   DK 1 2 3 4

Our staff/leadership team has strategies for advocacy.

- We have an advocacy plan in place.   DK 1 2 3 4

- We implement the advocacy plan.   DK 1 2 3 4

- We gauge the effectiveness of our advocacy strategies and   DK 1 2 3 4
  revise our plan as necessary.

- ELLs and their parents become advocates on their own behalf.   DK 1 2 3 4

Advocacy Strengths

1. _____

2. _____

3. _____

Future Possibilities

1. _____

2. _____

3. _____

Action steps

1. _____

2. _____

3. _____

GLOSSARY

Words in *italics* within a definition are defined in another entry in this glossary.

Academic language proficiency The type of language proficiency required to participate and achieve in content area instruction (contrast *conversational fluency*). There are different varieties of academic English associated with different content areas (such as the language of science, of social studies, of math). According to research, it may take at least five to seven years and up to eleven years for ELLs to acquire the academic English proficiency they need for academic success in U.S. schools. Cummins used the term cognitive academic language proficiency (CALP) in his earlier work to refer to this idea.

Additive bilingualism The process by which or context in which a second (or third or fourth) language is added without the loss of proficiency in the first language (contrast *subtractive bilingualism*). Our use of this term assumes a dynamic, developmental, recursive notion of bilingualism.

Bilingual education A well-planned educational program that uses two languages for instructional purposes. All bilingual programs in the United States aim for high levels of proficiency in English and academic achievement in English as important goals (some bilingual programs have additional goals). A program that is taught exclusively through English but that includes some *primary language support* is not a bilingual program (contrast *English-medium program*). There are several different types of bilingual education programs (see *transitional bilingual education, dual language education, developmental bilingual education, two-way immersion, immersion*).

Bilingual learner A student who draws on two (or more) languages in his or her linguistic repertoire to learn. All *English language learners* are bilingual learners.

Conversational fluency The type of English that is acquired through everyday social interaction. It generally takes English language learners approximately one to two years to acquire conversational fluency. Contrast *academic language proficiency*. Cummins used the term basic interpersonal communication skills (BICS) to refer to this concept in his earlier work.

Data-driven decision making The use of any form of evidence or information (i.e., data) for any type of decision making (e.g., on the classroom, program, school, program, district, community, state, Federal levels for summative and/or formative purposes). Our broad use of this term stands in contrast to a narrow notion of data-driven decision making using the results of standardized test results in English for all types of education decision making.

Developmental bilingual education (DBE) program A type of *bilingual education* that targets *English language learners* and/or *heritage language speakers* and aims for high levels of proficiency in English and in the students' home language and strong academic development. Students generally participate in these programs for at least five to six years, receiving content area instruction in English and in their home language. Developmental bilingual programs are also sometimes referred to as one-way developmental bilingual programs, maintenance bilingual programs, or late-exit bilingual programs. This guide considers one-way developmental bilingual programs to be a type of *dual language education* because they share the goals of *additive bilingualism* with other types of dual language programs.

Dual language A model of bilingual education that aims for (1) bilingualism, (2) biliteracy, (3) strong academic development, and (4) positive cultural understanding and intercultural communicative competence. Students generally participate in dual language programs for at least five to six years. They receive content-area instruction in two languages; at least 50 percent and up to 90 percent of that content-area instruction is through the minority language (language other than English in the United States). Under the broad definition of dual language programs used in this guide, we find three types: *one-way developmental bilingual education, two-way immersion,* and *second/ foreign language immersion* that differ in terms of their target populations.

ELL program Tradtionally this term has been used to refer narrowly to specially designed *English-as-a-second-language programs* as well as *bilingual education programs.* In this book, we use the terms "ELL program" or "program for ELLs" more broadly to refer to all aspects of the educational programming for ELLs at school, including the time ELLs spend in general education classes. This broader use of the term ELL program reflects an assumption of shared responsibility for ELL education among all educators who have ELLs in their classes and schools, not only the ESL and bilingual education specialists.

Emergent bilingual Students who are becoming proficient in a second or additional language. All *English language learners* are emergent bilinguals, regardless of whether they are in a *bilingual education* or *English-medium program.* The term "emergent bilingual" makes visible all of the languages in the learners' linguistic repertoire, highlighting the developmental nature of and potential for *additive bilingualism.*

English as a second language (ESL) Developmentally appropriate English language instruction tailored for English language learners' level of English proficiency; also known as English language development (ELD). While English language learners receive ESL/ELD instruction, they also receive content instruction from other sources (for example, in a bilingual program, in mainstream classes). There are different types of ESL classes, including *pull-out, push-in,* or *self-contained. Sheltered instruction programs* are another type of English-only program associated with the term ESL.

English language learner (ELL) A student who is in the process of learning English as a second/additional language. In the U.S., this term is an official designation for a bilingual learner who is identified by English language proficiency tests as in need of further English language proficiency development; this term is increasingly replacing the term "limited English proficient." All ELLs are *emergent bilinguals* or *bilingual learners.*

English-medium program A program for English language learners that uses English as the exclusive language for instructional purposes (contrast *bilingual education program*). English-medium programs, however, can and should offer *primary language support* to ELLs as appropriate.

Fully English proficient (FEP) An official designation for a former English language learner who has met all exit criteria of an ESL or bilingual program and is considered ready for participation in the all-English academic mainstream. However, because many districts use inappropriate exit criteria, we find many ELLs who have developed *conversational fluency* in English but who are still acquiring *academic language proficiency* in English.

Heritage language program A language program for *heritage language speakers* that aims to broaden the linguistic repertoire of these students. Heritage language programs may be offered by community-based institutions (such as Chinese programs at Saturday schools or Korean programs at church) or by public schools (such as a world language for these students). The most common heritage language programs offered in public schools are *Spanish for Spanish speakers* or *Spanish for Native Speakers* (*SNS*) programs. We also find programs that promote Native American languages or other less commonly taught languages.

Heritage language speaker A student who speaks a language other than English (their heritage language) at home. Heritage language speakers, as a collective, have a wide range of expertise in their heritage language. Some heritage language speakers may be able to speak, understand, read, and write for a wide range of purposes, while others may only be able to understand their heritage language when they are spoken to by a family or community member about a familiar topic.

Home language This term is generally used to refer to the languages other than English that are used in bilingual or multilingual households.

Immersion program A type of *dual language program* that exclusively targets *language majority students* (such as English speakers in the United States). These programs provide content area instruction through English and another language (for example, French, Spanish, Chinese) and aim for bilingualism, biliteracy, academic achievement in two languages, and positive cultural understanding and intercultural relations. They are sometimes referred to as second or foreign language immersion programs. NOTE: Sometimes the term immersion is used to describe all-English programs for *language minority students;* however, when schools do not structure the learning environment of English language learners (by, for example, using *sheltered instructional* strategies), this experience is better understood as submersion, or sink-or-swim. Contrast this with *sheltered English programs* or *specially designed academic instruction in English/SDAIE programs,* that is, *English-medium programs* that are specially designed to meet the language and learning needs of ELLs.

Language majority student A student who speaks the dominant societal or *majority language*. In the United States, this refers to a speaker of standard English.

Language minority student A student who speaks a language other than the dominant societal language, or a *minority language*. In the United States, this refers to a speaker of any language or variety of language other than standard English (for example, black vernacular English or Ebonics, Spanish).

Limited English proficient (LEP) An official designation for students who are designated as in need of instruction in English. This term has been criticized because it defines the student in terms of a deficit, namely, limited English proficiency. The term *English language learner* is increasingly used.

Majority language The dominant societal language (e.g., English in the United States). This language is the higher status, more powerful language in society and often is used for official or public purposes (e.g., education, government, mainstream media).

Minority language Any language or variety of a language other than the *majority language*. These languages are lower status, less powerful languages in society and are generally used for more private or unofficial purposes (e.g., home, local community religious and secular institutions).

Newcomers Students who have just arrived in the United States, typically with limited formal instruction. Most newcomers, as a result of their interrupted or limited schooling, have no or low levels of literacy in their native language.

Newcomer programs Specially designed programs for *newcomers* (recent arrivals to the United States who have no or low English proficiency and often have limited literacy in their native language). The goal is to accelerate their acquisition of language and academic skills and to orient them to the United States and to U.S. schools. Some follow a *bilingual education* approach and others focus on *sheltered English*.

Primary language The stronger language in a bilingual learner's linguistic repertoire; the term "dominant language" is often used in the field to refer to this notion. Although the terms "first language," "native language," and "mother tongue" are also often used to refer to this notion, these terms obscure the fact that a bilingual learner may be acquiring more than one language at a time (see also *sequential language acquisition* vs. *simultaneous language acquisition*) as well as the fact that a person's "first" or "native" language may not be their stronger language.

Primary language support Using students' *primary language* during *sheltered English instruction* to support and scaffold students' content-area learning in English.

Pull-out A teaching arrangement whereby a specialist teacher (such as ESL or bilingual) takes small groups of students out of the mainstream classroom for short periods of time to give them specialized support (such as ESL or native language instruction).

Push-in A teaching arrangement whereby a specialist teacher (such as ESL or bilingual) comes into the mainstream classroom to give specialized support to a small number of students, or to help the mainstream teacher who has those students in her or his classroom.

Sequential language acquisition The process through which a language learner first acquires one language and later acquires a second or additional language; this stands in contrast to the notion of *simultaneous language acquisition*.

Sheltered English immersion A program model for ELLs that combines *English-as-a-second language instruction, sheltered content-area instruction,* and *primary language support*. Sometimes called structured English immersion.

Sheltered content-area instruction Offers English language learners grade-level core content courses taught in English using instructional strategies that make the content concepts accessible while students are acquiring English as a second language. These programs and courses are sometimes referred to as sheltered English *immersion* or *specially designed academic instruction in English (SDAIE)*. The term sheltered instruction may also be used to describe pedagogy rather than a program design. Sheltered instruction practices and individual sheltered instruction courses can be and often are implemented in conjunction with other program alternatives.

Sheltered Instruction Observation Protocol (SIOP) model A research-based approach for *sheltered instruction* that helps English language learners develop oral language proficiency while building academic English literacy skills and content area knowledge. The SIOP Institute, trademark, and copyright are owned by LessonLab/Pearson Education.

Simultaneous language acquisition The process by which a learner acquires more than one language at the same time (contrast *sequential language acquisition*).

Spanish for Spanish/Native Speakers (SNS) A *heritage language program* for students who speak Spanish as a home or *heritage language*. These programs aim to broaden the linguistic repertoire of Spanish speakers, and they often focus on ensuring that Spanish speakers learn to read and write in Spanish (while not stigmatizing the vernacular variety of Spanish that the students speaks at home and in the community).

Specially designed academic instruction in English (SDAIE) Another term for *sheltered instruction*.

Subtractive bilingualism The process by which or context in which a second language is learned, but at the expense of the first one. As a person becomes more proficient in the new language, proficiency in the first language diminishes, or worse, the person loses that first language altogether (contrast *additive bilingualism*).

Transitional bilingual education (TBE) A model of *bilingual education* that provides content-area instruction to English language learners (ELLs) in their native language while they learn English (to varying extents for varying lengths of time). As the ELLs acquire English, they move to all-English mainstream classes, typically after one to three years (also known as early-exit bilingual programs).

Two-way immersion (TWI) A type of *dual language education* that targets balanced numbers of English language learners and English speakers and aims for (1) bilingualism, (2) biliteracy, (3) academic achievement in two languages, and (4) positive cultural understanding and intercultural communication. TWI programs provide content-area instruction through two languages to students in integrated classes, and they typically last for five to seven years. There is considerable variation across TWI programs in terms of how they allocate languages for instructional purposes. NOTE: The term *dual language* is sometimes used as a synonym for two-way immersion programs. This guide takes a broad view of dual language education, by which we mean any bilingual program that promotes bilingualism and biliteracy (that is, *additive bilingualism*), academic achievement in two languages, and positive cross-cultural understanding for its target populations. Under this broad view, a two-way immersion program is one type of dual language program.

REFERENCES

Abedi, J. (Ed.). (2007). *English language proficiency assessment in the nation: Current status and future practice*. Davis: University of California.

Alvarez, L. (2004). Suutarila journal; Educators flocking to Finland, land of literate children. *The New York Times*, April 9. (http://www.nytimes.com/2004/04/09/world/suutarila-journal -educators-flocking-to-finland-land-of-literate-children.html).

Artiles, A., Klingner, J., Sullivan, A., & Fierros, E. (2010). Shifting landscapes of professional practices: English learner special education placement in English-only states. In P. Gándara, & M. Hopkins, (Eds.), *Forbidden language: English learners and restrictive language policies* (pp. 102–117). New York: Teachers College Press.

August, D., & Shanahan, T. (Eds.). (2006). *Developing literacy in second-language learners: Report of the National Literacy Panel on language-minority children and youth*. Mahwah, NJ: Lawrence Erlbaum Publishers.

August, D., & Shanahan, T. (2010). Effective English literacy instruction for English learners. In *Improving education for English learners: Research-based approaches* (pp. 209–250). Sacramento, CA: California State Department of Education.

Baker, C. (2006). *Foundations of bilingual education and bilingualism*. Clevedon, UK: Multilingual Matters.

Baker, C., & Jones, S. P. (1999). *Encyclopedia of bilingualism and bilingual education*. Clevedon, U.K.: Multilingual Matters.

Baker, E. L., Barton, P. E, Darling-Hammond, L., Haertel, E., Ladd, H. F., Linn, R. L., Ravitch, D., Rothstein, R., Shavelson, R. J., & and Shepard, L. A. (2010). *Problems with the use of student test scores to evaluate teachers*. Washington, DC: Economic Policy Institute (http://epi.3cdn .net/37677c6d5a2153548f_7sm6iiwnl.pdf).

Banks, J., & McGee Banks, C. (2009). *Multicultural education: Issues and perspectives*. New York: John Wiley & Sons.

Beeman, K., & Urow, C. (in press). *Teaching literacy in Spanish and English in the United States: A handbook for teachers*. Philadelphia, PA: Caslon.

Bialystock, E. (2001). *Bilingualism in development: Language, literacy and cognition*. Cambridge, UK: Cambridge University Press.

Boyle, A., Taylor, J., Hurlburt, S., & Soga, K. (2010). Title III accountability: Behind the numbers. *ESEA evaluation brief: The English Language Acquisition, Language Enhancement, and Academic Achievement Act*. Washington, DC: American Institutes for Research.

Brisk, M. E., Burgos, A., & Hamerla, S. R. (2004). *Situational context of education: A window into the world of bilingual learners*. Mahwah, NJ: Lawrence Erlbaum Publishers.

Brown, J. E., & Doolittle, J. (2008). A cultural, linguistic, and ecological framework for response to intervention with English language learners. *TEACHING Exceptional Children*, *40* (5), 66–72.

Cardénas-Hagan, E., Carlson, C. D., & Pollard-Durodola, S. C. (2007). The cross-linguistic transfer of early literacy skills: The role of initial L1 and L2 skills and language of instruction. *Language, Speech, and Hearing Services in Schools*, *38*(3), 249–259.

Carlisle, J. F. & Katz, L. A. (2005). Word learning and vocabulary instruction. In Birsch, J. (Ed.), *Multisensory teaching of basic language skills* (pp. 345–376). Baltimore: Paul H. Brookes.

Castañeda v. Pickard, 648 F2d 989 (5th Cir 1981).

Castek, J., Leu, D. J. Jr., Coiro, J., Gort, M., Henry, L., & Lima, C. (2008). Developing new literacies among multilingual learners in the elementary grades. In L. Parker (Ed.),

Chamot, A. U. (2009). *The CALLA handbook: Implementing the cognitive academic language learning approach*. Boston: Pearson.

Chapelle, C. A. (2001). *Computer applications in second language acquisition: Foundations for teaching, testing, and research*. New York: Cambridge University Press.

Cloud, N. (2002). Culturally and linguistically responsive instructional planning. In A. J. Artiles & A. A. Ortiz (Eds.), *English language learners with special education needs: Identification, assessment, and instruction* (pp. 107–132). Washington, DC: ERIC Clearinghouse on Languages and Linguistics, Center for Applied Linguistics.

Cloud, N. (2005). Including students who are culturally and linguistically diverse. In D. Schwartz (Ed.), *Including children with special needs: A handbook for educators and parents*. Westport, CT: Greenwood Publishing Group.

Cloud, N., Genesee, F., & Hamayan, E. (2000). *Dual language instruction: A handbook for enriched education*. Boston: Heinle & Heinle.

Cloud, N., Genesee, F., & Hamayan, E. (2009). *Literacy instruction for English language learners: A teacher's guide to research-based practices*. Portsmouth, NH: Heinemann.

Cloud, N., Lakin, J., Leininger, E., & Maxwell, L. (2010). *Teaching adolescent English language learners: Essential strategies for middle and high school.* Philadelphia: Caslon.

Cole, M. (1996). *Cultural psychology: A once and future discipline.* Cambridge, MA: Belknap Press of Harvard University Press.

Collier, V. P., & Thomas, W. P. (2004). The astounding effectiveness of dual language education for all. *NABE Journal of Research and Practice, 2*(1), 1–20 (http://njrp.tamu .edu/2004.htm).

Collier, V. P. & Thomas, W. P. (2009). *Educating English learners for a transformed world.* Albuquerque, NM: Fuente Press.

Commins, N. L. (2011). Meaning is everything: Comprehension work with second language learners. In H. Daniels, H. (Ed.), *Comprehension going forward: Where we are and what's next.* Portsmouth NH: Heinemann.

Commins, N. L., & Miramontes, O. (2005). *Linguistic diversity and teaching.* Mahwah, NJ: Lawrence Erlbaum Publishers.

Cook, H. G., Boals, T., Wilmes, C., & Santos, M. (2008). *Issues in the development of annual measurable achievement objectives for WIDA consortium states (WCER Working Paper No. 2008-2)*. Madison: University of Wisconsin–Madison, Wisconsin Center for Education Research.

Corson, D. (1999). *Language policy in schools: A resource for teachers and administrators.* Mahwah, NJ: Lawrence Erlbaum Publishers.

Corson, D. (2001). *Language diversity and education.* Mahwah, NJ: Lawrence Erlbaum Publishers.

Crandall, J.A. (2000). The role of the university in preparing teachers for a linguistically diverse society. In J. W. Rosenthal (Ed.), *Handbook of undergraduate second language education* (pp. 279–299). Mahwah, NJ: Lawrence Erlbaum Publishers.

Crandall, J. A. (2003). They DO speak English: World Englishes in U.S. schools. *ERIC/ CLL News Bulletin,* Summer/Fall.

Crandall, J. A., & Greenblatt, L. (1999). Teaching beyond the middle: Meeting the needs of underschooled and high-achieving immigrant students. In M. R. Basterra (Ed.), *Excellence and equity in education for language minority students: Critical issues and promising practices* (pp. 43–80). Washington, DC: Mid-Atlantic Equity Center, American University.

Crawford, J. (1992). *Hold your tongue: Bilingualism and the politics of English-only.* Reading, MA: Addison-Wesley.

Crawford, J. (1999). *Bilingual education: History, politics, theory and practice.* Los Angeles: Bilingual Education Services.

Crawford, J. (2000). At war with diversity: US language policy in an age of anxiety. Clevedon, UK: Multilingual Matters.

Crawford, J. (2009). *No Child Left Behind: A Failure for English language learners.* Washington, DC: Institute for Language Education Policy. (www.elladvocates.org).

Cuevas, G. J. (1994). Mathematics learning in English as a second language. *Journal for Research in Mathematics Education, 15,* 134–144.

Cummins, J. (1979). Linguistic interdependence and the educational development of bilingual children. *Review of Educational Research, 49,* 221–251.

Cummins, J. (1981). The role of primary language development in promoting educational success for language minority students. In *Schooling and language minority students: A theoretical framework* (pp. 1–50). Los Angeles, CA: Evaluation, Dissemination, and Assessment Center.

Cummins, J. (2000). *Language, power and pedagogy: Bilingual children in the crossfire.* Clevedon, UK: Multilingual Matters.

Cummins, J. (2001). *Negotiating identities: Education for empowerment in a diverse society.* Los Angeles: California Association for Bilingual Education.

Cummins, J. (2006). Identity texts: The imaginative construction of self through multiliteracies pedagogy. In O. García, T. Skutnabb-Kangas, & M. Torres-Guzmán (Eds.), *Imagining multilingual schools: Languages in education and glocalization* (pp. 51–68). Clevedon, UK: Multilingual Matters.

Cummins, J., & Early, M. (2011). *Identity texts: The collaborative creation of power in multilingual schools.* Stoke-on-Trent, England: Trentham Books.

Darling-Hammond, L., & McLaughlin, M. W. (1995). Policies that support professional development in an era of reform. *Phi Delta Kappan, 76,* 597–604.

De Jong, E. (2011). *Foundations for multilingualism in education: From principles to practice.* Philadelphia: Caslon.

Díaz-Rico, L. T. (2004). *Teaching English learners: Strategies and methods.* Boston: Pearson.

Díaz-Rico, L. T., & Week, K. Z. (2006). *The cross-cultural language and academic development handbook: A complete K–12 reference guide.* Boston: Pearson/Allyn & Bacon.

DuFour, R., & Eaker, R. (1998). *Professional learning communities: Best practices for enhancing student achievement.* Bloomington, IN: National Education Service.

Echevarria, J., & Graves, A. (1998). *Sheltered content instruction: Teaching English-language learners with diverse abilities.* Boston: Allyn & Bacon.

Echevarria, J., & Short, D. (2010). Programs and practices for effective sheltered content instruction. In *Improving education for English learners: Research-based approaches* (pp. 251–321). Sacramento, CA: California State Department of Education.

Echevarria, J. E., Vogt, M., & Short, D. J. (2008a). *Making content comprehensible for English language learners: the SIOP model.* Boston: Pearson.

Echevarria, J., Short, D., & Vogt, M. (2008b). *Implementing the SIOP® model through effective professional development and coaching.* Boston: Allyn & Bacon.

Echevarria, J., Vogt, M. E. & Short, D. (2010a). *Making content comprehensible for elementary English learners: the SIOP® model.* Boston: Allyn & Bacon.

Echevarria, J., Vogt, M. E. & Short, D. (2010b). *Making content comprehensible for secondary English learners: the SIOP® Model.* Boston: Allyn & Bacon.

Edwards, V. (2009) *Learning to be literate: Multilingual perspectives.* Clevedon: Multilingual Matters.

Egbert, J., & Ernst-Slavit, G. (2010). *Access to academics: Planning instruction for K-12 classrooms with ELLs.* Upper Saddle River, NJ: Pearson.

Epstein, J., Sanders, M., Simon, B., Salinas, K., Jansorn, N., & Voorhis, F. (2002). *School, family and community partnerships: Your handbook for action.* Thousand Oaks, CA: Corwin Press.

Ehri, L. C., Nunes, S., Stahl, S., & Willows, D. (2001). Systematic phonics instruction helps students learn to read: Evidence from the National Reading Panel's meta-analysis. *Review of Educational Research, 71,* 393–448.

Escamilla, K., & Hopewell, S. (2010). Transitions to biliteracy: Creating positive academic trajectories for emerging bilinguals in the United States. In J. Petrovic (Ed.), *International Perspectives on Bilingual Education: Policy, Practice, and Controversy* (pp. 65–90). Raleigh, NC: Information Age Publishing.

Fairbairn, S., & Jones-Vo, S. (2010). *Differentiating instruction and assessment for English language learners: A guide for K-12 teachers.* Philadelphia: Caslon.

Fashola, O. S., Drum, P. A., Mayer, R. E., & Kang, S.-J. (1996). A cognitive theory of orthographic transitioning: Predictable errors in how Spanish-speaking children spell English words. *American Educational Research Journal, 33*(4), 825–843.

Feyer, T. (2004). The Letters Editor and the reader: Our compact, Updated. *The New York Times,* May 23, 2004. (Available at http://www.nytimes.com/2004/05/23opinion/23READ.html?ex=1098781586&ei=1&en=167fb22576f65f52).

Fielding, L. G., & Pearson, P. D. (1994). Reading comprehension: What works. *Educational Leadership, 51*(5), 62–68.

Figueroa, R. A. (2004). *Migrant students' achievement in language arts in California: A historical and contemporary analysis.* California State University, Sacramento: The Migrant/OLE Project.

Fillmore, L. W. (1991). When learning a second language means losing the first. *Early Childhood Research Quarterly, 6*(3), 323–346.

Fisher, D., Frey, N., and Rothenberg, C. (2011). *Implementing RTI with English learners.* Bloomington, IN: Solution Tree Press.

Freeman, D. E., & Freeman, Y. S. (2009). *Academic language for English language learners and struggling readers.* Portsmouth, NH: Heinemann.

Freeman, D. E., & Freeman, Y. S. (2011). *Between worlds: Access to second language acquisition.* Portsmouth, NH: Heinemann.

Freeman, Y. S., & Freeman, D. E. (2002). *Closing the achievement gap: How to reach limited formal schooling and long-term English learners.* Portsmouth, NH: Heinemann.

Freeman, Y. S., Freeman, D. E., & Ebe, A. (2011). Using culturally relevant Spanish/English bilingual books with emergent bilinguals. *NABE News* (January/February), 11–13.

Freeman, R. (2004). *Building on community bilingualism.* Philadelphia: Caslon.

Freire, P. (1993). *Pedagogy of the oppressed* (20th Anniversary ed.). New York: Continuum.

Friend, M., & Cook, L. (2000). *Interactions: Collaboration skills for adult professionals.* White Plains, NY: Longman.

García, E. (2002). *Student cultural diversity: Understanding and meeting the challenge.* Boston: Houghton Mifflin.

García, E. (2004). *Writing instruction for English language learners.* Carmel, CA: Hampton-Brown.

García, E. 2006. What is the role of culture in language learning? In E. Hamayan & R. Freeman (Eds.), *English language learners at school: A guide for administrators* (pp. 61–62). Philadelphia, PA: Caslon.

García, O. (2009a). *Bilingual education in the 21st century: Global perspectives.* Malden, MA: Wiley/Blackwell.

García, O. (2009b). Emergent bilinguals and TESOL. What´s in a name? *TESOL Quarterly, 43*(2), 322–326.

García, O. & Kleifgen, J. (2010). *Educating English language learners as emergent bilinguals. Policies, programs and practices for English language learners.* New York: Teachers College Press.

Genesee, F. (2003). Rethinking bilingual acquisition. In J. M. deWaele (Ed.), *Bilingualism: Challenges and directions for future research* (pp. 158–182). Clevedon, UK: Multilingual Matters.

Genesee, F., & Hamayan, E. (1994). Classroom-based assessment. In F. Genesee (Ed.), *Educating second language children: The whole child, the whole curriculum* (pp. 212–239). New York: Cambridge University Press.

Genesee, F., & Nicoladis, E. (2007). Bilingual acquisition. In E. Hoff & M. Shatz (Eds.), *Handbook of language development,* (pp. 324–342). Oxford: Blackwell.

Genesee, F., & Riches, C. (2006). Instructional issues in literacy development. In F. Genesee, K. Lindholm-Leary, W. Saunders, & D. Christian, (Eds.), *Educating English language learners: A synthesis of research evidence* (pp. 109–175). NY: Cambridge University Press.

Genesee, F., Lindholm-Leary, K., Saunders, W. M., & Christian, D. (2006). *Educating English language learners: A synthesis of research evidence* New York: Cambridge University Press.

Gholamain, M., & Geva, E. (1999). Orthographic and cognitive factors in the concurrent development of basic reading skills in English and Persian. *Language Learning, 49*(2), 183–217.

Gibbons, P. (2002). *Scaffolding language, scaffolding learning: Teaching second language learners in the mainstream classroom.* Portsmouth, NH: Heinemann.

Goldenberg, C. (2008). Teaching English language learners: What the research does—and does not—say. *American Educator,* /32(2), 8–23, 42–44.

González, N., Moll, L. C., & Amanti, C. (Eds.). (2005). *Funds of knowledge: Theorizing practices in households, communities, and classrooms.* Mahwah, NJ: Lawrence Erlbaum Publishers.

Gottlieb, M. (2006). *Assessing English language learners: Bridges from language proficiency to academic achievement.* Thousand Oaks, CA: Corwin Press.

Gottlieb, M. (2007). *English language proficiency standards and resource guide.* Board of Regents of the University of Wisconsin/WIDA Consortium.

Gottlieb, M., & Nguyen, D. (2007). *Assessment & accountability in language education programs: A guide for administrators and teachers.* Philadelphia, PA: Caslon.

Gottlieb, M., Katz, A., & Ernst-Slavit, G. (2009). *Paper to practice: Using the TESOL English language proficiency standards in Pre-K-12 classrooms.* Alexandria, VA: Teachers of English to Speakers of Other Languages.

Graves, M. (2006). *The vocabulary book: Learning and instruction.* New York: Teachers College Press.

Greene, J. 1997. A meta-analysis of the Rossell and Baker review of bilingual education research. *Bilingual Research Journal, 21*:103–122.

Hakuta, K. (1986). *Mirror of language: The debate on bilingualism.* New York: Basic Books.

Hakuta, K. (2000). *How long does it take English learners to attain proficiency?* UC Berkeley: University of California Linguistic Minority Research Institute.

Hall, C. J. (2005). *An introduction to language and linguistics. Breaking the language spell.* London and New York: Continuum.

Hamayan, E. (1994). Language development of low-literacy students. In F. Genesee (Ed.), *Educating second language children: The whole child, the whole curriculum, the whole community* (pp. 278–300). Cambridge, UK: Cambridge University Press.

Hamayan, E., Marler, B., Sanchez-Lopez, C. & Damico, J. (in press). *Special education considerations for English language learners: Delivering a continuum of services.* Philadelphia, PA: Caslon.

Hearne, J. D. (2000). *Teaching second language learners with disabilities: Strategies for effective practice.* Oceanside, CA: Academic Communication Associates.

Heath, S. B. (1983). *Ways with words: Language, life, and work in communities and classrooms.* New York: Cambridge University Press.

Howard, E. R., Sugarman, J., & Christian, D. (2003). *Trends in two-way immersion education: A review of the research.* Washington, DC: Center for Applied Linguistics.

Hudelson, S. (1989). *Write on: Children writing in ESL.* Englewood Cliffs, NJ: Prentice Hall Regents.

Illinois Resource Center (1997). *The iceberg model of culture.* Desplaines, IL: Illinois Resource Center.

Illinois Resource Center (1999). *Learning English: The stages.* Desplaines, IL: Illinois Resource Center.

International Reading Association. (2001). *Second language literacy instruction: A position statement of the International Reading Association.* Newark, DE: IRA.

Jimenez, R. T., García, G. E., & Pearson, D. P. (1996). The reading strategies of bilingual Latina/o students who are successful English readers: Opportunities and obstacles. *Reading Research Quarterly, 31*(1), 90–112.

Kopriva, R. (2008) *Improving testing for English language learners.* New York: Routledge.

Krashen, S. (1982). *Principles and practices in second language acquisition.* Oxford, UK: Pergamon Press.

Krashen, S. (1992). *Fundamentals of language education.* Torrance, CA: Laredo.

Krashen, S. (2000). What does it take to acquire language? *ESL Magazine, 3*(3), 22–23.

Krashen, S. (2004). *The power of reading: Insights from the research.* Portsmouth, NH: Heinemann.

Krashen, S., &. Terrell, D. (1983). *The natural approach: Language acquisition in the classroom.* Hayward, CA: Alemany Press.

Kuhl, P. K. (2004). Early language acquisition: Computational strategies, social influences, and neural commitment in the developing brain. *Nature Reviews Neuroscience, 5,* 831–843.

Lanauze, M., & Snow, C. E. (1999). The relation between first- and second-language writing skills: Evidence from Puerto Rican elementary school children in bilingual programs. *Linguistics and Education, 4,* 323–339.

Lindholm-Leary, K. (2001). *Dual language education.* Clevedon, UK: Multilingual Matters.

Lindholm-Leary, K. J. (2005). The rich promise of two-way immersion. *Educational Leadership. 62*(4), 56–59.

Lindholm-Leary, K. (in press). Student outcomes in Chinese two-way immersion programs: Language proficiency, academic achievement, and student attitudes. In D. Tedick, D. Christian, & T. Fortune, (Eds.), *Immersion education: Practices, policies, possibilities.* Clevedon, UK: Multilingual Matters.

Lindholm-Leary, K., & Genesee, F. (2010). Alternative educational programs for English language learners. In California Department of Education (Eds.), *Improving education for English learners: Research-based approaches.* Sacramento: CDE Press.

Lindholm-Leary, K., & Hernandez, A. (2009). *Disaggregating background factors in the achievement and attitudes of Hispanic students in dual language programs.* Paper presented at the American Educational Research Association Annual Meeting, San Diego, CA.

Lindholm-Leary, K. J., & Howard, E. (2008). Language and academic achievement in two-way immersion programs. In T. Fortune & D. Tedick (Eds.), *Pathways to bilingualism: Evolving perspectives on immersion education.* Clevedon, UK: Multilingual Matters.

Mahoney, K., MacSwan, J., Haladyna, T., & Garcia, D. (2010). Castañeda's third prong: Evaluating the achievement of Arizona's English learners under restrictive language policy. In P. Gándara, & M. Hopkins, (Eds.), *Forbidden language: English learners and restrictive language policies* (pp. 50–64). New York: Teachers College Press.

Manis, F.R., Lindsey, K. A. & Bailey, C. F. (2004). Development of reading in grades K-12 in Spanish-speaking English-language learners. *Learning Disabilities Research and Practice, 19*(4), 214–224.

Marshall, E., & Toohey, K. (2010). Representing family: Community funds of knowledge, bilingualism, and multimodality. *Harvard Educational Review, 80*(2), 221–241.

Marzano, R., Waters, T. & McNulty, B. A. (2005). *School leadership that works: from research to results.* Alexandria, VA: Association for Supervision and Curriculum Development.

Menken, K. (2008). *English learners left behind: Standardized testing as language policy*. Clevedon, UK: Multilingual Matters.

Menken, K. (Ed.). (2011). From policy to practice in the multilingual apple: Bilingual education in New York City. *International Journal of Bilingual Education and Bilingualism, 14*(2), March 2011.

Migrant/OLE Project. (2004). Available at http://edweb.csus.edu/Projects/ole.

Miller, E., & Almon, J. (2009). *Crisis in the kindergarten: Why children need to play in school*, College Park, MD: Alliance for Childhood.

Miramontes, O. F., Nadeau, A., & Commins, N. L. (2011). *Restructuring schools for linguistic diversity: Linking decision making to effective programs* New York: Teachers College Press.

Moll, L. C., Amanti, C., Neff, D., & González, N. (1992). Funds of knowledge for teaching using a qualitative approach to connect homes and classrooms. *Theory into Practice, 31*(2), 132–141.

Mora, J. K. (2008). Vocabulary development for English language learners: The language-concept connection. *Ideas for English Language Educators* (Spring) 1–4.

Nagy, W. E., McClure, E. F., & Mir, M. (1997). Linguistic transfer and the use of context by Spanish-English bilinguals. *Applied Psycholinguistics, 18*(4), 431–452.

Nakamoto, J., Lindsey, K. A, Manis, F. R. (2008). A cross-linguistic investigation of English language-learners' reading comprehension in English and Spanish. *Scientific Studies of Reading, 12*(4), 351–371.

National Foreign Language Center. (1995). *Heritage languages in the national interest*. Washington, DC: NFLC.

Neill, M.. (2005). Assessment of ELL students under NCLB: Problems and solutions. Jamaica Plain, MA: National Center for Fair and Open Testing (Fair Test). (http://fairtest.org/nclb-assessing-bilingual-students).

Neill, M., Guisbond, L., & Schaeffer, B., with Madson, J., & and Legeros, L. (2004). *Failing our children*: How "No Child Left Behind" undermines quality and equity in education, an accountability model that supports school improvement. Jamaica Plain, MA: National Center for Fair and Open Testing (Fair Test). (http://www.fairtest.org/node/1778).

No Child Left Behind (NCLB) Act of 2001, Pub. L. No. 107-110, § 115, Stat. 1425 (2002).

North Carolina Department of Public Instruction. (2003). *Spanish for Native Speakers Curriculum*. (Available at www.learnnc.org/dpi/instserv.nsf/category9.)

Office of Bilingual Education and Minority Language Affairs. (1995). *Model strategies in bilingual education: Professional development*. Washington, DC: U.S. Department of Education.

Ohanian, S. 2002. *What happened to recess and why are our children struggling in kindergarten?* New York: McGraw-Hill.

Olsen, L. (2010). *Reparable harm: Fulfilling the unkept promise of educational opportunity for California's long term English learners*. Long Beach, CA: Californians Together.

O'Malley, J. M., & Valdez Pierce, L. (1996). *Authentic assessment for English language learners: Practical approaches for teachers*. New York: Addison-Wesley.

Parrish, T., Linquanti, R., Merickel, A., Quick, H., Laird, J., & Esra, P. (2006). *Effects of the implementation of Proposition 227 on the education of English learners, K-12*. Palo Alto: American Institutes for Research.

Peyton, J. K., Ranard, D. A., & McGinnis, S. (2001). *Heritage languages in America: Preserving a national resource*. McHenry, IL: Center for Applied Linguistics and Delta Systems.

Ramirez, D. J., Yuen, S. D., Ramey, D. R., & Pasta, D. J. (1991). *Final report: National longitudinal study of structured English immersion strategy, early-exit, and late-exit transitional bilingual education programs for language-minority children*, Vols. I and II. San Mateo, CA: Aguirre International.

Reese, L., Garnier, H., Gallimore, R., & Goldenberg, C. (2000). Longitudinal analysis of the antecedents of emergent Spanish literacy and middle-school English reading achievement of Spanish-speaking students. *American Educational Research Journal, 37*(3), 633–662.

Rogers, E. (1983). *Diffusion of innovations*. New York: Free Press.

Rogoff, B. (2003). *The cultural nature of human development*. New York: Oxford University Press.

Rolstad, K., Mahoney, K., and Glass, G. (2005). The big picture: A meta-analysis of program effectiveness research on English Language Learners. *Educational Policy 19*, 572–594.

Rosenthal, J. W. (1996). *Teaching science to language minority students*. Clevedon, UK: Multilingual Matters.

Ruiz, R. (1984). Orientations in language planning. *NABE Journal: Journal of the National Association for Bilingual Education, 8*(2), 15–34.

Ruiz, N. T., & Figueroa, R. A. (2004). *"Scientifically-based reading research": The definitional dilemma for California migrant education students.* California State University, Sacramento: The Migrant/OLE Project.

Ruiz, N. T., García, E., & Figueroa, R. A. (1996). *The OLE curriculum guide: Creating optimal learning environments for bilingual students in general and special education.* Sacramento, CA: State Department of Education Publications Bureau.

Sargent, Judy K. (2007). *ELL data retreat and improvement planning workbook.* Green Bay, Wisconsin: Cooperative Education Service Agency 7.

Saunders, W., & Goldenberg, C. (1999). The effects of instructional conversations and literature logs on the story comprehension and thematic understanding of English proficient and limited English proficient students. *Elementary School Journal, 99*(4), 277–301.

Saunders, W., & Goldenberg, C. (2010). Research to guide English language development instruction. In *Improving education for English learners: Research-based approaches* (pp. 21–82). Sacramento, CA: California State Department of Education.

Schecter, S. A., & Cummins, J. (2003). *Multicultural education in practice. Using diversity as a resource.* Portsmouth, NH: Heinemann.

Schmidt, K., Greenough, R., & Nelson, S. R. (2002). *Designing state and local policies for the professional development of instructional paraeducators.* Portland, OR: Northwest Regional Educational Laboratory.

Short, D. J., & Boyson, B. (2004). *Creating access: Language and academic programs for secondary school newcomers.* McHenry, IL, and Washington, DC: Delta Systems and Center for Applied Linguistics.

Slavin, R., & Cheung, A. (2005). A synthesis of research on language of reading instruction for English Language Learners. *Review of Educational Research, 75,* 247–281.

Smith, P. H., Jiménez, R. T., & Martínez-León, N. (2003). Other countries' literacies: What U.S. educators can learn from Mexican schools. *Reading Teacher, 56*(8), 772–781.

Snow, C., Burns, M. S., & Griffin P. (Eds.). (1998). *Preventing reading difficulties in young children.* Washington, DC: National Academy Press.

Stefancic, J., & Delgado, R. (1996). *No mercy: How conservative think tanks and foundations changed America's social agenda.* Philadelphia: Temple University Press.

Street, B. (1984). *Literacy in theory and practice.* Cambridge: Cambridge University Press.

Swanson, C. B. (2009). *Perspectives on a population: English language learners in American schools.* Bethesda, MD: Editorial Projects in Education.

Taberski, S. (2000). *On solid ground.* Portsmouth, NH: Heinemann.

Taylor, R. (1980). *The computer in the school: Tutor, tool, tutee.* New York: Teachers College Press.

Teachers of English to Speakers of Other Languages. (2006). *PreK-12 English language proficiency standards.* Alexandria, VA: TESOL.

Thomas, W.P., & Collier, V.P. (1997). *School effectiveness for language minority students.* Washington, DC: National Clearinghouse for Bilingual Education.

Thomas, W.P., & Collier, V.P. (2002). *A national study of school effectiveness for language minority students' long-term academic achievement.* Santa Cruz, CA: Center for Research, Education, Diversity and Excellence, University of California, Santa Cruz.

Uriarte, M., Tung, R., Lavan, N., & Diez, V. (2010). Impact of restrictive language policies on engagement and academic achievement of English learners in Boston Public Schools. In P. Gándara, & M. Hopkins, (Eds.), *Forbidden language: English learners and restrictive language policies* (pp. 65–85). New York: Teachers College Press.

U. S. Commission on Civil Rights (1973). *Teachers and students: Differences in teacher interaction with Mexican-American and Anglo students.* Washington, DC: U.S. Government Printing Office.

Valdes, G. (2000). *Spanish for native speakers: AATSP professional development series handbook for teachers K-16.* Orlando, FL: Harcourt College.

VanPatten, B. (2003). *From input to output: A teacher's guide to second language acquisition.* Boston: McGraw Hill.

Wagner, S., & King, T. (in press). *Implementing effective instruction for English language learners: Twelve key practices for systemic and strategic action.* Philadelphia: Caslon.

Walker, S., Edwards, V., & Blacksell, R. (1996). Designing bilingual books for children. *Visible Language, 30*(3), 268–283.

Wentworth, L., Pellegrin, N., Thompson, K., & Hakuta, K. (2010). Proposition 227 in California: A long-term appraisal of its impact on English learner student achievement. In P. Gándara &

M. Hopkins, (Eds.), *Forbidden language: English learners and restrictive language policies* (pp. 37–49). New York: Teachers College Press.

Wiggins, G., & McTighe, J. (2006). *Understanding by design*. Alexandria, VA: Association for Supervision and Curriculum Development.

Wiley, T. G. (2005). *Literacy and language diversity in the United States*. Washington, DC: Center for Applied Linguistics.

Willig, A. 1985. A meta-analysis of selected studies on the effectiveness of bilingual education. *Review of Educational Research 55*, 269–317.

Wink, J. (2000). *Critical pedagogy: Notes from the real world*. New York: Addison Wesley Longman.

Wolf, M. K., Kao, J. C., Herman, J., Bachman,L. F., Bailey, A. L., Bachman, P. L., Farnsworth, T., & Chang, S. M. (2008). Issues in assessing English language learners: English proficiency measures and accommodations uses. *CRESST Reports 731–733.* Los Angeles: National Center for Research on Evaluation, Standards, and Student Testing, University of California, Los Angeles.

Wright, W. E. (2004). What English-only really means: A study of the implementation of California language policy with Cambodian American students. *International Journal of Bilingual Education and Bilingualism, 7*(1), 1–23.

Wright, W. E. (2005). English language learners left behind in Arizona: The nullification of accommodations in the intersection of federal and state policies. *Bilingual Research Journal, 29*(1), 1–30.

Wright, W. E. (2007). Heritage language programs in the era of English-only and No Child Left Behind. *Heritage Language Journal, 5*(1), 1–26.

Wright, W. E. (2010). *Foundations for teaching English language learners: Research, theory, policy, and practice*. Philadelphia: Caslon.

Wright, W. E., & Choi, D. (2006). The impact of language and high-stakes testing policies on elementary school English language learners in Arizona. *Education Policy Analysis Archives, 14*(13), 1–56. (Available at http://epaa.asu.edu/epaa/v14n13/).

Xu, Y., & Drame, E. (2008). Culturally appropriate context: Unlocking the potential of response to intervention for English language learners. *Early Childhood Education Journal, 35*, 305–311.

Zehr, M. A. (2010). Few states meeting goals of NCLB for English-learners. *Education Week, 29*(32), 10.

INDEX

Note: Page numbers followed by f refer to figures; page numbers followed by t refer to tables.